STATISTA
Towards a Statecraft of the Future
Staatskunst am Haus der Statistik
ZK/U – Zentrum für Kunst und Urbanistik
KW Institute for Contemporary Art

Towards a Statecraft of the Future

Staatskunst am Haus der Statistik

Zentrum für Kunst und Urbanistik ZK/U
KW Institute for Contemporary Art

PARK BOOKS

STATISTA
Towards a Statecraft of the Future
Staatskunst am Haus der Statistik
ZK/U – Zentrum für Kunst und Urbanistik
KW Institute for Contemporary Art

Editors/Herausgeber: ZK/U – Zentrum für Kunst und
Urbanistik and/und KW Institute for Contemporary Art
Translations/Übersetzung: Jill Denton, Good & Cheap
Copyediting English/Lektorat deutsch: Miriam Seifert-Waibel
Proofreading English / Korrektorat deutsch:
Liz Allan, Miriam Seifert-Waibel
Design: anschlaege.de
Pre-press/Lithografie: et boum c'est le choc
Printing/Druck: Oktoberdruck
Binding/Bindung: Reinhart & Wasser

Project imprint: see p. 199 / Impressum Gesamtprojekt:
siehe S. 199

© 2020 ZK/U – Zentrum für Kunst und Urbanistik,
KW Institute for Contemporary Art and/und
Park Books AG, Zürich

© for the texts: the authors / für die Texte:
die Autorinnen und Autoren
© for the pictures: see credits p. 199 / für die Bilder:
siehe Bildnachweise S. 199

Park Books
Niederdorfstrasse 54
8001 Zürich
Schweiz/Switzerland
www.park-books.com

Park Books is being supported by the Federal Office of Culture
with a general subsidy for the years 2016–2020. / Park Books
wird vom Bundesamt für Kultur mit einem Strukturbeitrag für
die Jahre 2016–2020 unterstützt.

All rights reserved; no part of this publication may be
reproduced, stored in a retrieval system or transmitted in any
form or by any means, electronic, mechanical, photocopying,
recording, or otherwise, without the prior written consent
of the publisher. / Alle Rechte vorbehalten; kein Teil dieses
Werks darf in irgendeiner Form ohne vorherige schriftliche
Genehmigung des Verlags reproduziert oder unter
Verwendung elektronischer Systeme verarbeitet, vervielfältigt
oder verbreitet werden.

ISBN 978-3-03860-188-3

Introduction
Einleitung

p. 6 AllesAndersPlatz
Dr. Klaus Lederer, Senator für Kultur und Europa Berlin

p. 10 Prelude
ZK/U – Zentrum für Kunst und Urbanistik
KW Institute for Contemporary Art

p. 14 Satan's Lust Garden – An Introduction to STATISTA
Tirdad Zolghadr

p. 30 Haus der Stadtistik – A Chronological Scenario
Harry Sachs, Philip Horst

Essays

p. 42 Donkey Paths & Pigeon Towers
Marion von Osten

p. 55 Capitalising Antigentrification
Suhail Malik

p. 68 **Berlin and the Blockchain**
Matthias Einhoff

Artwork Aktionsfelder

p. 78 **Allesandersplatz**
ZK/U

p. 84 **fallingwild**
Labor k3000

p. 88 **Pigeon Towers**
KUNSTrePUBLIK

p. 94 **Voices – First Recording**
raumlaborberlin

p. 100 **Musterhaus der Statistik**
openBerlin & KUNSTrePUBLIK

p. 106 **STATISTA Coin**
Economic Space Agency

p. 112 **Beecoin/Bee-DAO**
KUNSTrePUBLIK

p. 121 **Image series**
Documentation

p. 154 **Unser Leben 2020**
Image-Shift & anschlaege.de

p. 157 **Ishtar Gate**
Penny Rafferty

p.166 Conference Introduction
Tirdad Zolghadr

p.170 CATPC
p.176 Chto Delat
p.178 Campus in Camps
p.180 ExRotaprint
p.184 Nachbarschafts-akademie Prinzessin-nengärten
p.186 PlanBude
p.188 MACAO
p.190 Khalil Sakakini Cultural Center
p.192 ruangrupa

p.194 Contributors Index

AllesAndersPlatz

The Haus der Statistik (HdS) is a huge architectural ensemble that served as the Central Office of Statistics of the GDR from the early 1970s on—and has meanwhile been standing vacant for years. On Alexanderplatz in Berlin, an extraordinary group has come together in order to save the ensemble and lend it a new lease of life on behalf of civil society. Under the name „Koop5", the group has been working since 2018 to develop the HdS with and for the community.

The five cooperation partners in the group—the Senate for Urban Development and Housing, the Berlin-Mitte district administration, the real estate agencies WBM Wohnungsbaugesellschaft Berlin-Mitte mbH and BIM Berliner Immobilienmanagement GmbH (both owned by the State of Berlin), and the ZUsammenKUNFT Berlin eG—are jointly accountable for the project. This is why existing space at the HdS is to be converted and an additional 65,000 m^2 to be newly built, so as to accommodate the arts, cultural and social projects, education and training, affordable housing and the local administration on one and the same site.

The kickstarter for this urban rapprochement process, underway since 2015, was an art intervention: by unfurling a fake construction site banner announcing 'Under Development Here for Berlin: Space for Cultural Affairs, Education, and Social Projects,' the artists did more than provoke a rethink of the planned sale and demolition of the building. It culminated in realistic planning and development proposals in which even art, no less, would have its place. The current temporary use of the HdS is paving the way for the venue's long-term survival, and its upgrade for the common good. The crucial art action staged by AbBA, the Berlin Alliance of Artists' Studios *Under Threat*, was followed by several more, thanks to the various protagonists from the cultural sector, now united by the 'Initiative Haus der Statistik / ZUsammenKUNFT Berlin eG,' who ensure that public events, discussions, and the like all take place with increasing regularity.

Their current phase of creative endeavor, as presented in this catalog, revolves around *art in public space* that uses temporary interventions in existing neighborhoods to spark new concepts and approaches. STATISTA is the name—and STATISTA stands for an artistic pilot project at the heart of Berlin, which expands the reach of familiar terms such as *art in public space* or *urban art*, and challenges them too. The exhibition makers' thesis, 'Haus der Statistik plus contemporary art', is a sort of statecraft, as well as a pioneering art, of the future.

Here, experimental processes raise the question of how cooperation in the spirit of the commons, urban development and art can best succeed; they also ask whether such cooperation can be considered a matter of the state—or of statecraft—in the positive sense of the term. This is the fundamental question: of how contemporary art (in public space) can position itself sustainably within the realm of urban politics. How can art make a discursive and intellectual, perhaps even material and infrastructural, contribution to policy-making on urban issues? And can its involvement and solidarity with initiatives that are already active in urban politics be a means to critically question, and refresh, or even broaden its scope?

AllesAndersPlatz
Dr. Klaus Lederer

Answers to these questions are still being sought ... and here, I believe, the path is also the goal. STATISTA is a pilot project, a springboard to viable future options. The experimental and urban development potential unleashed exceeds by far the regular definition of *art in public space*, and marks a groundbreaking move towards further research into forms of art and urban culture that are of relevance to urban politics.

One thing is for sure: cooperation between two brilliant Berlin art institutions, the KW Institute for Contemporary Art and the ZK/U Center for Art and Urbanistics, has given rise to a trendsetting mix. Two years of preparation—and then an opening during Berlin Art Week 2019 that really did make everything 'AltogetherDifferent' on Alexanderplatz. Visitors were confronted with the HdS as an urban wasteland, in which animals, a choir, a defunct bumper car facility, and a variety of other initiatives have found a home.

Across ten different fields of activity, STATISTA developed artistic prototypes for a civil society based on the spirit of the commons. The artist groups invited to take part engaged in unusual experiments with the broadest possible range of urban dwellers: from a crypto-currency that is index-linked to the welfare of bees to a façade design that includes 'housing' for birds and insects, from a pigeon tower to neighborhood cooperative ventures, to an international congress devoted to exploring the sustainability of participatory art interventions in public space, also specifically in relation to certain areas of Mitte.

I believe that the participating artists' confrontation with difficult urban, social, and aesthetic questions was truly worthwhile, and I wish everyone concerned many more creative ideas and much success.

I thank the untiring and also undaunted creative minds at both the KW—director Krist Gruijthuijsen and curator Tirdad Zolghadr—and at ZK/U—the director trio and founding members of KUNSTrePUBLIK, Matthias Einhoff, Philip Horst, and Harry Sachs. And I wish everyone who comes upon this catalog an instructive and inspiring read.

Dr. Klaus Lederer, Senator for Culture and Europe, Berlin

AllesAndersPlatz

Das Haus der Statistik ist ein sehr großer Gebäudekomplex, der seit den 1970er Jahren Sitz der Staatlichen Zentralverwaltung für Statistik der DDR war – und seit Jahren leer steht. Am Alexanderplatz in Berlin hat sich eine ungewöhnliche Gruppe zusammengefunden, um das Gebäude für die Stadtgesellschaft zu retten und wieder mit Leben zu füllen: Seit 2018 arbeitet die sogenannte Koop5 an der gemeinwohlorientierten Entwicklung des Hauses der Statistik.

Die fünf Kooperationspartner*innen – Senatsverwaltung für Stadtentwicklung und Wohnen, das Bezirksamt Berlin-Mitte, die landeseigenen Gesellschaften Wohnungsbaugesellschaft Berlin-Mitte mbH (WBM) und Berliner Immobilienmanagement GmbH (BIM) sowie die ZUsammenKUNFT Berlin eG – werden in gemeinsamer Verantwortung arbeiten. So werden Raum für Kunst, Kultur, Soziales und Bildung, bezahlbares Wohnen, ein neues Rathaus für Mitte sowie Verwaltungsnutzungen in den Bestandsgebäuden und durch 65.000 Quadratmeter Neubau auf dem HdS-Areal geschaffen.

Ausschlaggebend für diesen seit 2015 andauernden Prozess der städtischen Verständigung war eine Kunstaktion, die mit der Aufstellung eines nicht regulären Bauschildes – „Hier entstehen für Berlin: Räume für Kultur, Bildung und Soziales" – mehr als nur den Anstoß zum Überdenken des geplanten Verkaufs beziehungsweise Abrisses des Hauses gab. Es führte zu realistischen Planungen des Gebäudekonzepts, in dem – nicht zuletzt – auch die Kunst ihren Platz haben wird. Aus der laufenden HdS-Zwischennutzung wird Verstetigung und Aufwertung im Interesse aller. Der ausschlaggebenden künstlerischen Aktion von der Allianz bedrohter Berliner Atelierhäuser (AbBa) sollten noch mehrere folgen – die in der Initiative HdS / ZUsammenKUNFT Berlin eG zusammengeschlossenen kunst- und kulturnahen Gruppierungen sorgen mit schöner Regelmäßigkeit für Aktionen, Akademien und Angebote.

Aktuell ist es die in diesem Katalog vorliegende Station der künstlerischen Beschäftigung mit Kunst im Stadtraum, die, temporär angelegt, durch Eingriffe in bestehende Quartiere neue Denkbewegungen auslösen will: STATISTA. Es geht bei STATISTA um eine künstlerische Versuchsanordnung im Zentrum Berlins, die bekannte Begriffe wie Kunst im Stadtraum oder Urban Art erweitert und diese infrage stellt. Die These der Ausstellungsmachenden: „Haus der Statistik plus Gegenwartskunst" sei eine Art Staats- und Pionierkunst der Zukunft.

In experimentellen Prozessen wird der Frage nachgegangen, wie gemeinwohlorientierte Zusammenarbeit in den Bereichen der Stadtentwicklung und der Kunst gelingen kann und ob dies im positiven Sinne ein staatlicher Auftrag sein könnte. Es ist die grundsätzliche Frage, wie sich die zeitgenössische Kunst (im öffentlichen Raum) innerhalb einer stadtpolitischen Landschaft nachhaltig positionieren kann. Wie kann die Kunst einen diskursiven und intellektuellen, vielleicht sogar materiellen und infrastrukturellen Beitrag leisten? Und kann sie sich mittels der Rückbindung an und Verbindung mit stadtpolitisch arbeitende(n) Initiativen kritisch hinterfragen, erneuern, gar erweitern?

AllesAndersPlatz
Dr. Klaus Lederer

Antworten auf diese Fragen werden weiter gesucht ... und ich glaube, der Weg ist hier das Ziel. STATISTA ist ein Versuch, ein Beginn, von dem aus man weitergehen kann. Das experimentelle und stadtpolitisch relevante Potenzial, das von dieser Kunstaktion weit über die reguläre Definition von Kunst im Stadtraum ausgeht, kann ein Weg sein, der in weitere Erforschung von stadtpolitisch relevanter Kunst und urbaner Kultur führt.

Eins ist sicher: Aus der Zusammenarbeit von zwei großartigen Berliner Kunsteinrichtungen, dem KW Institute for Contemporary Art und dem Zentrum für Kunst und Urbanistik (ZK/U) ist eine Gemengelage mit zukunftsweisendem Charakter entstanden. Zwei Jahre Vorbereitung – und dann eine Eröffnung der *Berlin Art Week* 2019, die wirklich „AllesAnders" machte am Platz: Das Publikum wurde mit der Stadtbrache des HdS konfrontiert, in der Tiere, ein Chor, eine verwaiste Autoscooterbahn und diverse Aktionen ein Zuhause gefunden haben.

In zehn Aktionsfeldern entwickelte STATISTA künstlerische Prototypen für eine auf Gemeingütern basierende Stadtgesellschaft. Die eingeladenen Künstler*innengruppen führten ungewöhnliche Experimente aller Art mit unterschiedlichsten Stadtbewohner*innen durch: von einer auf dem Wohlergehen von Bienen basierenden Kryptowährung über einen Entwurf für eine Fassadengestaltung, die „Wohnräume" für Vögel und Insekten bietet, von einem Taubenturm bis hin zu nachbarschaftlichen Kooperationen und einem internationalen Kongress mit der Frage nach einer Nachhaltigkeit künstlerisch-partizipativer Interventionen im öffentlichen Raum, auch für die konkreten Quartiere in Mitte.

Ich meine, die Auseinandersetzung mit virulenten städtischen, gesellschaftlichen und ästhetischen Problemstellungen aller beteiligten Kunstschaffenden hat sich gelohnt, und ich wünsche allen Beteiligten weiterhin gute, schöpferische Ideen und viel Erfolg.

Ich danke dem KW und dem ZK/U und ihren unermüdlichen und auch unerschrockenen Betreibern, Direktor Krist Gruijthuijsen und Kurator Tirdad Zolghadr, sowie den Direktoren des ZK/U und den Mitgliedern der KUNSTrePUBLIK, Matthias Einhoff, Philip Horst und Harry Sachs. Allen Leser*innen dieses Katalogs wünsche ich eine aufschlussreiche und anregende Lektüre.

Dr. Klaus Lederer, Senator für Kultur und Europa Berlin

Prelude

Berlin is the city with the second highest density of artists in the world after New York City. According to current estimates there are about 8000 professional artists living in Berlin. Of those artists, 1.3 percent state that they have NO need for working space. Nevertheless, 12 million tourists cite art and culture as the second most important reason for visiting Berlin.

Berlin's very own history of change since the fall of the Berlin Wall, the lack of role models for economic and spatial development, the merging of two administrations, the debt crisis and the search for an identity that emerged from two contrary identities has led to a 'Berlin Melange' of epic-fail developments and showcase projects.

In the meantime, the city has developed into a 'global player'. In the struggle for sovereignty over identity and space, the private and public stakeholders are becoming more organized, larger and more powerful in their positions. Cultural workers and artists have been pioneers in the historical development since the fall of the Berlin Wall and have played a major role in shaping the city's image as a creative city. They invested a great deal – but their cultural capital was increasingly proving worthless in urban policy debates. The model project Haus der Statistik (HdS) reacts to this discrepancy between the investment and return among artists.

KUNSTrePUBLIK, as a collective, has for several years now been successfully pursuing the questions of space, art and social change in the form of new collective infrastructures and a programming oriented towards the urban environment. In 2006, it founded Skulpturenpark Berlin_Zentrum on the former Wall strip dividing east and west at Spittelmarkt – not far from Alexanderplatz – and, in several series of site-specific artistic projects in the still-young Berlin urban discourse, formulated a scepticism towards the appropriation of art by speculative urban development. In 2012, the collective founded the Center for Art and Urbanistics (ZK/U) in the former freight station Moabit and established a long-term sustainable basis for artists and local formats via a heritable building right, positioning itself as a political and neighborhood platform against displacement and speculation. The ZK/U quickly sensed that it can only escape the embracing global real estate capital if it not only critically questions the rules of urban production but also actively participates in shaping them and providing a roof over the heads of the protagonists of change. Since its foundation, the ZK/U has been the interface of representation, transformation and information of a critical urban discourse.

From 2015 to 2017, regular network meetings constituted a public sphere here, which emphatically brought about the repurchase of the HdS in 2017 and brought together political and civil society actors in a previously unknown way.

For its part, KW Institute for Contemporary Art aims to approach the central questions of our times through the production, display, and dissemination of contemporary art. Since its inception more than 25 years ago, KW has established itself, not only as an institution, but also as a dynamic and lively space for progressive practices within the Berlin art scene, as well as in an international context. By means of exhibitions and various event formats, KW has aligned itself towards the current tendencies of the national and international art and cultural discourse, and has actively developed them on a collaborative level with artists, institutions, and by means of commissioned works, maintaining a high degree of flexibility in creating its programs and addressing its audience.

The current program evolves around the central objective of using the participating artists' perspective as a starting point, entailing their subjects and points of view as ways to reflect on social and political issues. The institution is thereby conceived as a social space that facilitates contemplation and exchange between different protagonists and cultures, consistently challenging its audience.

In 2015, KW launched the REALTY program, a critical reflection process on the alliances between art and real estate capital in the new Berlin-Mitte, in the course of which an examination of the process at the HdS, in which the ZK/U was involved, became decisive. STATISTA is a logical consolidation of the discourses pursued at both institutions and combines the questioning of the representative aspects of art with a practice of inclusive urban production.

What was achieved with the KW in the Scheunenviertel in the 1990s, and the ZK/U in Moabit in the 2010s (albeit from very different perspectives on art), is to be developed with the HdS in the 2020s, as a long-term secure cultural venue in a trans-sectoral cooperation. Civil society and cultural and public actors are working on a common vision for a diverse and imaginative Berlin. STATISTA is a speculative prelude to this ongoing process.

STATISTA would like to take this opportunity to thank all contributors and participants. Without the tenacious and humble commitment of all those involved, today's constructive process would never have come about. We would like to thank all the participating artists and collectives, and all colleagues at the Initiative Haus der Statistik, as well as all partners in conversation, from the neighbor next door to the district mayor, and the backstage team, whose brilliant support made all this possible to begin with. We would also like to thank the five local cooperation partners, the Berlin Art Week team, and Krist Gruijthuijsen, director of the KW Institute for Contemporary Art. Their cooperative spirit has made new paths possible. Finally, we thank the Senate Department for Culture for their belief in our project, and their consistent financial and non-material support.

Matthias Einhoff, Philip Horst, Harry Sachs, Tirdad Zolghadr

Präambel

Berlin ist die Stadt mit der weltweit zweithöchsten Dichte von Kunstschaffenden nach New York City. Gemäß aktueller Schätzungen leben in Berlin ca. 8000 professionell arbeitende Künstler*innen. 1,3 Prozent davon geben an, *keinen* Bedarf an Arbeitsraum zu haben. Gleichwohl führen zwölf Millionen Tourist*innen Kunst und Kultur als zweitwichtigsten Grund ihres Besuchs in Berlin an.

Berlins sehr eigene Geschichte des Wandels seit dem Mauerfall, der Mangel an *role models* für eine wirtschaftliche und raumpolitische Entwicklung, die Zusammenlegung von zwei Verwaltungen, die Schuldenkrise und die Suche nach einer Identität, die aus zwei konträren Identitäten hervorging, hat zu einer eigenen Berliner Melange von Fehlentwicklungen und Vorzeigeprojekten geführt.

Inzwischen hat sich die Stadt zu einem *global player* entwickelt. Beim Ringen um die Hoheit über Identität und Raum werden die privaten und öffentlichen Beteiligten organisierter, größer und meinungskräftiger. Kultur- und Kunstschaffende waren Pionier*innen in der historischen Entwicklung seit dem Fall der Mauer und prägten das Image Berlins als kreative Stadt wesentlich mit. Sie investierten viel – doch ihr kulturelles Kapital sollte sich in den stadtpolitischen Debatten zunehmend als wertlos erweisen. Das Modellprojekt Haus der Statistik (HdS) reagiert auf diese Diskrepanz von Investition und Rendite von Kunstschaffenden.

KUNSTrePUBLIK geht als Kollektiv seit mehreren Jahren den Fragen nach Raum, Kunst und sozialen Veränderungen in Form neuer kollektiver Infrastrukturen und einer am urbanen Umfeld ausgerichteten Programmierung nach. Es gründete 2006 den Skulpturenpark Berlin_Zentrum auf dem ehemaligen Mauerstreifen am Spittelmarkt – unweit des Alexanderplatzes – und formulierte in mehreren Reihen ortsbezogener künstlerischer Projekte im noch jungen Berliner Stadtdiskurs eine Skepsis gegenüber der Vereinnahmung von Kunst durch spekulative Stadtentwicklung. 2012 gründete das Kollektiv im ehemaligen Güterbahnhof Moabit das Zentrum für Kunst und Urbanistik (ZK/U) und stellte eine langfristige, nachhaltige Basis für Kunstschaffende und lokale Formate her, die sich als politische und nachbarschaftliche Plattform gegen Verdrängung und Spekulation positioniert. Das ZK/U erkannte, dass es den Umarmungen des globalen Immobilienkapitals nur entkommen kann, wenn es die Regeln der Stadtproduktion nicht nur kritisch hinterfragt, sondern aktiv mitgestaltet und den Protagonist*innen der Veränderung ein Dach über dem Kopf ist. Seit seiner Gründung versteht sich das als ZK/U Schnittstelle von Repräsentation, Transformation und Information eines kritischen Stadtdiskurses. Von 2015 bis 2017 konstituierte sich hier über regelmäßige Netzwerktreffen eine Öffentlichkeit, die den Rückkauf des HdS im Jahr 2017 mit Nachdruck erwirkte und politische und zivilgesellschaftliche Akteur*innen in zuvor unbekannter Weise zusammenführte.

Die KW Institute for Contemporary Art widmen sich durch die Produktion, Präsentation und Vermittlung zeitgenössischer Kunst zentralen Fragen unserer Gegenwart. Seit ihrer Gründung vor mehr als 25 Jahren haben sich die KW als Institution und lebendiger Ort für progressive

Präambel
ZK/U & KW

künstlerische Praktiken in der Berliner und internationalen Kunstszene etabliert. Mittels Ausstellungen und unterschiedlichster Veranstaltungsformate greifen die KW stets aktuelle Tendenzen aus dem nationalen und internationalen zeitgenössischen Kunst- und Kulturdiskurs auf und entwickeln diese in Zusammenarbeit mit Künstler*innen, mit Institutionen sowie durch Auftragsarbeiten aktiv weiter. Das gegenwärtige Programm der KW entwickelt sich stets aus dem Anliegen heraus, von den beteiligten Künstler*innen, deren Themen und Arbeitsweisen auszugehen und über politische und gesellschaftliche Fragestellungen zu reflektieren. Dabei wird die Institution als sozialer Raum begriffen, der Reflexion und den Austausch zwischen unterschiedlichen Akteur*innen und Kulturen ermöglicht und seine Besucher*innen stets aufs Neue herausfordert.

2015 startete KW mit dem REALTY Programm einen kritischen Reflektionsprozess der Allianzen von Kunst und Immobilienkapital in der neuen Berliner Mitte, in dessen Verlauf eine Auseinandersetzung mit dem vom ZK/U mitgeprägten Prozess am HdS unabdingbar wurde. STATISTA ist eine folgerichtige Zusammenführung der an beiden Häusern geführten Diskurse und verbindet das Hinterfragen der repräsentativen Aspekte von Kunst mit einer Praxis der inklusiven Stadtproduktion.

Was mit dem KW im Scheunenviertel in den 1990er und dem ZK/U in Moabit in den 2010er Jahren mit unterschiedlichen Kunstauffassungen gelang, soll mit dem HdS in den 2020er Jahren als langfristig gesicherter Kulturort in einer transsektoralen Kooperation entstehen. Zivilgesellschaftliche, kulturelle und öffentliche Akteur*innen arbeiten an einer gemeinsamen Vision für ein vielfältiges und ideenreiches Berlin. STATISTA bildet den spekulativen Auftakt in diesem andauernden Prozess.

STATISTA möchte an dieser Stelle allen Mitwirkenden und Mitstreitenden danken. Ohne das zähe und uneitle Engagement aller Beteiligten wäre der heutige konstruktive Moment nie zustande gekommen. Unser großer Dank geht an alle Künstler, Kollektive und Diskussionspartner im Gesamtprozess, von den Nachbar*innen nebenan bis zum Bezirksbürgermeister, und insbesondere an das Team im Hintergrund, ohne deren brillanter Mithilfe das Projekt nicht zu Stande gekommen wäre. Wir danken den fünf Partner*innen vor Ort, aber auch Krist Gruijthuijsen, Direktor des KW Institute for Contemporary Art, und dem gesamten Berlin Art Week Team, durch deren kooperativen Geist neue Wege möglich wurden. Ein besonderer Dank gilt der Senatsverwaltung für Kultur, für das große Vertrauen in das Projekt und die konsequente Unterstützung.

Matthias Einhoff, Philip Horst, Harry Sachs, Tirdad Zolghadr

Satan's Lust Garden – An Introduction to STATISTA

In September 2015, during the Berlin Art Week, AbBA, the Allianz bedrohter Berliner Atelierhäuser (Alliance of Berlin Artists' Studios Under Threat), initiated an art intervention near Alexanderplatz, at Haus der Statistik (HdS). A large banner especially commissioned for the occasion was unfurled on the façade, to choral accompaniment, announcing the opening of a new public center for all manner of social and cultural purposes.

The event was essentially symbolic—demolition of the HdS had long since been approved. Yet within only a few years its prophecy turned out to be self-fulfilling. Today, the HdS is a unique pilot project collectively defined and steered by a broad coalition of actors in the interests of a pioneering urban development.

Thanks to AbBA, the sale and demolition of the 40,000 m² building have been prevented, and a new 65,000 m² addition is soon to be built. The venture will provide space for the arts, culture, social projects, education and outreach, and low-cost housing, as well as a new city hall and administrative offices for the Berlin-Mitte district.

Four years after the AbBA event, and once again in sync with Art Week, art is back on the agenda—though not

Satan's Lust Garden — An Introduction to STATISTA
Tirdad Zolghadr

as a pointed provocation directed at the state but as a public art venture that seeks to position the pioneering spirit of 2015 as the statecraft of the future. A blueprint for civic and civil cooperation in the interests of the common good, far removed from the rivalry of 'Creative City' schemes. Perhaps Berlin-Mitte can remain just as attractive, entertaining, and spectacular as it is today, even without degenerating into a doormat for tourists and property investors.

Human settlement on what is now Alexanderplatz began around 1400. The first example of state infrastructure in the neighborhood were a set of gallows. Which is

[1]
View of HdS Werkstatt from OASE fast food establishment / Sicht auf HdS Werkstatt und OASE Imbissbude

Satan's Lust Garden — An Introduction to STATISTA
Tirdad Zolghadr

why, at least according to Wikipedia, the spot was first known as 'Devil's Lust Garden' (Teufels Lustgarten). The gallows were soon followed by jails, courthouses, military barracks and quarantine facilities, while the square's name officially became 'King's Gate' (Königs Thor Platz), later followed by 'Alexanderplatz' when Tsar Alexander I visited in 1805. One would be forgiven for assuming the square's genius loci is of a harsh, aristocratic type. After all, the House of Statistics itself, seat of data accumulation on all East German citizenry, was an unapologetic tool of state surveillance.

After the fall of the Berlin Wall, the Kollhoff Plan for Alexanderplatz continued this royal tradition of top-down decision-making—albeit, of course, in a radically different vein. The said plan is a brash attempt to Manhattanize the Berlin skyline by means of a string of high-rises, cheerfully ignoring all lessons learned from gentrification patterns of recent decades.

On the other hand, there is also, of course, another subtext to the Devil's Lust Garden. A genealogy of black markets, illicit construction, persistently disproportionate crime rates and the famous armed barricades of 1848, not to mention the epochal mass demonstrations that precipitated the fall of the communist government in 1989. Thus, a hopeful side to an otherwise grim history. One which we cultural worker types are always eager to side with; keen, as we are, to echo the voice of grassroots multitudes, wholly and unreservedly. After all, what are we if not critical? Allow me to return to this collective professional desire in just a moment's time.

During the era of the Cold War, West Berlin was peddled as an insular beacon of freedom, a gentle historical experiment, braving the communist apparatchiks in polyester suits, peering grimly from the rooftop of the House of Statistics. Later, over the 1990s, this dimly libertarian fantasy—Berlin as the weird and wonderful oasis of creative flux—morphed into rather more ambitious visions for the city. This took the shape of the monumental Kollhoff Plan, and other urban planning adventures. While at the same time, the freedom fantasy did persist, in the desire to make the very best of the countless empty lots and venues the post-Berlin Wall city had to offer. Countless cultural workers invested blood, sweat, and tears for the sake of appropriating a space for only one year, one week, one single night, before moving on to the next. These temporary usages of Berlin's vast panorama of empty spaces made it a hub of spatial creativity, a legacy it still builds on to this day.

The 2000s brought with them the realization that this celebration of haphazard flux was, in point of fact, one colossal urban renewal plan. To what degree the upshot was premeditated is anyone's guess the fact is that temporary usage proceeded to devour its own children (as Berlin architect Robert Huber shrewdly puts it). And the only ones to benefit from all the sweat equity invested, over the course of the 90s, were the legal proprietors and the faraway investors, not the culturati who made the neighborhoods feel safe, special, and creative, let alone the local tenants, old and new, who resided there.

One rare survivor from that heady scramble for gentrification is KW itself. The venue persisted to become what is arguably, in some ways, the topmost German institution in the contemporary artscape. In terms of financial

Satan's Lust Garden — An Introduction to STATISTA
Tirdad Zolghadr

clout, it remains a dwarf, but in terms of sociocultural capital, KW clearly has the patient ear of policymakers who wish to keep Berlin as attractive as it is today. To its detractors, it is a classic tale of institutionalization, from Rock 'n' Roll to Prada. To its supporters, KW has saved a patch of land from yet another cheesecake cappuccino nightmare. Even its harshest critics will find it hard to deny that KW is a dazzlingly successful case of the possibilities of *Verstetigung*, of digging in one's heels, using the means and methods of Contemporary Art, and as such offers a lot to learn from. To ask more of the venue is not entirely fair, as it is to blame the player for the game: to shift the use of art as a vessel for urban renewal is to demand another mode of cultural production altogether.

To be sure, Berlin has indeed generated such models too; it has spawned structures that benefit constituencies beyond cultural workers themselves, driven by hopes of collectivization, redistribution, democratization. HdS stands on the shoulders of these extensive local histories, which over the decades have contributed decisively to keeping Berlin accessible, unpredictable, and great, all throughout the rude awakening of last decade. ZK/U has been pursuing this very premise of collective infrastructures for a number of years, with considerable success. From a KW perspective, STATISTA was an opportunity to collaborate with ZK/U, one that emerged from REALTY, a program curated by Tirdad Zolghadr (and commissioned by KW and other institutions), which pursues very similar art-political parameters on its own behalf.[1]

From the vantage point of an artist or curator of the KW mold, doing justice to such traditions demands more than merely testifying to those structures, and to the histories of resistance around us. Speaking for my own field (as opposed to the Berlin culturati at large), Contemporary Art has long entered the corridors of power. Within the processes of urban renewal alluded to above, and that are taking our cities by storm, it plays a small but proactive, prescient and fascinating role. All of which makes solidarity with the victims of city development an even more complicated affair than it always is to begin with. Hence the insistence, on the following pages, on leverage, speculative scenarios, statecraft.

At this point, power has become more art-like (Josephine Berry). This does not only mean the powerful appreciate art, but that they operate by means of open questions and adaptability, and a claim to powerlessness—much as Contemporary Art itself does. Herein lies an awkward common ground. By and large, policymakers of all possible leanings have long been doing the bidding of the real estate sector, claiming they have few other options unfortunately, unfortunately. For its part, Contemporary Art forever insists on standing outside power, speaking truth to it, critically and unpredictably; this even as it caters to the exact same stakeholders as the said policymakers themselves.

To this day, forms of empowerment of (and through) art remain undertheorized, to the benefit of speaking truth TO power, and critical tricksterism, as art's moral horizon. This slippage translates into many things, including awkward positions vis-à-vis positions of power, especially

1   realtynow.online

Satan's Lust Garden — An Introduction to STATISTA
Tirdad Zolghadr

art's very own commissioners, public and private. STATISTA, rather typically for KW and ZK/U, is entirely funded by the Berlin Senate for Culture and Europe. To be publicly funded comes with stipulations and paperwork, but it is also empowering. To name but one example, few of the permits which were eventually granted to STATISTA would have materialized without discreet senatorial backing. As an entirely government-funded operation, the team attempted from the get-go to take its place in the urban cycle of 'Hotspot' value creation more seriously than is commonly the case. It is important to clarify that temporary cultural usage at the HdS 2019 is not 90s flippancy revisited. Instead, it partakes in creating hard facts on the ground, helping to make HdS a political promise that is very difficult to break.

In Berlin specifically, *die Zweckfreiheit der Kunst*—art's freedom from purpose—remains a decisive rallying cry, as jarring as that may seem to many. To propose statecraft as a leitmotif is to break with this tradition, to the best of one's abilities. The German *Staatskunst* offers a pun the English translation is lacking here; meaning both the art of governance, famously discussed by Plato, Machiavelli, Locke, Rousseau, Hegel, Marx and others, but also government-commissioned art. STATISTA is no critique, and harbors no pretense at autonomy—strategic, engaged, quasi-autonomy, or otherwise—it's an attempt to embody a modus operandi firmly embedded within a broader state of affairs, one that consolidates and accelerates the HdS project as it goes along.

Many of the stated objections to STATISTA (and there are many) argued that we were venturing onto toxic historical ground. The HdS postal address, Karl-Marx-Allee 1, they would argue, is cause for caution, not adventurism. In a neighborhood such as this, statecraft is nothing to mess with. Although none of the critics mentioned as much, the roots of left-wing malaise[2] in matters of statecraft are tied to geopolitical stakes that reach well beyond recent urban histories. The suspicions of the progressive left are historically informed by state violence of all possible political stripes, causing staggering numbers of casualties over the course of the 20th century, including in nations well-represented by STATISTA itself (Iran, Palestine, Indonesia, Russia, etc.).

In light of this backdrop, the easy tourism of the artworld becomes a cause for concern, to say the least. The question is whether a political tradition, a cityscape, or a cultural movement can be reclaimed and consolidated by caution alone. What makes the temperament of HdS so encouraging is that it lays claim to a vision for the city itself, not just the Alexanderplatz neighborhood. One that can be contested, but also, in the best of cases, referenced, theorized, and scaled. The HdS is no safe space for grassroots ideas, or niche oasis of self-governance. As a proposal, it hopes to be disseminated and scaled. It represents a coalition of interests tackling the actual infrastructural needs of the city, here and now, as opposed to banking on those needs being covered via a return on private investment at some point in the future.

At the risk of sounding dramatic, STATISTA's wager is that HdS offers a blueprint for a statecraft for future

---

2   I owe the following point to curator Katharina Morawek.

Satan's Lust Garden — An Introduction to STATISTA
Tirdad Zolghadr

occasions. A helpful reference here is theorist Keller Easterling's oft-quoted term 'extrastatecraft'. As a contemporary form of governance, extrastatecraft relies on complex infrastructures that embody multiple agendas, some of them openly declared, only to be indefinitely postponed, some of them surreptitiously active from the get-go. Alexanderplatz offers a rather didactic example, with the declared intentions ('quality of life', 'urban renewal') remaining completely extraneous to the policy's long-term efficacy, and its material effects on the ground. HdS, by contrast, immediately protagonizes unconventional players, and openly allows for synergies of use between them.

For once, in a city where the competition for resources is nothing less than ferocious, refugee shelters are not pitted against social housing and artists' studios. Instead, a situation arises where various agendas can lend each other leverage and legitimacy. Here, the institutionalization process that at times compromises other initiatives will be mitigated by a cohabitation of wildly different usages—social facilities, cultural facilities, social housing, policymaking, technocracy. As described in the essay penned by ZK/U, a large portion of the HdS will be devoted to bureaucracy. (It bears mentioning that a typical obstacle to progressive housing policy is not the law but its implementation and supervision, and Berlin bureaucracy is desperately understaffed and starved of space.)

If artists play an unusually promising role here, the art they bring to the table is at one remove from Contemporary Art in the orthodox sense of the term. Beginning with AbBA itself, alongside the Berlin collectives that authored the work on ➤ p. 78 – p. 120, not to mention the conference invitees from further afield, the collectives featured in this book exemplify what some might term 'speculative' practices. To get things done these practitioners eagerly resort to the devices of Contemporary Art, but they consider these their strategic means, the aesthetico-conceptual tools not the ethical end, of the exercise at hand. And these ethical ends are clarified by openly stated agendas, not submerged in playful opacities. The aim is not to raise critical questions alone, but to venture hypotheses, however tentative, that might be proven wrong. It is to generate knowledge, and working models.

All of which require ambitious time frames, and strength in numbers. It takes team spirit, divisions of labor, collective grit, nerves of steel.

Needless to say, there are few options available for disseminating this kind of speculative work. After half a century of dematerialization, deskilling, and institutional critique, we are still very much married to museums as our 120-year-old gateways to the public. As curator Victoria Ivanova eloquently argues, what is urgently required is not more art infrastructure, doing more of the same in new urban settings, but organizational protocols beyond the show and the catalog, permitting new interfaces with non-traditional partners.

Perhaps it is no coincidence STATISTA unfolded in the shadow of the Bauhaus centenary. A movement which set a lasting benchmark in terms of simultaneously commodifying, institutionalizing, and experimenting with one's own work, this in the interest of both circulation and longevity. For all its shortcomings, the Bauhaus remains a helpful reference for any speculative temperament, and

Satan's Lust Garden — An Introduction to STATISTA
Tirdad Zolghadr

a clear alternative to the critical tricksterism that remains far more common in Contemporary Art today.[3]

STATISTA harnessed its energies to the very cause of HdS. It contributed with artworks that can be refashioned, over time, as rooftop message boards, event platforms, façade designs and more. Its more speculative scenarios embody conceptual pointers for potential use in the near future. Its prerequisite onsite fixtures (electricity, safety, lighting, etc.) are now part of the HdS structure itself. We also opened legal doors, securing permits which proved essential to other usages in turn (see, for example, Making Futures, ► p. 166), and by establishing working relationships with technocrats in key positions.

When it comes to the commissions themselves, although boundaries are never clear-cut, the material contributions, or *Aktionsfelder* ('playing fields'), were focused largely on parameters such as international outreach, local communities, or on research-intensive proposals along biospheric or crypto-experimental lines of inquiry.

The commissions ALLESANDERSPLATZ (► p. 78) and Unser Leben 2020 (► p. 154), but also the conference program (► p. 166 – p. 171) and the documentation room (the STATISTA exhibition showcasing all collectives participating in the conference)—as well as this very book—are all propagandistic attempts to get the word out, to gather kindred spirits in a long-term conversation. Meanwhile, commissions such as Musterhaus (► p. 100) and Voices - first recording (► p. 94) focused primarily on neighborhood interactions. To a large extent, the credibility and legitimacy of HdS depend on anchoring the colossal building within its complex immediate environs. Both Musterhaus and Voices succeeded in mobilizing participation in the shorter term; ongoing efforts are devoted to keeping the newfound momentum alive over years to come.

Other commissions, meanwhile, devised scenarios for making the HdS more sustainable, inclusive, and efficient as a future-oriented endeavor. Two of these—Pigeon Towers (► p. 88) and fallingwild (► p. 84) – addressed the exigencies of interspecies cohabitation. The essay in this publication by founding Labor k3000 member Marion von Osten, demonstrates how ecological intelligence implies not only better techniques of building and planning but also an effort to surpass anthropocentric routines on all levels. (As a case in point, my own history of Alexanderplatz begins at 1400, omitting millennia of marshlands that preceded human settlement.) How to plot scenarios beyond the extractivist forms of modern societal organization?

The Beecoin commission combines the above set of ecological questions with a second strand of speculative inquiry: cryptocurrencies and the distributed ledger technologies known as Blockchain. Matthias Einhoff's contribution 'Berlin and the Blockchain' explains the promise of new tech for a context such as HdS, as exemplified not only by Beecoin but also by STATISTA commissions Ishtar Gate (► p. 157) and STATISTA Coin (► p. 106). At their best,

---

3   See the Yes Men appearances in the mainstream media, or iconic interventions in public space, e.g. the 0100101110101101 collective renaming the Karlsplatz Vienna 'Nikeplatz' in 2003.

Satan's Lust Garden — An Introduction to STATISTA
Tirdad Zolghadr

these experiments represent groundbreaking attempts to render data flows transparent, to redistribute socio-financial capital, and to allow for value creation along criteria determined by respective microeconomic communities themselves.

By way of a clarification of terms, Suhail Malik's contribution to this book is decisive. The piece insists on the necessity of urban development, and painfully reveals the self-interest of artists who consider anti gentrification a sufficient tactic in and of itself. To be fair, radical opposition to any and all forms of redevelopment stems from a long history of broken promises (often in the guise of the extra-statecraft described above). But as Malik argues, to accept urban poverty as it currently stands can only be in the artist's interest, at best. For all the well-documented risks, there are few viable alternatives to programmatic, unapologetic public investment in infrastructure, and a developmental agenda of redistribution, one that is protracted and open-ended enough to reflect the interests of an existing neighborhood constituency.

Finally, another key contribution to STATISTA was a year-long collective research project that materialized as a student blog, hosted on allesandersplatz.berlin. In close collaboration with Stephan Lanz, Professor of Urban Studies at Viadrina University in Frankfurt (Oder), students contributed glossary definitions, interviews, and case studies. Also contributing to the blog were students at the Institut Kunst im Kontext, University of the Arts Berlin, under the auspices of Professor Jörg Heiser. All materials were organized around the idea of *Verstetigung* as artistic practice. The German term corresponds loosely to 'consolidation', 'entrenchment', or 'steadifying'.

The term *Verstetigung* touches on a particularly difficult aspect of the HdS trajectory. For now, with elections looming and the right wing on the rise, the project as currently defined remains a precarious endeavor. However, even when the new institution has finally secured its survival, a new set of problems will arise. Can a dynamic be steaded? How can a colossus like HdS avoid becoming a caricature of itself? The risks of becoming part of the broader problem, over future generations to come, are as obvious as they are inevitable. If we're looking for a project without any such risks involved, we can always curate group exhibitions. As for the HdS experiment, for all the minor miracles and lucky breaks that have brought it this far, some of the biggest risks still lie ahead, just around the corner. Much to look forward to.

The author wishes to thank the HdS Werkstatt for their untiring support. But also Penny Rafferty and Paul Seidler for their patience and composure in the wake of unrelenting complications. Many thanks also to Martin Heller for an enthusiasm and input far beyond his legal remit.

Teufels Lustgarten. Eine Einführung zu STATISTA

Im September 2015, während der *Berlin Art Week*, führte AbBA, die Allianz bedrohter Berliner Atelierhäuser, eine Kunstintervention am Haus der Statistik (HdS) durch. Ein eigens angefertigtes Banner wurde auf der Fassade entrollt und kündigte, zu chorischer Untermalung, die Eröffnung eines neuen öffentlichen Zentrums für vielfältige soziale und kulturelle Zwecke an.

Das Ereignis ist als rein symbolischer Akt zu deuten, da der Abriss des HdS längst beschlossen war. Doch binnen weniger Jahre sollte sich das Ereignis als selbsterfüllende Prophezeiung erweisen. Heute ist das HdS ein einzigartiges Pilotprojekt, das von einem breiten Bündnis Beteiligter im Interesse der städtebaulichen Entwicklung betrieben und gesteuert wird.

Dank AbBA konnten der Verkauf und Abriss des 40.000 Quadratmeter großen Gebäudes verhindert und der baldige Bau eines 65.000 Quadratmeter großen Anbaus durchgesetzt werden. Das Vorhaben bietet Raum für Kunst-, Kultur- und Sozialprojekte, für Bildung und Öffentlichkeitsarbeit, für preiswerten Wohnraum sowie für ein neues Rathaus und Verwaltungsbüros im Bezirk Berlin-Mitte.

Vier Jahre später und abermals zeitgleich mit der *Art Week* steht Kunst erneut auf der Tagesordnung – allerdings nicht als an den Staat gerichtete Provokation, sondern in Form eines Versuchs, die Aufbruchsstimmung 2015 in Form einer Staatskunst der Zukunft zu etablieren. Das Modellprojekt setzt sich für zivile Zusammenarbeit im Interesse des Gemeinwohls ein – weitab der Rivalitäten um die „Creative City"-Pläne. Vielleicht kann Berlin-Mitte genauso attraktiv, unterhaltsam und eindrucksvoll bleiben, wie es heute der Fall ist, ohne dabei zum Fußabtreter für Urlaubsreisende und Immobilieninvestierende zu werden.

Die Besiedlung des heutigen Alexanderplatzes begann um 1400. Als erste staatliche Infrastruktur in der Nachbarschaft wurde ein Galgen errichtet. Deshalb war der Ort, zumindest laut Wikipedia, als „Teufels Lustgarten" bekannt. Auf den Galgen folgten bald Gefängnisse, Gerichtsgebäude, Kasernen und Quarantänestationen. Nachdem der Platz offiziell zunächst den Namen „Königs Thor Platz" erhielt, wurde er anlässlich eines Besuchs von Alexander I. im Jahre 1805 in „Alexanderplatz" umbenannt. Wollte man dem Platz einen brutalen und aristokratischen Genius Loci unterstellen, wäre das durchaus nachvollziehbar, denn schließlich war das HdS, als Sammelstelle für die Erfassung von Daten über die gesamte Bevölkerung der DDR, ein unverhohlenes Instrument staatlicher Überwachung. Nach dem Fall der Mauer führte der Kollhoff-Plan die königliche Tradition der Top-down-Entscheidungen am Alexanderplatz fort – obschon mit völlig anderen staatspolitischen Vorzeichen. Hier geht es um den Versuch, die Berliner Skyline mittels einer Reihe von Hochhäusern zu „manhattanisieren" und dabei alles, was uns die Gentrifizierungsmuster der letzten Jahrzehnte gelehrt haben, in Bausch und Bogen zu ignorieren.

Teufels Lustgarten — Eine Einführung zu STATISTA
Tirdad Zolghadr

Dabei besitzt des Teufels Lustgarten natürlich auch einen anderen Subtext: eine Genealogie der Schwarzmärkte, illegales Bauprojekt, anhaltend überproportionale Kriminalitätsraten, die berühmten bewaffneten Barrikaden von 1848, ganz zu schweigen von den epochalen Massendemonstrationen 1989. Die Lichtseite einer ansonsten eher düsteren Geschichte – auf diese Seite schlagen wir Kulturschaffenden uns immer gern, brennen wir doch darauf, die Stimmen der Entmachteten wiederhallen zu lassen. Denn wenn wir eines sind, dann kritisch. Auf dieses kollektive professionelle Anliegen wollen wir später zurückkommen.

 Während der Ära des Kalten Krieges war Westberlin als isoliertes Leuchtfeuer der Freiheit angepriesen worden, eine Oase der Freigeister, die den Apparatschiks trotzen, die mit ihren Polyesteranzügen grimmig vom HdS herabblickten. Später, während der 1990er Jahre, verwandelte sich diese libertäre Fantasie – Berlin als kreativer Tummelplatz – nicht nur in Beispiele städtebaulicher Grandezza. Vielmehr lebte die Fantasie auch im Grassroots-Impuls weiter, das Beste zu machen aus den unzähligen unbebauten Grundstücken und Veranstaltungsorten, die das Post-Mauer-Berlin zu bieten hatte. Unzählige Kulturschaffende vergossen Blut, Schweiß und Tränen, um sich einen Raum für die Dauer eines Jahres, einer Woche oder einer einzigen Nacht anzueignen, bevor sie kurz darauf den nächsten Raum bezogen. Diese temporäre Nutzung von Berlins breitem Angebot an leer stehenden Räumen machte die Stadt zu einem Hotspot räumlicher Kreativität – ein Ruf und ein Erbe, auf die sie bis heute baut.

 Die 2000er Jahre brachten langsam, aber sicher die Vermutung mit sich, dass es sich bei diesem scheinbar ungesteuerten Pioniergeist womöglich um einen Stadterneuerungsplan mit kolossalen Ausmaßen handelte. Die Frage der systemimmanenten Planung sei dahingestellt, Tatsache ist, dass die temporäre Nutzung begann, ihre eigenen Kinder zu fressen (wie es Berliner Architekt Robert Huber scharfsinnig bemerkt). Bekanntermaßen profitierten von der kulturellen beziehungsweise finanziellen Aufwertung der Kieze nunmehr ausschließlich Privatbesitzende. Die Ortsansässigen und die Kulturschaffenden, die im Laufe der 1990er Jahre das genannte Schweiß-Kapital (*sweat equity*) investiert hatten, gingen leer aus.

 Die KW-Institute für Contemporary Art selbst zählen zu den wenigen Überlebenden des heftigen Ringens um die Gentrifizierung. International ist die KW zur wohl prominentesten Institution in der zeitgenössischen deutschen Kunstlandschaft geworden. Was die Finanzkraft angeht, ist sie ein Zwerg, aber aufgrund ihres soziokulturellen Kapitals haben Lokalpolitiker*innen, die den Standort Berlin erhalten wollen, ein offenes Ohr für sie. Kritische Stimmen sehen darin eine typische Geschichte der Instrumentalisierung und der Institutionalisierung, von Rock 'n' Roll zu Prada. In den Augen ihrer Unterstützenden dagegen haben die KW ein Stück Land davor bewahrt, in einen weiteren Cheesecake-Cappuccino-Albtraum verwandelt zu werden. Dabei werden auch die härtesten Kritiker*innen kaum leugnen, dass die KW ein überwältigendes Beispiel für die Verstetigung mit den Mitteln und Methoden der zeitgenössischen Kunst sind – ein Beispiel, von dem sich viel lernen lässt.

Teufels Lustgarten — Eine Einführung zu STATISTA
Tirdad Zolghadr

Größere Erwartungen an die Institution zu stellen, hieße, die Spielerin für die Spielregeln verantwortlich zu machen. Zwar kann man sehr wohl verlangen, dass die Kunst zu einer Trägerin der nachhaltigen, basisdemokratischen, urbanen Erneuerung werden muss, was jedoch wiederum der Forderung einer vollkommen anderen Produktionsweise gleichkommt. ZK/U geht als Kollektiv seit mehreren Jahren dieser Prämisse in Form neuer kollektiver Infrastrukturen erfolgreich nach. Aus Sicht der KW war STATISTA *die* Gelegenheit für eine Zusammenarbeit mit ZK/U, basierend auf dem REALTY-Programm (kuratiert von Tirdad Zolghadr, in Auftrag der KW und anderen Institutionen), das seinerseits diesem kunstpolitischen Ansatz langfristig folgt.

Berlin hat eine Vielzahl solcher Modelle hervorgebracht, von denen nicht nur Kulturschaffende profitieren – Strukturen, die von der Hoffnung auf Kollektivierung, Umverteilung, Demokratisierung angetrieben werden. Das HdS steht sprichwörtlich auf den Schultern dieser langjährigen lokalen Geschichte, die im Laufe der Jahrzehnte entscheidend zu Berlins offenem, unberechenbarem und unterhaltsamem Charakter beigetragen hat – ungeachtet des bösen Erwachens der letzten Jahre.

Will man dieser Tradition gerecht werden, bedarf es vom Standpunkt der Kunstschaffenden aus mehr als eines bloßen Bekennens zu Geschichten des Widerstands (*speaking truth to power* usw.). Denn die zeitgenössische Kunst genießt schon seit Langem Zugang zu den Schalthebeln der Macht. Innerhalb der oben erwähnten Prozesse der Stadterneuerung, die unsere Städte im Sturm erobern, kommt ihr eine zwar kleine, aber proaktive, vorausschauende und attraktive Rolle zu. All dies macht die kuratorische Solidarität mit den Opfern der Stadtentwicklung zu einer noch gespreizteren Angelegenheit, als sie es ohnehin schon ist. Gerade daher beharre ich im Folgenden auf spekulativen Szenarien, taktischer Hebelkraft und Staatskunst.

Laut Josephine Berry ist die Macht inzwischen „künstlerischer" geworden (*power has become more art-like*). Was nicht bloß bedeutet, dass die Mächtigen die Kunst schätzen, sondern auch, dass sie – wie die zeitgenössische Kunst selbst – mit angeblicher Offenheit, radikaler Anpassungsfähigkeit und einem lauten Anspruch auf Machtlosigkeit agieren. Meist rechtfertigen sich politisch Entscheidungsbefugte, die zu treibenden Kräften des Immobilienmarktes geworden sind, mit der Behauptung, dass uns keine Wahl bleibe, als innerhalb des Standortwettbewerbs intelligente und kritische Akzente zu setzen. Ihrerseits behauptet die zeitgenössische Kunst, jenseits der Macht zu stehen, ihr gegenüber kritisch, bauernschlau und unberechenbar die Wahrheit zu sagen; selbst dann, wenn sie im Dienst derselben Interessengruppen steht wie die offiziellen Verfechter*innen des Standortwettbewerbs. Innerhalb der Kunst mündet dieses machtpolitische Paradox mitunter in die Unmöglichkeit, eine klare Position gegenüber jenen einzunehmen, die uns Aufträge erteilen.

STATISTA wird – wie es auch für die KW und das ZK/U eher typisch ist – vollständig von der öffentlichen Hand finanziert. Obwohl öffentliche Förderungen mit besonderen Bestimmungen und Formalitäten einhergehen, schaffen sie Privilegien, Vorrechte, neue Möglichkeiten. So wären vermutlich, etwa seitens Berliner Denkmalschutz und Kunstkommission, nur wenige der nötigen

Teufels Lustgarten – Eine Einführung zu STATISTA
Tirdad Zolghadr

Genehmigungen erteilt worden, hätte STATISTA nicht den Segen der Berliner Senatsverwaltung für Kultur und Europa genossen.
So war unser gänzlich aus staatlichen Mitteln gefördertes Unternehmen von Anfang an darum bemüht, seinen Platz im urbanen Zyklus der Hotspot-Wertschöpfung ernster zu nehmen, als es sonst üblich ist. STATISTAs Zwischennutzung des HdS sollte an keiner Stelle mit einer Neuauflage der 1990er-Jahre-Frivolität vergleichbar sein. Stattdessen trägt sie vor Ort dazu bei, das HdS zu einem gemeinwohlorientieren Versprechen zu machen, das sich schwerlich brechen lässt.
Wie lässt sich eine solche kuratorische Haltung auch kunsttheoretisch klarstellen? Leider bleibt, gerade in Berlin, die traditionalistische „Zweckfreiheit der Kunst" eine entscheidende Parole – nach wie vor. Staatskunst als Leitmotiv vorzuschlagen, impliziert, mit dieser Tradition nach besten Kräften zu brechen. Der deutsche Begriff Staatskunst bietet hierbei ein Wortspiel, das der englischen Übersetzung (*statecraft*) abgeht: Staatskunst bezeichnet sowohl die Kunst des Regierens, wie sie bekanntermaßen von Platon, Machiavelli, Locke, Rousseau, Hegel, Marx und anderen erörtert wurde, als auch die seitens Regierung in Auftrag gegebene Kunst. STATISTA versteht sich nicht als Kritik und erhebt keinen Anspruch auf Autonomie. Vielmehr versucht STATISTA einen Modus Operandi zu verkörpern, der fest in die äußeren Umstände eingebettet ist und das HdS-Projekt auf dieser Weise realpolitisch konsolidiert, propagiert und beschleunigt.
Einer der am häufigsten erklärten Einwände gegen STATISTA (und es gab derer durchaus viele) lautete, dass wir uns auf toxischem historischen Boden bewegten. Die Postanschrift des HdS, Karl-Marx-Allee 1, solle einen zu Zurückhaltung veranlassen, und nicht zu Spitzfindigkeiten. In einer solchen Nachbarschaft treibe man mit Staatskunst keine Späße. Obgleich keine der skeptischen Stimmen es erwähnte, hängt das linke Unbehagen[1] gegenüber der Staatskunst mit geopolitischen Herausforderungen zusammen, die weit über die jüngeren Stadthistorien hinausgehen. Die Vorbehalte der progressiven Linken werden auch historisch durch den Staatsterrorismus jeglicher politischer Couleur während des 20. Jahrhunderts begründet. Eine Epoche, die unzählige Opfer forderte, mitunter in Staaten, die in STATISTA selbst stark vertreten sind (Iran, Palästina, Indonesien, Russland usw.).
Vor diesem Hintergrund gibt der intellektuelle Tourismus der Kunstwelt großen Anlass zur Sorge. Die Frage ist jedoch, ob eine politische Tradition, eine Stadtlandschaft oder eine Kulturbewegung durch Zurückhaltung zurückgewonnen werden kann. Der Ansatz der HdS-Initiative wirkt als Beispiel ermutigend, weil es einen übermütigen Entwurf für die Stadt geltend macht, nicht bloß für die unmittelbare Nachbarschaft des Alexanderplatzes – ein visionäres Stadtbild, das angefochten, aber auch zitiert, theoretisiert und in größerem Maßstab umgesetzt werden kann. Das HdS ist weder ein *safe space* für gute Ideen noch eine Nische der Selbstverwaltung. Als Vorschlag erhofft es sich, in größerem Maßstab umgesetzt zu werden.

---

1 Folgendes Argument verdanke ich der Kuratorin Katharina Morawek.

Teufels Lustgarten – Eine Einführung zu STATISTA
Tirdad Zolghadr

Auf die Gefahr hin, dramatisch zu klingen, geht STATISTA die Wette ein, dass das HdS ein Modellprojekt für eine zukünftige Form von Staatskunst bietet. Das HdS ist ein Interessenverbund, der die realen infrastrukturellen Bedürfnisse der Stadt hier und jetzt proaktiv angeht, statt darauf zu setzen, dass diese Bedürfnisse irgendwann durch Rückgriff auf Privatinvestitionen erfüllt werden. Der oft zitierte Begriff *extrastatescraft* der Theoretikerin Keller Easterling dient uns zugleich als wichtiger Bezugspunkt und hilfreicher Kontrapunkt, um Staatskunst *tout court* zum Leitmotiv erklären zu können. Als zeitgemäße Form der Realpolitik stützt sich *extrastatescraft* auf komplexe Infrastrukturen, die jeweils mehrere Agenden haben; diese werden zum Teil offen kundgetan und auf unbestimmte Zeit verschoben, während andere von Beginn an im Verborgenen wirken. Der Alexanderplatz bietet ein eher didaktisches Beispiel: Hier bleiben die erklärten Absichten Lebensqualität und Stadterneuerung völlig irrelevant für die langfristige Wirksamkeit der Stadtpolitik und ihre physischen Auswirkungen vor Ort.

Das HdS macht hingegen unkonventionelle Agierende zu politischen Schlüsselfiguren, und ermöglicht auch Nutzungssynergien zwischen ihnen. In einer Stadt, in der mit aller Heftigkeit um Ressourcen gekämpft wird, werden hier Geflüchtetenunterkünfte nicht gegen sozialen Wohnungsbau und Ateliers ausgespielt. Stattdessen entsteht eine Situation, in der unterschiedliche Agenden sich gegenseitig bestärken und legitimieren. (Ein wesentlicher Teil des HdS wird der Berliner Bürokratie gewidmet sein. Diesbezüglich muss erwähnt werden, dass einer fortschrittlichen Wohnungspolitik typischerweise nicht das Gesetz im Wege steht, sondern dessen Umsetzung und Kontrolle – und gerade in Berlin herrscht hochgradiger Personal- und Ressourcenmangel.)

Auch wenn den Kunstschaffenden hier eine vielversprechende Rolle zukommt, fällt die von ihnen eingebrachte Kunst streng genommen nicht mehr unter den Begriff der zeitgenössischen Kunst. Angefangen bei AbBA selbst, über die Berliner STATISTA-Partner*innen bis hin zu den Konferenzteilnehmenden, die in ganz anderen Kontinenten tätig sind: Die in diesem Buch vertretenen Kollektive sind beispielhaft für das, was manche als „spekulative" Praxis bezeichnen würden. Um etwas zu erreichen, greifen sie auf Methoden der zeitgenössischen Kunst zurück, aber sie betrachten diese als strategisches Mittel, als ästhetischkonzeptionelles Werkzeug, nicht als den ethischen Zweck der Übung. Zudem wird der tatsächliche jeweilige Zweck nicht spielerisch verschleiert, sondern als Zielsetzung klar offengelegt. Letztlich geht es nicht bloß darum, kritische Fragen zu stellen, sondern auch um Wissensproduktion, um Vorsätze und um Hypothesen, die falsifiziert werden können. All dies erfordert ehrgeizige Zeitpläne und viele helfende Hände. Es braucht Teamgeist, Arbeitsteilung, kollektiven Schneid und starke Nerven.

Selbstverständlich ist es nicht ganz leicht, sich an dieser Art spekulativer Arbeit zu beteiligen. Nach einem guten Jahrhundert der stetigen konzeptuellen Entmaterialisierung, des *Deskilling* und der Institutionskritik sind wir noch immer an die Museen als unsere Pforten zur Öffentlichkeit gebunden. Wie die Kuratorin Victoria Ivanova treffend argumentiert, mangelt es nicht an Infrastruktur, die an neuen urbanen Settings das immer gleiche Programm bietet,

Teufels Lustgarten — Eine Einführung zu STATISTA
Tirdad Zolghadr

sondern an organisatorischen Protokollen jenseits der Ausstellung und des Katalogs, die neue Schnittstellen zu nicht traditionellen Partnerschaften ermöglichen.

Vielleicht ist es kein Zufall, dass STATISTA im Schatten des Bauhaus-Jubiläums umgesetzt wurde – einer Bewegung, die dauerhaft Maßstäbe hinsichtlich der gleichzeitigen Kommodifizierung, Institutionalisierung und dem Experimentieren mit der eigenen Arbeit gesetzt hat. Trotz aller Mängel bietet das Bauhaus einen verlässlichen Bezugsrahmen für alle spekulativen Ansätze und eine klare Alternative zur Zweck- und Narrenfreiheit, die in der zeitgenössischen Kunst noch immer weit verbreitet ist.[2]

STATISTA hat die eigenen Energien für die Sache des HdS gebündelt, und Kunstwerke beigesteuert, die sich zu Schriftzügen, Veranstaltungsplattformen, Fassadengestaltungen und vielem mehr umfunktionieren lassen. Unsere spekulativeren Szenarien enthalten Anhaltspunkte für mögliche räumliche und finanzielle Nutzungen in naher Zukunft. Und manch eine Onsite-Infrastruktur von STATISTA (Strom, Sicherheit, Beleuchtung usw.) ist nun Bestandteil des HdS-Gebäudes. Darüber hinaus haben wir juristische Türen geöffnet, indem wir Genehmigungen eingeholt haben, die sich als unerlässlich für andere Nutzungen erweisen sollten (siehe z.B. *Making Futures*, ▶ p. 167) und ein Arbeitsverhältnis mit der lokalen Verwaltung aufgebaut haben.

Was die eigentlichen Arbeiten angeht, konzentrierten sich die physischen Beiträge oder Aktionsfelder vor allem auf Parameter wie internationale Sichtbarkeit, lokale Gemeinschaften oder forschungsintensive Vorhaben zu

---

2 Siehe die *Yes-Men*-Auftritte in den Mainstream-Medien oder ikonische Interventionen im öffentlichen Raum, beispielsweise die kollektive Umbenennung des Wiener Karlsplatzes zu „Nikeplatz" durch das Kollektiv 0100101110101101 im Jahr 2003.

1
STATISTA conference as seen from rear HdS courtyard / Blick auf die STATISTA-Konferenz vom Innenhof aus

ökologischen beziehungsweise krypto-experimentellen Fragestellungen.

Die Arbeiten *ALLESANDERSPLATZ* (► p. 80) und *Unser Leben 2020* (► p. 156), aber auch das Konferenzprogramm (► p. 167) und der Dokumentationsraum (im STATISTA-Dokumentationsraum wurden Arbeiten aller Konferenzteilnehmenden ausgestellt) – ebenso wie dieses Buch – sind semi-propagandistische Versuche, die HdS-Nachricht zu verbreiten und einen langfristigen Dialog mit Gleichgesinnten aufzunehmen.

Unterdessen konzentrierten sich Arbeiten wie *Musterhaus* (► p. 102) und *Voices. Stimmen – first recording* (► p. 96) vor allem auf Interaktionen mit der Nachbarschaft. Die Glaubwürdigkeit des HdS ist darauf angewiesen, dass das kolossale Gebäude in seiner komplexen unmittelbaren Umgebung verankert wird. Während es den Beiträgen *Musterhaus* und *Voices* sehr wohl gelungen ist, eine stadtweite Partizipation zu erwirken, zielen langfristige Bemühungen inzwischen darauf ab, diese Dynamik in den kommenden Jahren aufrechtzuerhalten.

Indessen veranschaulichen andere Arbeiten, wie sich das HdS als zukunftsorientiertes Unterfangen nachhaltiger, inklusiver und effizienter gestalten lässt. Zwei dieser Arbeiten – *Taubentürme* (► p. 90) und *fallingwild* (► p. 85) – thematisieren die Anforderungen des Zusammenlebens verschiedener Spezies. Der Aufsatz der Labor-k3000-Mitbegründerin Marion von Osten demonstriert, inwiefern ökologische Intelligenz nicht nur bessere Bau- und Planungstechniken impliziert, sondern auch den Versuch, anthropozentrische Strukturen auf allen Ebenen zu überwinden. (Meine Geschichte des Alexanderplatzes setzt beispielsweise im Jahr 1400 an und lässt die Jahrtausende aus, die von Sumpflandschaften geprägt waren und der menschlichen Besiedlung vorausgingen.) Wie lassen sich gesellschaftliche Zukunftsszenarien jenseits extraktivistischer Formen der modernen Organisation entwerfen?

Die Arbeit Beecoin kombiniert die oben aufgeführten ökologischen Fragestellungen mit einem zweiten thematischen Strang: Kryptowährungen und *Distributed-Ledger*-Technologien, die allgemein als Blockchain bekannt sind. In seinem Beitrag erörtert Matthias Einhoff am Beispiel von *Beecoin* und den STATISTA-Arbeiten *Ishtar Gate* (► p. 160) und *STATISTA Coin* (► p. 108), welche Bedeutung neue Technologien für einen Kontext wie das HdS haben. Es handelt sich hier um Versuche, Datenflüsse transparent zu machen, soziales Kapital umzuverteilen und Wertschöpfung nach Kriterien zu ermöglichen, die von den jeweiligen mikroökonomischen Gemeinschaften selbst festgelegt werden.

Suhail Maliks Begriffsbestimmungen sind ein entscheidender Beitrag zu diesem Buch. Mit seinem Essay insistiert er auf der Notwendigkeit einer „linken Stadtentwicklung" und führt uns schmerzlich das Eigeninteresse von Kunstschaffenden vor Augen, die die Anti-Gentrifizierung an sich als effiziente Strategie betrachten. Natürlich geht der radikale Widerstand gegen jedwede Form der baulichen Neuentwicklung auf eine langjährige Geschichte gebrochener Versprechen zurück (oftmals in Form der oben beschriebenen *extrastatecraft*). Doch laut Malik ist es bestenfalls im Interesse der Kunstschaffenden, die gegenwärtige strukturelle Armut in den Städten hinzunehmen. Trotz der gut dokumentierten Risiken, die diese bergen, gibt

Teufels Lustgarten — Eine Einführung zu STATISTA
Tirdad Zolghadr

es nur wenige tragfähige Alternativen zu programmatischen öffentlichen Investitionen in die Infrastruktur, und auch keine Entwicklungsagenda der Umverteilung, die vorausschauend und offen genug ist, um die Interessen einer bestehenden Nachbarschaft widerzuspiegeln.

Ein weiterer wichtiger Beitrag zu STATISTA ist ein einjähriges kollektives Forschungsprojekt in Form eines Studierendenblogs, der auf allesandersplatz.berlin gehosted wurde. In enger Zusammenarbeit mit Stephan Lanz, Professor für Urban Studies an der Europa-Universität Viadrina in Frankfurt (Oder), trugen die Studierenden Glossardefinitionen, Interviews und Fallstudien bei. Auch Studierende des Instituts für Kunst im Kontext der Universität der Künste in Berlin unter der Leitung von Professor Jörg Heiser trugen zu dem Blog bei. Im Zentrum der Beiträge stand die Formel der „Verstetigung als künstlerische Praxis". Der Begriff Verstetigung tangiert einen schwierigen Aspekt der Zukunft des HdS. Angesichts der bevorstehenden Wahlen und des zunehmenden Rechtsdrucks bleibt das Projekt ein prekäres Unterfangen. Hat eine Institution ihr eigenes Überleben jedoch gesichert, entsteht eine Reihe neuer Fragestellungen. Lässt sich eine Dynamik verstetigen? Wie lässt sich vermeiden, dass ein Koloss wie das HdS zu einer Karikatur seiner selbst wird?

Das Risiko, im Laufe der kommenden Generationen zu einem Teil des Problems zu werden, ist unvermeidlich. Sollten wir ein Projekt vorziehen, das keine solchen Risiken birgt, steht es uns jederzeit frei, Gruppenausstellungen zu kuratieren und dabei die Keule der radikalen Kritik zu schwingen. Was das HdS-Experiment betrifft, so stehen trotz all der kleinen Wunder und Glücksfälle, die zum Erfolg des Projekts beigetragen haben, einige der größten Risiken unmittelbar bevor.

Der Autor dankt der HdS-Werkstatt für ihre Unterstützung. Aber auch Penny Rafferty & Paul Seidler für ihre Fassung und ihre Geduld, angesichts den schier unendlichen Komplikationen. Zudem tausend Dank an Martin Heller für den enthusiastischen Input, der weit über jegliche legalen Verpflichtungen hinausging.

Haus der Stadtistik
Harry Sachs, Philip Horst

Haus der Stadtistik – A Chronological Scenario

1968–2008: Prologue
From 1970 on, technocrats at the Haus der Statistik (HdS) analyzed all available data on everyday life under socialism, drawing up five-year plans for the German Democratic Republic's centralized command economy. Propaganda experts then glossed the data and the state-controlled TV newscast *Aktuelle Kamera* presented it monthly, not least in order to demonstrate the superiority of an anti-capitalist form of society. Other data analysts in the high-rise ensemble at the corner of Otto-Braun-Straße and Karl-Marx-Allee worked on behalf of the 'Stasi,' East Germany's secret police or Ministry for State Security (MfS). Following German reunification in 1990, a branch of the Federal Republic of Germany's statistics office, Destatis, moved into the building, followed by the BStU or 'Stasi archive,' under successive directors Joachim Gauck (the future Federal President) and Marianne Birthler.

From 2008 on, the building stood vacant, and was carefully combed and stripped bare by scroungers and thieves. It also proved very popular as an adventure playground, emergency shelter, and pigeon loft. By and by, a development plan was drawn up, which foresaw the demolition of the entire ensemble, and sale of the site to the highest bidder. Progress was slow, however, and had the HdS not been jointly owned by the federal government and the State of Berlin at the time, it probably would have long since been torn down and disappeared.

2015: The Initiative
On 16.9.2015, during Art Week, the 'Berlin Alliance of Artists' Studios Under Threat' (AbBA) unfurled a huge banner on the façade. 'Coming Soon: spaces for art, social needs and cultural facilities' it announced, along with an ambiguously phrased claim that could be read as 'demanded of" or 'funded by' the State of Berlin, the Federal Republic of Germany, and the European Union ('*Gefordert von Land Berlin, Bundesrepublik Deutschland, Europäische Union*').

The press and other visitors were invited to attend. Following an official speech, and some orchestrated, performative chanting, the state authorities realized that the action was a stunt, so the State Office of Criminal Prosecutions (State Security Department) pressed charges, and had the banner removed the following day. Happily, the prosecuting attorney dropped the charges some months later.

Independent artist studios and groupings had all decided to join forces on account of the increasing risk of eviction at the hands of profit-hungry speculators. For many years now, all over the city, leases are being terminated, and vital cultural infrastructure is disappearing fast, without any adequate alternatives being put in place.

The ZK/U, which evolved from the longstanding collective studio project 'Köpi36–ExBau Ateliergemeinschaft,' is a founding member of the AbBA alliance, and actively participated in the intervention. Immediately

Haus der Stadtistik
Harry Sachs, Philip Horst

1
HdS construction works 1969 / HdS Bauarbeiten 1969

2
HdS Foyer ca. 1970

Haus der Stadtistik
Harry Sachs, Philip Horst

following the hugely successful media splash, the ZK/U also played host as a venue to the founding of the HdS Initiative. A concept was collectively hammered out, politicians were lobbied, and only two months later, in December 2015, a press conference was held, whereupon the Berlin-Mitte district administration (BVV) passed a resolution—with broad support from all parties—to put the plan into action, and to seek the support of the Berlin Senate.

From early 2016 on, the first major 'networking councils' (*Vernetzungsratschläge* or brainstorming sessions), were held at the ZK/U, attracting hundreds of representatives from associations, initiatives, and institutions all over the city. This strong (and, to this day, sustained) level of interest speaks volumes about the urgent need for space and collective action on urban development issues. A broad campaign was launched, the Initiative grew, and funding applications were made for various educational and artistic projects. In parallel, since the aim was to win the Berlin Senator of Finance's support, and prevent the proposed sale of the HdS to the highest bidder, the Initiative's core group set up a legal entity that would be able to purchase and manage the building. In April, the most active coalition partners founded a registered, not-for-profit umbrella organization, 'ZUsammenKUNFT Berlin eG"[1]—a Cooperative for Urban Development, which serves as the legal representative of the grassroots HdS Initiative. The Cooperative will also be at the disposition of future Berlin initiatives, as a partner in developing real estate for the common good.

In Summer 2016, two more pilot projects joined the fray. The 'ZUsammenKUNFT Academy' was founded primarily to network with other players in the arts, the goal being to work not in parallel with one another, but together, on joint projects, events, and workshops. The Academy aimed to attract any independent artists, new Berliners, university seminar groups, initiatives, and associations with a declared interest in issues such as refugee rights, migration society, urban development, integrative housing schemes, education, and the arts. It invited them to share questions, insights, and working knowledge pertaining to public space, at the HdS as well as neighboring venues.

'ZUsammenKUNFT' (2015–19) was located across two penthouse floors of an emergency refugee shelter, located near Berlin's Parliament, where cultural and social initiatives, artist collectives, and NGOs spent four years exploring how to put into practice their ideas of 'inclusionary and solidary coexistence' with refugee 'new Berliners.' These activities fostered a lively exchange, also pertaining to future societal scenarios, between the building's users and civil society at large. Beyond providing emergency accommodation, ZUsammenKUNFT enabled a large group of participants to engage at length in learning from one another, and to identify issues that are crucial to any successful mix of different constituencies. The initiative was a prime example of what a 'project of the people, for the people' can be, and sought to anchor its experience of diversity and inclusion in longer-term urban development projects.

---

1   The name combines the German words for 'the future' and 'together.'

Haus der Stadtistik
Harry Sachs, Philip Horst

From 2018 on: Cooperation
Beginning in 2018, the campaign further evolved as a commons-oriented model of co-produced urban development. The concept proposed by the HdS Initiative was mentioned in the coalition agreement of the ruling Red-Red-Green Berlin Senate. In late 2017, the State of Berlin had already bought the HdS building from the Bundesanstalt für Immobilienaufgaben (BImA; Institute for Federal Real Estate), thus paving the way for the implementation of the community-oriented project. It was agreed that the existing surface area, plus a 65,000 m² new-build, would accommodate art, culture, social facilities, education, and affordable housing, as well as a new district city hall for Mitte and other administrative functions. Lending great significance to the slogans on the banner unfurled in 2015: 'demanded of' truly was becoming a case of 'funded by....'

To consolidate this success, a new organizing principle was needed. Since January 2018, under the name 'Koop5,' five cooperation partners have been working side by side to develop the HdS: the Senate for Urban Development and Housing, the Berlin-Mitte district administration, the real estate agencies WBM Wohnungsbaugesellschaft Berlin-Mitte mbH and BIM Berliner Immobilienmanagement GmbH (both owned by the State of Berlin), and ZUsammenKUNFT Berlin eG.

To acquire planning permission for the new buildings, an urban development workshop tailored precisely to the needs of the project was held regularly from September 2018 until February 2019. The draft development proposal, maximizing the input on behalf of civil society, foresees the following:

Berlin-Mitte is to build its new district city hall in a high-rise on the site of the former computer center. Existing buildings are to be allotted largely to the BIM and the Mitte district tax office, and 20 percent—mostly ground level spaces and Haus A (Karl-Marx-Allee 1)—to the HdS Initiative. Several new buildings, with a total floor area of ca. 50,000 m², are planned for the vacant lot to the rear of the ensemble. The WBM is to build *several* seven-story blocks and one fifteen-story high-rise comprising 300 affordable apartments overall, to be completed by 2024. A total footprint of ca. 15,000 m², housed in two experimental new-builds, and possibly in sections of the WBM buildings, is earmarked for the Initiative's purposes.

The planning process continues to this day. Under the aegis of Koop5, all the ground level spaces have been devoted to the first so-called 'pioneer uses.' These are developing on a small scale what are later to become the defining features of the neighborhood. Research into collective formats, cooperative issue clusters, leisure facilities, alternative operating systems, and circular solidary economies is underway, and feeds directly into the ongoing planning process. Reflection, further development, and education and outreach in all disciplines remain the major challenges being handled daily by the ZUsammenKUNFT eG.

Various legal instruments were also brought into play, in order to consolidate the long-term collective usage that is at the heart of the HdS. Firstly, a comprehensive Quarter Charta, which continues to be discussed and amended, serves as a constitution governing the tenets of the neighborhood and its users. The approved development plan stipulates not only actual construction and infrastructure, but also the proposed commons-oriented uses thereof. The latter are more closely defined in respective urban development contracts. The new buildings are to be leased in perpetuity for specific uses. For the already existing buildings, a general rental agreement is drafted for the maximum period possible (currently thirty years); and its signatory, a not-for-profit association that is yet to be founded, will be legally liable for management of the attendant infrastructure. Above all, transparency and public accountability, the main 'capital' or 'floating assets' of the HdS, will serve as a blanket guarantee for the stability and constancy of the Initiative's ideals.

2030: Vision and Potential
Since *nomen est omen*, the ZK/U Center for Art and Urbanistics saw fit to turn the name Haus der Statistik into Haus der '*Stadtistik*' (or the House of Urbanistics): a grassroots venue that works bottom-up, at the interface of city and society. A social laboratory where issues are identified, reflected on, negotiated, and constantly questioned in light of current developments. The HdS is a place for lively discussion, for local practice in combination with global discourse, a place forged by the community, for the community: for transdisciplinary players who work for the common good, assembling at a single site a spectrum of community-oriented projects, with as many overlaps and intersections as possible. From art and culture to education, from social projects to inclusive housing, from nutrition to the climate, in endless variations, together with temporary initiatives as well as established institutions. Spatial interfaces are designed as hybrid formats, and widely shared, by experimental means, and in multiple 'languages.' Open participatory formats enable the public to become active co-producers themselves.

In association with the administrative partners, multiple surplus values are generated, along with new forms of governance, such as Public Civil Partnerships for civil society, policymaking, and administration. The Berlin-Mitte tax office, which happens to be a neighbor at the site, proves an interesting partner. How to identify potential added values, how to define which tax cycles or funding mechanisms might best facilitate sustainable production? Since development here is geared toward the needs of the local community—indeed, it has been in community hands from the start—the rise in living standards benefits the actual users of the new HdS and its surroundings, and not only a handful of investors and property magnates, as is generally the case. Non-monetary values are created and secured, and a pioneering legal framework is put in place to link net value added in the HdS to its users, whereby the users themselves become a prototypical part of the improved quality of life, yet without being squeezed out. The Quarter Charta effectively steers the 'market forces' inherent to capitalism, so as to facilitate an 'AltogetherDifferentSquare'': a place of innovation, inclusion, and circular solidarity, and hence a model for the city of tomorrow.

The HdS is being discussed and further developed worldwide, in various contexts, as a model of sustainable urban development and inclusionary culture: 'inclusive production of space' with maximal cooperation as an economic alternative to the inflationary market for 'exclusive space production.' It operates as a collectively authored

Haus der Stadtistik
Harry Sachs, Philip Horst

'production strip,' and thus as a contrast to the Alexanderplatz opposite, with its privately curated 'consumerism strip.' The 'Alexanderplatz Master Plan' (1991) is redrawn as the 'AltogetherDifferentSquare Plan' (2025): vital social needs are acknowledged, and integrated within a dynamic blueprint for land-use. Inclusion and diversity are comprehensively assured, at all levels of representation, and become visible also in urban development terms. Socially relevant infrastructure programs are defined as construction tasks, statistically scaled, and projected onto future new buildings.

From its bottom-up grassroots aspirations to the experimental prototypes of the pioneering phase, art at the HdS is attuned to the material realities of the architectural ensemble. The initial artistic gesture thus becomes a state-supporting pillar for an entire new neighborhood: art becomes statecraft, and the art of state(-making) comes into focus as a new artistic discipline. After long years of critical discourse comes the co-productive synthesis. The state, in other words, is investing in the development of effective artistic models. Art production takes on responsibilities and is regarded as a relevant social laboratory. From the fragments of the Haus der Statistik as 'real estate,' there emerges a cooperative 're-state": a place where the art of statecraft is tried and tested, hands-on, and where best practice models propel the long-term evolution of the state apparatus itself.

Haus der Stadtistik. Chronologisches Szenario

1968 — 2008: Prolog

Im Haus der Statistik (HdS) analysieren ab 1970 Mathematiker*innen sämtliche verfügbaren Daten des sozialistischen Alltags, um unter anderem die mehrjährigen Wirtschaftspläne der DDR zu erarbeiten. Propagandafachleute verarbeiteten die Zahlen zu Meldungen, die monatlich in der *Aktuellen Kamera* verlesen werden und die Überlegenheit des antikapitalistischen Gesellschaftssystems belegen sollen. Auch Auswertungsoffizier*innen der Stasi sitzen in dem neun- bis elfgeschossigen Gebäude an der Ecke Otto-Braun-Straße/Karl-Marx-Allee. Nach der Wende ist eine Außenstelle der Bundesbehörde für Statistik in Teilen des Gebäudes angesiedelt sowie die Stasiunterlagenbehörde mit ihren damaligen Leitenden Joachim Gauck (späterer Bundespräsident) und Marianne Birthler.

Ab 2008 steht das Gebäude komplett leer und wird von Materialdieb*innen minutiös durchkämmt und zerlegt. Als Abenteuerspielplatz, Notunterkunft und Taubenschlag erfährt der Gebäudekomplex große Beliebtheit. In der Folgezeit wird ein Bebauungsplan erarbeitet mit dem Ziel, das Gebäude abzureißen und an die höchstbietende Person zu verkaufen. Der Prozess ist langwierig und die geteilten Eigentumsverhältnisse zwischen Bund und Land sind wahrscheinlich der wesentliche Hintergrund, warum der Gebäudekomplex seinerzeit nicht schon lange abgerissen ist und meistbietend vermarktet wird.

2015: Initiative

Die Allianz bedrohter Berliner Atelierhäuser (AbBA) hängt flankierend zur *Art Week* am 16. September 2015 ein doppeldeutiges großformatiges Werbebanner an die Fassade mit der Botschaft: „Hier entstehen für Berlin Räume für Kunst, Kultur und Soziales. *Gefordert* von Land Berlin, Bundesrepublik Deutschland, Europäische Union".

Presse und Besucher*innen werden eingeladen. Nach offizieller Rede und performativem Sprechchor entdeckt die Staatsmacht den Fake, es folgen eine Anzeige durch das Landeskriminalamt (Abteilung Staatsschutz) und ein Abhängen des Banners am nächsten Tag. Das folgende Strafverfahren wird Monate später von der Staatsanwaltschaft eingestellt. Das ZK/U unterstützt die Aktion aktiv und ist mit seinem alten Atelierhaus (Köpi36 – ExBau Ateliergemeinschaft) Gründungsmitglied und Ideengeber für die Aktion. Seit Jahren sind viele freie Berliner Atelierhäuser unter Verwertungsdruck und haben sich daher in der Allianz vernetzt. Reihenweise werden Verträge gekündigt und wichtige kulturelle Infrastruktur verschwindet ohne adäquate Alternativen.

Der medial sehr erfolgreichen Aktion folgt im direkten Anschluss die Gründung der Initiative HdS im ZK/U. Ein Konzept wird kollektiv erarbeitet, die Politik wird adressiert und zwei Monate später findet im Dezember 2015 eine Pressekonferenz statt, woraufhin die Bezirksverordnetenversammlung (BVV Mitte) einen Beschluss zur

Haus der Stadtistik
Harry Sachs, Philip Horst

Umsetzung des Konzepts mit der Unterstützung aller bezirklichen Parteien fasst und an den Senat weiterreicht.

In der Folge finden ab 2016 erste große Vernetzungsratschläge im ZK/U statt, es kommen Hunderte Interessierte aus Vereinen, Initiativen und Institutionen der ganzen Stadt. Dieses starke Interesse verleiht dem Bedarf an Raum und gemeinsamem Handeln im Sinne einer anderen Stadtentwicklung Ausdruck. Eine breite Kampagne wird gestartet und die Initiative wächst. Aus dem Bündnis entstehen Förderanträge für Bildungs- und Kunstprojekte. Zeitgleich entwickelt die Kerngruppe des Bündnisses eine Rechtskonstruktion für Kauf und Bewirtschaftung des Objekts – mit dem Ziel, den Berliner Finanzsenator für das Vorhaben zu gewinnen und den geplanten Verkauf abzuwenden. Im April konstituieren sich die aktivsten Bündnispartner*innen unter dem Dach einer Genossenschaft: ZUsammenKUNFT Berlin eG – Genossenschaft für Stadtentwicklung. Diese soll als Werkzeug der Initiative dienen und soll auch künftigen Berliner Initiativen als Partnerin für die Entwicklung von gemeinwohlorientierten Immobilien zur Verfügung stehen.

Im Sommer 2016 beginnen zwei Pilotprojekte zur weiteren Konkretisierung der Vision: Die Akademie der ZUsammenKUNFT will die Vernetzung vor allem künstlerisch Tätiger betreiben, um nicht nur *nebeneinander* zu arbeiten, sondern auch etwas *gemeinsam* in Projekten, Veranstaltungen oder Workshops zu schaffen. Die Plattform richtet sich an Kunstschaffende der freien Szene, Neu- und Alt-Berliner*innen, universitäre Seminargruppen, Initiativen und Vereine, die sich mit den Themen Flucht beziehungsweise Migrationsgesellschaft, Stadtentwicklung, integratives Wohnen oder Bildung und Kunst beschäftigen. Diese werden eingeladen, ihre Fragen und Kenntnisse im öffentlichen Raum und in benachbarten Einrichtungen des HdS zu vermitteln.

Im Rahmen des Modellprojekts ZUsammenKUNFT wird auf zwei Penthouse-Etagen einer Erstunterkunft für Geflüchtete nahe des Berliner Abgeordnetenhauses das inklusive solidarische Miteinander von kulturellen und sozialen Projekten, Initiativen, Kunstkollektiven und NGOs mit geflüchteten Neu-Berliner*innen vier Jahre lang erprobt. Es entstehen Aktivitäten, die den wechselseitigen Austausch der neuen und alten Gebäudebewohnerschaft sowie der Stadtgesellschaft fördern und einen Blick in die gesellschaftliche Zukunft erlauben: Jenseits der reinen Notunterkunft entfaltet sich in der ZUsammenKUNFT ein aktiver Prozess, in dem alle Beteiligte voneinander lernen und somit die Punkte einer gelingenden Inklusion ausgemacht werden können.

Die Initiative erarbeitet exemplarisch, was ein Projekt von Vielen für Viele bedeutet und versucht programmatische Inhalte, Diversität und Inklusion stadtplanerisch langfristig zu sichern.

Ab 2018: Kooperation

Aus der Kampagne wird ab 2018 ein gemeinwohlorientiertes Modellprojekt ko-produzierter Stadtentwicklung. Der Impuls der Initiative wird im Koalitionsvertrag der rot-rot-grünen Regierung Berlins aufgegriffen. Um das Modellprojekt zu realisieren wird das Gebäude Ende 2017 durch das Land Berlin von der Bundesanstalt für Immobilienaufgaben (BImA) erworben. Damit wird der Weg für eine

Haus der Stadtistik
Harry Sachs, Philip Horst

gemeinwohlorientierte Entwicklung auf dem Areal frei. Im Bestand und durch ca. 65.000 Quadratmeter Neubau entstehen Raum für Kunst, Kultur, Soziales und Bildung, bezahlbares Wohnen sowie ein neues Rathaus für Mitte und Verwaltungsnutzungen. Das Werbebanner von 2015 wird in ausdifferenzierter Form zum Leitbild erklärt, aus der Proklamation „gefordert von ..." wird faktisch ein „gefördert von ...".

Um dieses Ziel zu erreichen, wird eine neuartige Konstellation von Akteur*innen geschlossen. Die fünf Kooperationspartner*innen (Koop5) – Senatsverwaltung für Stadtentwicklung und Wohnen, das Bezirksamt Berlin-Mitte, die landeseigenen Gesellschaften Wohnungsbaugesellschaft Berlin-Mitte (WBM) und Berliner Immobilienmanagemetn (BIM) sowie die ZUsammenKUNFT Berlin eG als Werkzeug der Initiative – arbeiten seit Januar 2018 in gemeinsamer Verantwortung auf Augenhöhe an der Entwicklung des HdS.

Zur Schaffung des für die Neubauten benötigten Planungsrechts läuft von September 2018 bis Februar 2019 ein eigens dafür konzipiertes städtebauliches Werkstattverfahren. Der unter maximaler Mitwirkung der Stadtgesellschaft entwickelte Bebauungsplanentwurf sieht folgendes Nutzungskonzept vor: Auf der Fläche des ehemaligen Rechenzentrums baut das Bezirksamt sein neues Rathaus. In die Bestandsbauten ziehen als Verwaltungsnutzende das Finanzamt und die BIM sowie zu 20 Prozent Nutzungen der Initiative, konzentriert auf die Erdgeschosse und das Haus A (Karl-Marx-Allee 1).

Auf der Freifläche hinter dem Gebäudekomplex sind mehrere Neubauten mit insgesamt ca. 50.000 Quadratmeter Bruttogeschossfläche geplant. Die WBM errichtet in ihrem Programm günstigen sozialen Wohnungsbau mit siebengeschossigen Wohnhäusern und einem 15-geschossigen Wohnturm für insgesamt rund 300 Wohnungen. 2024 sollen die Wohnhäuser fertig sein.

Für die Nutzungen der Initiative entstehen zwei Experimentierhäuser sowie möglicherweise Teilflächen in den WBM-Gebäuden von insgesamt ca 15.000 Quadratmetern.

Der folgende mehrjährige Planungsprozess wird ergänzt durch eine innovative Praxisebene. Alle Erdgeschosse werden unter Federführung der Genossenschaft mit ersten sogenannten Pioniernutzungen belegt. Diese erarbeiten im Kleinen, was das spätere Quartier im Großen ausmachen soll. Gemeinschaftsformate, kooperative Themencluster, aktive Freiraumkonzepte, alternative Betriebssysteme und zirkuläre solidarische Ökonomien werden erforscht und fließen direkt in den laufenden Planungsprozess ein. Reflexion, Weiterentwicklung und Vermittlung in alle Fachrichtungen werden zentrale Herausforderungen der ZUsammenKUNFT eG.

Die langfristige Sicherung des Nutzungskonzepts ist elementar für das HdS und soll über verschiedene rechtliche Konstruktionen stattfinden. Zum einen ist da eine vollumfängliche Quartiers-Charta, welche laufend fortgeschrieben wird und wie eine Verfassung die Grundzüge des Quartiers und der dort Agierenden regelt. Im festgesetzten Bebauungsplan werden neben dem Städtebau auch die integrierten gemeinnützigen Nutzungen festgelegt, sowie gegebenenfalls über städtebauliche Verträge ergänzt. Im Neubau werden Erbbaurechte vergeben, mit eindeutig

Haus der Stadtistik
Harry Sachs, Philip Horst

AbBA banner in use during 2015 intervention / AbBa-Banner im Rahmen der Intervention 2015

definierten Nutzungen. Im Bestand wird ein Generalmietvertrag mit maximaler Laufzeit erstellt (aktuell 30 Jahre), der über eine noch zu gründende gemeinnützige Gesellschaft, als Trägerin des komplexen städtischen Bedarfsprogramms, gezeichnet wird. Über allem schwebt das einzige „Kapital" der Initiative: Transparenz und öffentliche Sichtbarkeit als Garanten für die Stabilität und langfristige Sicherung der Ideale der Initiative.

2030: Vision und Potenzial
Im Sinne des ZK/U-Begriffspaares Kunst & Urbanistik wird das Haus der Statistik zum Haus der Stadtistik transformiert. Es arbeitet als Bottom-up-Produktions- und Diskursort im Bereich der Schnittmenge von Stadt und Gesellschaft. Es werden Fragen erarbeitet, reflektiert, verhandelt und in einer Art Gesellschaftslabor fortwährend in der Praxis hinterfragt. Das HdS ist Ort aktiver Produktion und Diskussion – gelebte lokale Praxis mit globalem Diskurs. Ein Ort von Vielen für Viele: hybride kooperative Formationen transdisziplinärer zivilgesellschaftlicher Akteur*innen, die das Spektrum des Gemeinwohls/Gemeinbedarfs mit größtmöglichen Schnittmengen vor Ort versammeln; Kunst und Kultur, Bildung, Soziales, inklusives Wohnen, Ernährung und Klima in unterschiedlichen Ausprägungen, mit temporären Initiativen und festen institutionellen Trägerschaften. Räumliche und kommunikative Schnittstellen sind als hybride Formate angelegt und werden experimentell und „vielsprachig" vermittelt. Über Veranstaltungen und Beteiligungsformate können sich Stadtgesellschaft und Nachbarschaft in die Prozesse einklinken und selbst aktive Produzentinnen werden.

Im Verbund mit kooperativen Verwaltungsnutzungen im HdS-Quartier entstehen multiple Mehrwerte und neue Governance-Formen von Public Civil Partnerships für Stadtgesellschaft, Politik und Verwaltung. Das Finanzamt als zufälliger Nachbar im Quartier wird interessanter Partner bei der Frage, welche gesellschaftlichen Wertschöpfungen identifiziert werden könnten und welche Steuerkreisläufe und Fördersysteme nachhaltige gesellschaftliche Produktivkräfte freimachen. Wertschöpfungen der Quartiersentwicklung sind von gesellschaftlichem Bedarf und gesellschaftlicher Relevanz gesteuert, Aufwertung findet statt für die *vielen* aktiven Nutzer*innen des Quartiers und seiner Nachbarschaft, und nicht wie sonst, ausschließlich für die *wenigen* Investierenden und Eigentümer*innen. Nicht-monetäre Werte werden geschaffen und gesichert, die Wertschöpfung des Quartiers wird über ein modellhaftes juristisches Verfahren an die Nutzer gebunden, sodass diese Nutzerschaft prototypischer Teil der Aufwertung wird, ohne nachfolgende Verdrängung. Die kapitalbasierten marktimmanenten Kräfte werden durch eine Quartiers-Charta produktiv umgelenkt und ermöglichen einen *Allesandersplatz* als Ort innovativer, auf Inklusion basierender, zirkulärer Solidarmodelle für die Stadt von morgen.

Das HdS-Quartier wird als Modell für nachhaltige Urbanisierung und Inklusionskultur weltweit in unterschiedlichen Kontexten weiterentwickelt: *inklusive* Raumproduktion mit maximaler Kooperation als ökonomisches Gegenmodell zum inflationären Markt der *exklusiven* Raumproduktion. Das Quartier operiert als gemeinschaftlich kuratierte Produktionsmeile komplementär zum benachbarten Alexanderplatz, der in seiner Grammatik bestenfalls eine kuratierte Konsummeile mit exklusiven Konsumtempeln darstellt. Aus dem *Masterplan Alexanderplatz* (1991) wird der *Masterplan Allesandersplatz* (2025): Wichtige gesellschaftliche Bedürfnisse werden erkannt und in einen dynamischen Stadtentwicklungsplan integriert. Inklusion und vollumfängliche Diversität sind Teil der Repräsentationsebene und damit auch städtebaulich im Zentrum unserer Städte sichtbar. Gesellschaftlich relevante Bedarfsprogramme werden als bauliche Auflagen definiert, statistisch skaliert und auf zukünftige Neubauten projiziert.

Der Kunst am HdS, von der Bottom-up-Behauptung bis zu den experimentellen Prototypen der Pionierphase, folgt die gebaute Realität des HdS. Damit wird die initiierende künstlerische Geste zur staatstragenden Säule eines ganzen Quartiers: Kunst wird zur Staatskunst, und die Kunst des Staat(machen) erscheint als neue künstlerische Disziplin. Dem jahrelangen kritischen Diskurs folgt die ko-produktive Synthese. Der Staat investiert in der Folge in die Entwicklung künstlerisch-gesellschaftlich wirksamer Projekte und Modelle. Kunstproduktion übernimmt Verantwortung und wird als relevantes Gesellschaftslabor begriffen. Aus den Fragmenten des „Real Estate" HdS entsteht ein kooperativer „Re-State": ein Ort an dem die Kunst des Staats *hands-on* erprobt wird und langfristig über Best-Practice-Modelle den Staatsapparat evolutioniert.

[2]
Masterplan Allesandersplatz (2025):
AbBA banner in city model proclaims new use of planned high-rises at Alexanderplatz / AbBA Banner proklamiert im Stadtmodell neue Nutzungen der geplanten Hochhäuser am Alexanderplatz

Pigeon Towers and Donkey Paths

A brand-new pigeon tower stands by the River Thames; the New Tate Modern in London. A brick building with small recesses and niches, and masonry reminiscent of brick expressionism; both a modern industrial building and a medieval pigeon tower. The building was designed by Basel-based architects Herzog & de Meuron in 2007, and was planned to feature a glass façade, which one year later was converted into a perforated brick façade enclosing an ornamental glass body within. From the outside, the building looks like the ideal nesting and breeding site for city pigeons: once at home in rock faces, in latter-day city settings they need cornices and niches to survive.

The city pigeon is actually a feral domestic pigeon, a farm animal used as a messenger as well as for sustenance before the American broiler chicken challenged its spot in the food chain. Today, it is, above all, a stray cat of the air, a feral animal that found its ideal home in cities of stone, and making the most of *Gründerzeit* stucco, ornamental façades and wall crannies. Whooshing over our heads in swarms, in Venice they are to be seen on every photo, the epitome of a tourist picture trophy.

The pigeon flaunts so many connotations, good and bad, symbolic and emblematic, that you can fill entire books with it. Its excrements, said to be corrosive, are widely loathed, while in other segments of the garden market the excrements of Antarctic penguins offer salvation for balcony fauna. Today, the pigeon is the only species in Germany to breed in and around buildings without enjoying legal protection. Bats have it better, though of course they are not feral, but dutifully tick all the boxes of the threatened wild animal worthy of protection. (Statistically, things don't look too bright for the pigeon either.)

None of which is the bat's fault. The blame lies with the hierarchical order as defined by human beings. They are the ones who have a problem with the stray dogs of Moscow, who shrewdly cross the city by subway, but also with any cats or pigeons who have escaped domestication. Current polls suggest that city dwellers associate many of their everyday troubles with fellow inhabitants such as crows and magpies, rabbits and foxes, along with rats, of course, and show little interest in the species with which they share urban space today. Hygiene discourses, on a warpath with dirt and disease, do further disservice to those non-human city dwellers threatened with exile.

Over in London, one is not particularly pleased with the city pigeon either. The New Tate Modern's claim to be a pigeon tower is mere pretense. In fact, the architects went to great lengths to make the openings too small for pigeons to access. The openings in the outer façade refer to historical pigeon towers only symbolically; in reality, the façade does all it can to be a pigeon repellent. The New Tate Modern building, monument to contemporary art, unites everything contemporary art stands for today: global attention is garnered with enormous production budgets (the New Tate Modern boasts the biggest sponsoring project ever), and by quoting formats from a great diversity of contexts,

Pigeon Towers and Donkey Paths
Marion von Osten

but bereft of any genuine function. From a pigeon's perspective, the building perfectly epitomizes the gestural symbolism contemporary art and its architecture widely prefer: representing something one does not actually do.

The museum building in London is rooted in a long tradition of urban planning and architecture that expelled the animals the very moment they became obsolete. Up until the 19th century, cities were still the abode of farm animals – horse-drawn street carriages, along with backyard cows, pigs and chickens, shaped the everyday image of the city, even London's. Those sheds, dragoon areas and royal stables have now become objects of land speculation and gentrification. And yet, modern city development discourses addressing the animal are of key importance to the enforcement of urban modernity itself.

As philosopher Fahim Amir points out, this exclusion was already inscribed within the Athenian definition of the polis, as a place to which neither animals nor plants, slaves or women have access, but in which only free anthropodes may hang around, in that know-it-all style of theirs, while the others toil away at the margins, or are eaten wholesale. A vision not unfamiliar to modernism, as in, for example, Lewis Mumford's introduction to the International Congress of Architecture: 'The Heart of the City'. According to Mumford, the polis, as a city ideal, is not a cluster of houses, but a meeting place and a place of public affairs, and therefore a place of government in and of itself. Mumford contrasts urban citizens with the existence of peasants, who are still subject to the cultivation of plants. According to Mumford, it is the tradition of the Greco-Roman city that has radically detached itself from the geo-botanical cosmos. Mumford's ideal of the modern city deliberately turns its back on the countryside, 'to free man from the communion of plants and animals', as he puts it (Mumford 2000: 207).

The architect Le Corbusier also banned animal life from his vision of the modern city. In his 1925 text *The City of Tomorrow*, Le Corbusier describes the city dweller as a purposeful being: 'The human being walks in a straight line because he has a goal and knows where he is going. He has set himself the goal of reaching a certain place, and he is going there directly' (Le Corbusier 1967 [1925]: 11f). An assumption that later drove the Situationists up the wall, and had them pit 'traces' and 'derives' against the modernist fantasy of order. Corbusier contrasts the figure of the purposeful human being with that of a donkey, which boycotts the modernist fantasy with its supposed inertia, laziness, and stubbornness: 'The pack donkey wanders along, meditates in its absent-minded manner, and meanders to evade larger stones, or to facilitate the ascent, or to gain a little shade; it takes the line of least resistance [...] The path of the pack donkey is responsible for the map of every continental city' (Le Corbusier 1967 [1925]: 11f). As a farm animal, the donkey embodies a whole range of headaches for Le Corbusier, and his urban-architectural vision of a new human being. The donkey stands for the intricate, medieval and Mediterranean urban layout, which does not follow planned grids, but organic growth patterns, and which simply sidesteps a given obstacle – instead of attempting to overcome it by any engineering means necessary.

According to Catherine Ingraham, for Le Corbusier, the donkey is the 'recurring figure of resistance to modernity and of decorative froufrou and dilatory

Pigeon Towers and Donkey Paths
Marion von Osten

historicism' (Ingraham 1998: 65). While according to Fahim Amir, the donkey, a disorderly pack animal, becomes the saboteur of Le Corbusier's aesthetic politics of the straight line, methodical and abstract. This imago of an orderly, purified and sanitized city, bereft of any species but the anthropos itself, brings with
it the streamlined animal slaughterhouses, the mechanization of food production, the industrialization of agriculture and factory farming, but also the petting zoo, the zoo-at-large, the hamster wheel, the guinea pig cage and the terrarium. The violent fantasies and practices inherent to this system are mirrored in our fortified building façades, with their arsenal of quasi-military paraphernalia – nets, spikes, acoustics, predator dummies, dazzling mirrors and electric shocks.

The fact that the human animal has always created new habitats for non-human animals, through its buildings, houses, bridges and towers, remains an utterly subconscious, hidden reality. Think of the Norway rats in our sewers, the sparrow colonies on our roof tiles, or modernist columns serving as fox shelters. In Hamburg's Hafencity, real estate prices are falling, as the many glass façades along the Elbe – an ever-shimmering source of light, and therefore a perfect attraction for insects – have become home to an armada of spiders which residents can no longer control. Ideal for spiders, bad for rentals.

It's astonishing that neither architectural discourse nor political theory have paid much attention to nonhuman animals as spacemakers and city actors – in the sense of Donna Haraway's concept of 'companion species' – along the lines of an inter-species relation beyond containment and sadistic dominance.[1] This despite the introduction of animal protection laws as key leitmotifs in post-capitalist efforts and struggles. As in, for example, the Hermit Beetle leading to a short-term halt of the Stuttgart 21 development, or the horseshoe bat – also known as 'Hufi' – playing a similar role at the Dresden Waldschlösschenbrücke, or the many other construction blockades at the hands of environmental authorities, the new harbingers of investment horror and profit loss. The Hermit Beetle of Stuttgart now has its own website (eremit.net), and a reader of the *Stuttgarter Zeitung* daily demanded that the beetle be awarded the Nobel Peace Prize, since it achieved what so many protesters have been unable to do. The beetle was indeed successful because it didn't only crawl around in trees, but at the very edges of our legislation (life is sweet in prime locations such as the Stuttgart palace gardens). Studies have shown that the marked increase of wild animal migration into urban areas is due to a variety of causes. Animals are losing their habitats in the monocultures of industrialized agriculture, and food supply in the city is decent by comparison, if not better. This is not only on account of overflowing garbage cans, as is often claimed,

---

1   Donna Haraway is a biologist, science historian and feminist philosopher of science. In her writings, she questions the fixity of categories such as 'human being', 'nature', 'technology' or 'gender'. Her book *The Companion Species Manifesto* deals with the implosion of nature and culture in the joint life of dogs and people who are connected through their 'significant otherness'. She uses the term 'companion species' instead of (domestic) animals, as humans, being historical and social organisms, are affected by many species that do not fall into the animal category, such as insects and bacteria.

Pigeon Towers and Donkey Paths
Marion von Osten

but of the many parks, gardens, wastelands, abandoned ruins and construction sites, countless snack bars and food festivals, as well as our city architecture itself. In fact, for a variety of different species, a city is a decent habitat thanks to its nuanced spatial diversity, those many historical architectural phases and building types.

For the kestrel, a house can't be high enough. It loves the updrafts in the gorges of New York, and even three realtynow.online nests in balcony boxes. Other animals remain in the city because they are not hunted there. According to a study in Germany, deer increasingly settle on the outskirts of cities where hunters do not get to them. Sometimes, industrialization itself is the starting point for a better habitat, as in the case of the Sand Lizard, for which there could be no better place to settle than a railway track, with its hot sand, gravel beds and staggered side tracks.

But all these many examples cannot hide the fact that the very future of the wild animal is at stake: whatever doesn't go extinct is being eaten, usually by us humans. At the same time, with new urban developments and new animal protection laws, a new constellation of habitats has emerged, one that favours new forms of cohabitation. New forms of coexistence are already a reality. However, the new legal situation has also established a new hierarchy of protection, one that continues to hunt down city pigeons, even as it protects coal tits.

Setting aside the hands-on interventions within existing habitats, the above also implies a new spatial discourse, and a new approach to building design. Both of which became noticeable on the fringes of the 'Animal-Aided Design' conference in January 2019. On the one hand, one noticed a problematic contrast between the idea of 'target species', and a general normalisation of animal protection in building laws. On the other hand, housing cooperatives now combine post-capitalist goals with new green spaces, and with façade innovations in the name of animal protection, thereby inventing entirely new fields of activity for themselves. When an Ingoldstadt housing cooperative collaborated with immigrant tenants on hedgehog tunnels, bee hives and sparrow colonies, the euphoric applause suggested a new way of becoming human, and becoming animal at that.

Can we also think of human relations as relations between species (beyond the known concepts of ecological diversity) – as a condition without which humans ultimately cannot exist? According to Anna Löwenhaupt Tsing, human exceptionalism has blinded us to the manifold interspecies relationships from which we ourselves have emerged. Löwenhaupt Tsing critically suggests an idea of human supremacy that modern science has inherited from the great monotheistic religions, and which to this day regards human autonomy and the control of nature as a given.

One of the many limitations of this heritage is that it considers the human species as autonomous, i.e. as a constant throughout culture and history. The notion of being the dominator of all other species has been instrumentalized among social conservatives and socio-biologists in order to support the most autocratic and militaristic of tropes, from the Alpha Animal to the natural pecking order. In its place, Löwenhaupt Tsing calls for thinking and acting within and through the interdependence of species.

Pigeon Towers and Donkey Paths
Marion von Osten

Historically, relations between species have shifted continuously between different types of dependencies. The idea that humans can only evolve in relation to other species – i.e. through different forms of interaction and cooperation with other species around them – may in turn lead to new forms of politics and subjectification, far from neoliberal individualism. This approach would help us understand non-human animals as spacemakers together with whom we live, and to whom we owe not only construction delays, but also the very possibility of shaping our living spaces for a diversity of users, beyond pure exploitation, speculation and utilitarianism. Solidarity with the city pigeon, and the struggle against its expulsion, could in turn suggest that other stray, precarious, grimy city dwellers equally have a right to temporary housing, social relevance and respect. It could imply that it is indeed unacceptable that human and non-human animals are being displaced and persecuted – when all they need is protection, care and autonomous, uncontrolled places. To think of the city as an interspecies relationship is to throw the separation of nature and culture onto the garbage dump of history, and to instead think of wastelands and ruins, fox houses and skyscrapers, as interdependent urban spaces. As Donna Haraway insists, to think and act in our present time is to turn the socioeconomic and political contradictions of the modern city on their head. Inter-species spaces are created precisely to test new modes of subjectification and solidarity; after all, we already live together anyway.

Translated by Jana Thormälen

Taubentürme und Trampelpfade
Marion von Osten

Taubentürme und Trampelpfade

Ein neuer „Taubenturm" steht an der Londoner Themse, es ist die New Tate Modern: ein Backsteingebäude mit kleinen Aussparungen, Nischen, die durch eine spezielle Mauerung entstanden sind und an Backsteinexpressionismus, modernen Industriebau und einen mittelalterlichen Taubenturm erinnern. Der Bau wurde vom Basler Architekturbüro Herzog & de Meuron 2007 zunächst mit Glasfassade geplant. Diese wurde ein Jahr später zu einer perforierten Backsteinfassade umgearbeitet, die einen Glaskörper umschließt und so im Innenraum eine ornamenthafte Verschattung bietet. Von außen wirkt das Gebäude wie der ideale Nist- und Brutplatz für Stadttauben: Da ursprünglich ein Felsentier, benötigt sie in der Stadt zum Erhalt ihrer Art Simse und Nischen.

Die Stadttaube ist eigentlich eine verwilderte Haustaube, ehemals Nutztier als Briefbotin und auch Fleischtier, bevor das amerikanische Masthühnchen ihr diesen Rang streitig machte. Heute ist sie vor allem eine *stray cat* der Lüfte, ein verwildertes Tier, das von Gründerzeitstuck, Fassaden mit Ornamenten und Mauerspalten profitierte und in der steinernen Stadt sein ideales Habitat fand. Rauschend fliegen Tauben als Schwarm über unsere Köpfe. In Venedig ist der Vogel auf jedem Foto zu sehen, der Inbegriff einer touristischen Bildtrophäe.

Die Taube hat so vielfältige positive und negative, symbolische und metaphorische Zuschreibungen erfahren, dass man ganze Bücher damit füllen kann. Gehasst ist ihr Kot, der zersetzende Wirkung haben soll, während andernorts im Gartenmarkt jener von Pinguinen aus der Antarktis großes Heil für die Balkonpflanze verspricht. Die Taube ist heute auch die einzige Gebäudebrüterin, die in Deutschland nicht geschützt wird. Fledermäuse haben es da besser, sie sind aber natürlich auch nicht verwildert, sondern erfüllen brav die Kategorie vom zu schützenden bedrohten Wildtier, obwohl es auch für die Taube statistisch gesehen nicht rosig aussieht.

Dafür kann die Fledermaus nichts, aber das hierarchische Ordnungssystem des Menschen. Der hat ein Problem mit streunenden Hunden, die in Moskau mit der U-Bahn die Stadt klug durchqueren, aber auch in London ist man über die verwilderte Stadttaube nicht erfreut. Die Anmutung, ein Taubenturm zu sein, ist bei der New Tate Modern nur Schein. Tatsächlich waren die Architekten besonders bemüht, die Öffnungen für Tauben zu klein und damit unzugänglich zu gestalten. Die Öffnungen in der Fassadenhülle verweisen nur symbolisch auf historische Taubentürme, tatsächlich wehrt die Fassade die Taube bewusst ab. Das Gebäude der New Tate Modern als Monument der Gegenwartskunst vereint somit alles, was zeitgenössische Kunst heute ausmacht: global Aufmerksamkeit erregen, bestehende Formate ohne deren Funktion zitieren und auf unterschiedlichste Kontexte verweisen, aber auch große Geldsummen für die Produktion verschlingen (die New Tate Modern rühmt sich, das größte Sponsoringprojekt *ever* gewesen zu sein). Mit Blick auf die Tauben steht das Gebäude für jene symbolische Geste, mit der die Gegen-

Taubentürme und Trampelpfade
Marion von Osten

wartskunst und auch ihre Architektur es vorziehen, auszukommen: etwas darzustellen, was man nicht ist.

Das Londoner Museumsgebäude steht in einer langen Tradition von Architektur und Städtebau, die das Tier aus dem Stadtraum verbannt haben, da es hier obsolet wurde. Während im 19. Jahrhundert Städte noch Orte von unterschiedlichsten Nutztieren waren und Pferdekutschen auf den Straßen und Milchkühe, Schweine und Hühner im Hinterhof das Alltagsbild der Stadt – auch Londons – prägten, sind Remisen, Dragonerareale und Marställe heute Gegenstände der Bodenspekulation und Gentrifizierung geworden. Dabei ist gerade der Diskurs des modernen Städtebaus über das Tier von konstituierender Bedeutung für die Durchsetzung der Stadt und Stadtmoderne selbst.

Wie der Philosoph Fahim Amir hervorhebt, wurde bereits in der athenischen Definition der Polis diese Exklusion miteingeschrieben, als ein Ort, zu dem weder Tiere, Pflanzen, Sklav*innen noch Frauen Zugang haben, sondern an dem nur freie Anthroposse schlaumeiernd herumlungern, während die anderen an den Rändern schuften oder gefressen werden.[1] Diese Vorstellung spiegelt sich in der Moderne wider, etwa in der Einleitung von Lewis Mumford zum Internationalen Kongress für Architektur – *The Heart of the City*.

Die Polis, als Stadtideal, ist nach Mumford nicht eine Ansammlung von Häusern, sondern Treffpunkt und Ort öffentlicher Angelegenheiten und somit Ort der Regierung

---

[1] Vgl. Fahim Amir: Schwein und Zeit, Tiere, Politik, Revolte. Hamburg: Edition Nautilus, 2018.

Taubentürme und Trampelpfade
Marion von Osten

selbst. Den Stadtbürger*innen stellt Mumford die Existenz der Bauernschaft gegenüber, die dem Wachstum der Pflanze weiterhin unterworfen sei. Nach Mumford ist es die Tradition der greco-romanischen Stadt, die sich vom geo-botanischen Kosmos radikal gelöst hat. Mumfords Ideal der modernen Stadt kehrt dem Land bewusst den Rücken zu, um, wie er sagt, „den Menschen von der Gemeinschaft der Pflanzen und Tiere zu befreien".[2]

Auch der Architekt Le Corbusier verbannt das Tierleben aus seiner Vision der modernen Stadt. In seinem Text *The City of Tomorrow* aus dem Jahr 1925 beschreibt Le Corbusier den Stadtmenschen als zielgerichtetes Wesen: „Der Mensch läuft in einer geraden Linie, weil er ein Ziel hat und weiß, wohin er geht. Er hat sich vorgenommen, einen bestimmten Ort zu erreichen, und er geht direkt dorthin."[3]

[2] Eric Mumford: CIAM discourse on urbanism, 1928–1960. Cambridge Mass.: MIT Press, 2000, S. 207.
[3] Le Corbusier: The City of Tommorow. London: Architectural Press, 1967 [1925], S. 11f.

[1] Pigeons over HdS / Tauben über dem HdS

Eine Annahme, die die Situationisten später auf die Palme brachte; sie setzten *strayen* und *deriven* der modernistischen Ordnungsfantasie entgegen. Der Figur des zielgerichteten Menschen stellt Le Corbusier einen Esel gegenüber, der mit seiner vermeintlichen Trägheit, Faulheit und Sturheit die Modernefantasie boykottiert: „Der Packesel schlängelt sich dahin, meditiert in seiner zerstreuten Art und mäandert, um den größeren Steinen auszuweichen oder den Aufstieg zu erleichtern oder ein wenig Schatten zu gewinnen, er nimmt den Weg des geringsten Widerstands auf [...] Der Weg des Packesels ist für den Plan jeder kontinentalen Stadt verantwortlich."[4] Der Esel als ländliches Nutztier verkörpert eine ganze Reihe von Problemen für Le Corbusier, der seine städtische und architektonische Vision eines neuen Menschen durchsetzen will. Der Esel steht in diesem Diskurs für den verschlungen mittelalterlichen und mediterranen Stadtgrundriss, der keinem geplanten Raster, sondern einer gewachsenen Form entspricht und einem Hindernis ausweicht – statt es mit allen Mitteln moderner Ingenieurskraft zu überwinden.

Nach Catherine Ingraham ist der Esel bei Le Corbusier die „wiederkehrende Figur des Widerstandes gegen die Moderne und des dekorativen Froufrou und dilatatorischen Historismus".[5] Der Esel wird – so Fahim Amir – als unordentliches Lasttier zum Saboteur von Le Corbusiers geordneter und abstrakter ästhetischer Politik der geraden Linie. In dieser Imagination einer geklärten und gesäuberten, geordneten und speziesentleerten Stadt des Anthropos sind die rationelle Tötung von Tieren in Schlachthöfen enthalten wie auch die Mechanisierung der Lebensmittelproduktion, die Industrialisierung der Landwirtschaft und die Massentierhaltung, aber auch der Streichelzoo, der Zoo überhaupt und auch das Hamsterrad, die Meerschweinchenkäfige und das Terrarium. Auch die Abwehrinstrumente an Fassaden, die einem ganzen Arsenal von quasi-militärischem Samisdat ähneln – Netze, Stacheln, Beschallungsanlagen, Raubvögelattrappen, Blendspiegel und Stromstöße –, zeugen von den dieser Ordnung immanenten Gewaltfantasien und -praktiken.

Völlig ausgeblendet bleibt die Tatsache, dass das menschliche Tier konstant durch seine Gebäude, Häuser, Brücken und Türme neue Habitate für nicht menschliche Tiere geschaffen hat. Dies betrifft die Kanalisation für die Wanderratte ebenso wie den Dachziegel für Spatzenkolonien, oder modernistische Pilotigebäude als Schutz für den Fuchsbau. In der Hafencity Hamburg sinken schon die Immobilienpreise, da sich an den vielen Glasfassaden an der Elbe – eine stets schimmernde Lichtquelle und damit Anziehungspunkt für Insekten – eine ganze Armada von Spinnen angesiedelt hat, denen die Hausbewohnerschaft nicht mehr gewachsen ist – ideal für Spinnen, schlecht für die Mietpreise.

Es ist erstaunlich, dass nicht menschliche Tiere als Raumproduzenten und Stadtakteure auch im Sinne von Donna Haraways Konzept der *Companion Species* – das heißt einer anderen Form der Interspezies-Relation, jenseits der Einhegung und sadistischen Dominanz – bislang kaum

---

4 Ebd.
5 Catherine Ingraham: Architecture and the Burdens of Linearity. New Haven: Yale University Press, 1998, S. 65.

Beachtung im Architekturdiskurs oder in der politischen Theorie finden.[6] Dies obwohl mit der Einführung des Artenschutzes Tiere ständig in post-kapitalistische Aktionen und Reaktionen verwickelt sind. Wie etwa der Juchtenkäfer im Fall des kurzzeitigen Baustopps von Stuttgart 21 oder die Hufeisennasenfledermaus – auch Hufi genannt – an der Waldschlösschenbrücke in Dresden oder aber in den vielen weiteren Fällen von Baustopps, die von Umweltämtern ausgesprochen werden, als neue Figur des Grauens und Kapitalverlustes für investoriende. Dem Stuttgarter Käfer wurde sogar eine eigene Website gewidmet (eremit.net), und ein Leser der *Stuttgarter Zeitung* fordert, dem Käfer solle der Friedensnobelpreis verliehen werden, da er geschafft habe, was die vielen Demonstrierenden nicht erreichen konnten. Wahrscheinlich ist der Käfer auch deswegen so erfolgreich, weil er nicht nur in Bäumen, sondern auch an den Rändern unserer Gesetzgebung herumkrabbelt, und es sich hier, wie im Stuttgarter Schlosspark, ganz gut leben lässt.

Studien über Tiere in der Stadt haben gezeigt, dass die nachweislich zunehmende Migration von Wildtieren in den städtischen Raum unterschiedliche Gründe hat: Tiere verlieren ihren Lebensraum in den Monokulturen der industrialisierten Landwirtschaft, und das Nahrungsangebot in der Stadt ist gut, wenn nicht sogar besser. Was nicht allein – wie oft behauptet wird – an gefüllten Mülltonnen liegt, sondern an den vielen Parks, Gärten, Brachen, verwilderten Bauruinen und Baustellen, an den zahlreichen Imbissständen und Foodfestivals, und nicht zuletzt an der Stadtarchitektur selbst. Die Stadt ist tatsächlich ein sehr gutes Habitat für viele verschiedene Spezies aufgrund ihrer ausdifferenzierten räumlichen Vielfalt und der unterschiedlichsten historischen Architekturphasen und Gebäudetypen.

Dem Turmfalken kann ein Haus gar nicht hoch genug sein, er liebt die Aufwinde in den Schluchten New Yorks und nistet auch schon mal im Balkonkasten. Andere Tiere bleiben in der Stadt, da sie hier nicht gejagt werden, das zeigt etwa eine Studie über Rehe, die sich in Deutschland zunehmend an den Stadträndern angesiedelt haben, wo sie der Jäger nicht erwischt.

Manchmal ist auch die Industrialisierung selbst der Ausgangspunkt für ein besseres Habitat, wie im Fall der Zauneidechse, der nichts Besseres passieren konnte als die vielen Eisenbahnschienen mit ihren heißen Sand- und Schotterbetten und versteppten Nebengleisen, wo sie sich gut eingerichtet hat.

Aber all diese tierischen Stadtbewohner*innen können nicht darüber hinwegtäuschen, dass die Zukunft des Wildtieres infrage steht: Was nicht ausstirbt, wird gefressen – und zwar meistens von uns. Gleichzeitig hat sich mit dem städtischen Raum und der neuen staatlichen Regulierung

---

6   Donna Haraway ist Biologin, Naturwissenschaftshistorikerin und feministische Wissenschaftstheoretikerin. In ihren Schriften stellt sie die Geschlossenheit von Kategorien wie Mensch, Natur, Technik oder Geschlecht infrage. Ihr *Companion-Species*-Manifest handelt von der Implosion von Natur und Kultur im gemeinsamen Leben von Hunden mit Menschen, die in ihrem „signifikanten Anderssein" verbunden sind. Sie verwendet den Begriff *Companion Species* anstelle von (Haus-)tiere, da der Mensch als ein historischer und sozialer Organismus von vielen Arten betroffen ist, die nicht in die Tierkategorie fallen, wie Insekten und Bakterien. Vgl. Donna Haraway: The Companion Species Manifesto. Dogs, People, and Significant Otherness. Chicago: Prickly Paradigm Press, 2003.

des Artenschutzes eine neue Habitat-Konstellation ergeben, die neue Formen der Kohabitation begünstigt. Neue Formen des Zusammenlebens sind bereits Realität. Durch die neue Gesetzeslage hat sich aber auch eine neue Ordnung des Schutzes etabliert, der weiterhin Stadttauben verjagt und Kohlmeisen schützt.

Diese Tatsache wird, neben dem Eingriff in bestehende Habitat-Konstellationen, auch einen neuen Raumdiskurs und eine neue gestalterische Verfahrensweise in der Baupraxis nach sich ziehen, die am Rande einer Konferenz im Januar 2019 zur Methode des *Animal Aided Design* sichtbar wurde. Hier zeigte sich einerseits eine problematische Ausdifferenzierung in Zielarten und Normalisierung des Artenschutzes im Siedlungsbau; andererseits wurde auch deutlich, dass die involvierten Agierenden der Wohnungsbaugenossenschaften mit neuen Grünanlagen und Fassadenvorhaben zum Artenschutz auch post-kapitalistische Ziele verbinden konnten und für sich selbst neue Tätigkeitsfelder erfanden. Der euphorische Applaus, wenn eine Ingolstädter Wohnungsbaugenossenschaft mit ihrer post-migrantischen Mieterschaft gemeinsam an Igeltunneln, Bienenhäusern und Spatzenkolonien arbeitet, spricht auch für eine andere Art des Mensch- und Tierwerdens.

Können wir menschliche Beziehungen auch als Beziehungen zwischen den Spezies denken (über die bekannten Konzepte ökologischer Vielfalt hinaus) – als eine Bedingung, ohne die der Mensch letztendlich nicht existieren kann? Nach Anna Lowenhaupt Tsing hat uns der menschliche Exzeptionalismus blind gemacht für die vielfältigen Interspezies-Beziehungen, aus denen wir selbst hervorgegangen sind. Es ist nach Lowenhaupt Tsing die Vorstellung menschlicher Vorherrschaft, die die neuzeitlichen Wissenschaften von den großen monotheistischen Religionen geerbt haben, die bis heute die Annahme menschlicher Autonomie und Kontrolle der Natur als gegeben voraussetzt.[7]

Im Sinne dieses Erbes ist somit die menschliche Spezies als autonom zu betrachten, als konstant in Kultur und Geschichte. Die Idee, alle anderen Spezies zu beherrschen, wurde an Sozialkonservative und Soziobiolog*innen weitergegeben, um damit die autokratischsten und militaristischsten Ideologien zu unterstützen, vom Alphatier bis zur Hackordnung. Stattdessen fordert Lowenhaupt Tsing ein Denken und Handeln in und mit der Interdependenz der Arten.

Beziehungen zwischen den Spezies haben sich historisch in verschiedenen Arten von Abhängigkeiten kontinuierlich verschoben. Die Vorstellung, dass selbst der Mensch sich nur in Beziehung zwischen den Spezies herausbilden konnte, in jeweils unterschiedlichsten interaktiven und kooperativen Formen mit anderen Spezies, wäre ein Ansatz, eine neue Politik und Subjektivierung jenseits des neoliberalen Individualismus zu denken. Dies würde auch dazu führen, nicht menschliche Tiere als Raumproduzierende zu verstehen, mit denen wir zusammenleben und denen wir nicht nur einen Baustopp zu verdanken haben,

---

7 Anna Lowenhaupt Tsing: Der Pilz am Ende der Welt. Über das Leben in den Ruinen des Kapitalismus. Übersetzt von Dirk Höfer. Berlin: Matthes & Seitz, 2018.

sondern auch die Möglichkeit, unseren Lebensraum jenseits purer Verwertung, Spekulation und Utilitarismus für unterschiedlichste Nutzungen zu gestalten. Im solidarischen Kampf gegen die Vertreibung der Stadttaube könnte sich einschreiben, dass auch andere streunende, prekäre, schmuddelige Stadtakteur*innen ein Recht auf temporäre Behausung, soziale Relevanz und Respekt haben. Und dass wir nicht mehr akzeptieren können, dass menschliche und nicht menschliche Tiere verdrängt und verfolgt werden, sondern dass wir ihnen Schutz, Zuwendung und autonome, unkontrollierte Orte zukommen lassen. Die Stadt als Interspezies-Relation zu denken, heißt, die Trennung von Natur und Kultur auf die Müllhalde der Geschichte zu werfen und stattdessen Brache und Ruine, Fuchsbau und Hochhaus als interpendenten städtischen Raum zu denken. Denkend und gegenwärtig handeln, wie es Donna Haraway fordert, heißt, die sozialen, ökonomischen und politischen Widersprüche, die die moderne Stadt erschaffen hat, anders zu wenden: als einen Interspezies-Raum, der gerade dazu geschaffen ist, neue Subjektivierungsweisen und Solidaritäten zu erproben, gerade weil wir bereits zusammenleben.

Der Aufsatz „Taubentürme und Trampelpfade" wurde November 2018 vom KW-Programm REALTY in Auftrag gegeben.

Capitalising Antigentrification

City planners across the planet have recently adopted gentrification led by creatives as a development strategy for increasing the wealth of cities while also promoting inclusiveness, diversity and social integration, all of which are important to these cities' engagement in global networks, as well as increasing capital with minimum political objection. An all-round win. However, faced with growing socioeconomic inequalities within major cities over the same period—and between global urban hotspots, or what are called 'superstar cities', such as New York, London, Shanghai, Dubai and the rest—even Richard Florida, proselytiser-in-chief for creative gentrification as the path to urban 'renewal', has recanted his earlier prescriptions:[1]

our geography is splintering into small areas of affluence and concentrated advantage, and much larger areas of poverty and concentrated disadvantage. It became increasingly clear to me that the same clustering of talent and economic assets generates a lopsided, unequal urbanism in which a relative handful of superstar cities, and a few elite neighborhoods within them, benefit while many other places stagnate or fall behind. Ultimately, the very same force that drives the growth of our cities and economy broadly also generates the divides that separate us and the contradictions that hold us back.[2]

Gentrification is integral to a process that has led to the social entrenchment of income and wealth concentration, with increased spatial segregation of rich and poor *within* cities, *between* cities, and of cities against their surrounding regions. Along with that increasing disparity of inequality, interactions across different demographic categories are increasingly commercially organised rather than on the basis of social commonality or of equal claims to city use.
 Displacement, rent rises, privatisation, corporatisation, and cultural homogenisation by a transnational elite are part of this process, as then is the hegemonic and capital control by those elites. As Florida highlights, this means a reduction of social mobility and the reinforcement of poverty traps. And, whereas creatives were once the spontaneous frontline of gentrification, the art field is now fully programmed into the conversion mechanisms of urban and capital development. Contrary to the imperatives of an art field abiding by leftist-critical imperatives, as contemporary art mostly does, art—and contemporary art in particular—has for some time now been an attractor, not a spoiler, for capital and municipal investment formatted by gentrification.

---

1   'Superstar cities' is a phrase Florida adopts from Joseph Gyourko, Christopher Mayer & Todd Sinai, 'Superstar Cities', *American Economic Journal: Economic Policy* 5:4, 2013: pp. 167–99 [http://www.nber.org/papers/w12355.pdf].
2   Richard Florida, *The New Urban Crisis: How Our Cities Are Increasing Inequality, Deepening Segregation, and Failing the Middle Class and What We Can Do About It* (New York: Basic Books, 2017), p. xv.

Capitalising Antigentrification
Suhail Malik

This presents a formidable dilemma for the critically minded artworker. But help is now at hand to redress it. As noted, gentrification is now recognised as a core problem by urban policy makers, who insist that cities must protect spaces and rents for low-income sectors like artworkers (and other creative sector entrepreneurs) in order to maintain urban vitality, and mend cities from the pernicious effects of unhindered gentrification. Yet changing the policy agenda does not challenge the basic premise of a creative-led gentrification. Rather, checking back gentrification is a good result for the creative class, artists included, and may even be the optimal one: creatives can then maintain their role in converting cities to their own ends with the added advantage of subsequent development taking place *around* them.

Questions remain, however: what of those who also have claims—perhaps more trenchant, historically based claims—to urban sites but who are not creatives? How do the interests and material conditions of this population fare when the combination of creative-led gentrification and antigentrification shape policy? These concerns are taken up in the conclusion below, but first require elaboration of: the dynamic logic tying gentrification and antigentrification together; the advantages and quandaries faced by creatives in these restructuring dynamics; and the difficulty that it presents to those on the political left in particular. This elaboration will lead to prescriptions for how the art field can contribute to redressing entrenched poverty rather than its own interests. That's important because, as will be seen, the art field's interests lie more obviously in maintaining the poverty trap.

The basic terms for the present discussion are as follows:

Gentrification: Ruth Glass first defined gentrification as a term in 1964: referring to the changing social composition of specific areas in London, Glass describes how

> one by one, many of the working class quarters have been invaded by the middle class.... Shabby, modest mews and cottages ... have been taken over ... and have become elegant, expensive residences. [...] Once this process of 'gentrification' starts in a district it goes on rapidly.[3]

The chief characteristics of gentrification being that 'all or most of the working class occupiers are displaced and the whole social character of the district is changed'. Concomitantly, those displaced are left in a worse situation than they were before, including: travelling further to existing jobs and schools; losing jobs as a result and precarious re-employment; increased susceptibility of meaningful support structures, relatives and community to increased distance or dispersion of lived bonds; and the loss of familiarity by which daily life is routine, familiar and secure.

The rent gap: The economic driver for gentrification was theorised in the 1980s by Neil Smith's stylisation of the 'rent

---

3 Ruth Glass, 'Aspects of Change', in Centre for Urban Studies (ed.), *London: Aspects of Change* (London: MacGibbon and Kee, 1964): p. xvii.

gap'.[4] Smith proposes that as buildings get older and fall into disrepair, the amount of rent that can be extracted from them decrease. If, simultaneously, the amount of rent that could be extracted from new land and buildings continues to increase, then the owner of the land/building is making an effective loss compared to the potential income: this is the rent gap.[5]

If the owners are capitalists, they will increase revenues by one or more of the following: renewing the building or use of land, increasing rents, or selling it to another party who can buy the property at a price reduced from its market rates—and renovate it to restart the rent gap cycle (or by selling it on when market rates increase, 'flipping' or 'land-banking'). The net effect of closing the rent gap towards the higher market price of potential rent is in any case to evict those who cannot afford the increased rates and attract those who can, making explicit that gentrification is a dynamic social reordering, a wealth cleansing.

Neoliberalism and supergentrification: Gentrification understood via the rent gap has been theorised in one way or another since the 1920s, if not before. But, as Florida remarks, early twenty-first century gentrification is distinct from its precursors because of three characteristics of class recomposition and ownership structures specific to neoliberalism:

1. the increased concentration of the ownership of capital and wealth by a super minority;
2. the erosion of a middle class attainable by those from historically low-income backgrounds;
3. the extraction of income through various forms of leasing and rent from peripheral and poorer actors of any sector to the wealthier and therefore increasingly richer core who own key provisions and services.

Gentrification as a channel for neoliberal accumulation specifically leads to very rapid increases in rent and property prices, quicker turnover of increasingly concentrated ownership, more systemic rent extraction processes, and a correspondingly accelerated social restructuring. It's a gentrification on steroids, sometimes called supergentrification.[6]

Creatives with relatively low-income, typical of the art field, have an interest in this nexus of gentrification and supergentrification: gentrification, because that is how this sector takes advantage of the rent gap to inhabit dense urban spaces where art scenes have historically been concentrated in modernity; and supergentrification, because the art field is now economically structured around the consumption patterns of a neoliberal elite for its financial

---

4 Neil Smith, Toward a Theory of Gentrification: A Back to the City Movement by Capital, Not People', *Journal of the American Planning Association* 45, 1979: pp. 538–48. For the economic and explanatory importance of the rent gap to geosocially diverse conditions of gentrification, see Loretta Lees, Hyun Bang Shin and Ernesto López-Morales, *Planetary Gentrification* (Cambridge: Polity, 2016).
5 Adapted from Eric Clarke and Anders Lund Hansen, 'Financialization, Rescaling Rent Gaps and Land Grabbing', May 2012 [http://backdoorbroadcasting.net/2012/05/ eric-clarke-and-anders-lund-hansen-financializationrescaling- rent-gaps-and-land-grabbing/]
6 Loretta Lees, 'Super-gentrification: The Case of Brooklyn Heights, New York City', *Urban Studies* 40:12, 2003: pp. 2487–2509.

Capitalising Antigentrification
Suhail Malik

viability. Both of these conditions can serve creatives very well: artworks, designed objects and experiences, ideas and discourses, and general innovation are each and all key elements for the expansion of experience sought in creative-led gentrification, which relies on low-cost spaces in urban centres, consequently upgraded as service sites for elite enrichment.[7]

As is now well established, the continued celebration of what creatives do, while removing the material conditions enabling them to actually do so, leads to a closing of the rent gap and, accordingly, resentment and frustration within the creative sector. It's then consistent for creatives to join struggles against gentrification. But this indexes a third vector of advantage: antigentrification.

Creative-led antigentrification looks to block further development after the early-stage gentrification from which they benefit. And this means that the low-income creative sector in particular presents a twofold problem to others who are also casualties of gentrification.

—First: while alliances with local communities at risk of eviction, homelessness and displacement endorse the common interest in low-price rental and ownership of property, understood then as a public good, that alignment is not the optimal condition for the creative sector. It is instead best served in a sweet spot between supergentrifi-

---

[7] On financial and experiential enrichment structuring an elite-forging economy (paradigmatic for which is art collecting), see Luc Boltanski and Arnaud Esquerre, 'The Economic Life of Things. Commodities, Collectibles, Assets', *New Left Review* 98, March–April 2016: pp. 31–54; and *Enrichissement. Une critique de la marchandise* (Paris: Gallimard, 2017) for the full elaboration of the thesis.

[1]
Banner draped anonymously onto *fallingwild* model overnight / Über Nacht bedeckten Unbekannte das *fallingwild* Modell mit einem Banner

cation (products, sales), gentrification (urban existence) and antigentrification (property requirements) combined.
—Second: in their solidarity with the historically urban poor at risk of displacement, creatives endorsing antigentrification maintain and perpetuate the rent gap, which is also a proxy measure of relative impoverishment and disinvestment.

To elaborate: identifying any kind of development with gentrification, antigentrification of this kind stipulates the continued disinvestment in poor parts of the city where a substantial enough rent gap is to be had. In the name of such solidarity, antigentrification in cities that are otherwise increasing their overall capital base and productivity can thereby contribute 'from below' to the economic segregation entrenched by neoliberal gentrification. More alarmingly, given that neoliberal gentrification erodes social mobility and enforces urban segregation and wealth inequalities in cities, antigentrification can lock in the historically routine poverty trap by which the poor stay in poverty intergenerationally.

In order to serve their own needs of low rents and cheap property, creatives supporting antigentrification may (by accident or not) thereby be maintaining disinvestment, reinforcing the poverty of the poor. The direct benefit of antigentrification to creatives entrenches social hierarchy based on wealth, enforced through urban spatial organisation. This continued indirect exploitation of the poor, and entrenchment of economic-spatial stratification, can be called 'right antigentrification'. Right antigentrification supports neoliberal gentrification.

The exacerbation of economic and social segregation in cities presents an insurmountable problem for the political left, for whom societal organisation including cities should by contrast be just by virtue of increasing economic and political equality, socioculturally expansive, inclusive, in the collective interest, and socially liberal. Economic and experienced poverty are ameliorated by the improvement of services, provision, and infrastructure; from basic requirements of water and energy to affordable transport links to decent housing. The poverty trap is sprung open by investment in infrastructure and people, by transformation of their living conditions and material capacities. For this, a path distinct from the two standard options of gentrification and reactive right antigentrification needs to be set out.

Such a route is not hard to formulate: not all urban economic development is gentrifying, because it need not be led by exogenous interests or financially speculative developers. Indeed, this last term must be retrieved from its now near-exclusive connotations with capital concentration, associations entrenched by neoliberal doctrine. Development is necessary to meet the political imperative of social mobility from poorer to richer sections of the population. And it is such development that is thwarted by the reactive formation of right antigentrification.

But a leftist demand for development puts pressure not just on gentrification but on antigentrification too. Though the alleviation of poverty and hardship, and also, crucially, increasing access to higher living standards are common justifications for gentrification, the political left must also insist that improvements to income levels, infrastructure and services in poor areas do not force displacements (direct or indirect). Rather, they maintain provision for incoming people in need, as well as defend existing occupants and residents against expropriation. In the most general terms, what is required is a pro-development antigentrification (ProDAG).

ProDAG capitalises antigentrification: it re-quires channelling capital to the urban poor, who can be anyone: black or white, the established poor over two generations of deindustrialised surplus populations, or the new poor (such as the economic or political refugee), or the former middle classes. Instead of looking to only protect the interests of communities under threat from external price increase and land-grab pressures, ProDAG advances the claims of constituencies liable to be displaced by advocating the development of those areas for those who are there in the first instance. This antipoverty pro-development capitalization is an active left antigentrification. Against the reactive formation of reactive right antigentrification, which looks to maintain the rent gap, a ProDAG approach also looks to close or reduce the rent gap by these modes of intensively directed capitalisation:

1. blocking the possibility of increasing rent, or at least mitigating its rate of increase, meaning rent caps;
2. providing support for rent through state support;
3. reducing the market property rental price by distorting the price system, which is to introduce market controls.

These measures do not alone suffice to meet a ProDAG agenda: the first is an attenuated form of continued disinvestment and is an easy-to-hand but short-term variant of reactive antigentrification. The second proposal consolidates the dynamics of rent increases, securing revenues for owners of property and so further concentrating capital by state subsidy, while also deferring the standard operations of gentrification. Like state subsidy of housing, rent control can only contribute to ProDAG if it is accompanied by a redistribution of property ownership. That is, ProDAG must set up revised models and practices of financial, monetary and legal mechanisms if it is to countermand the displacement and continued degradation of the urban poor.

The closing proposal is that a revised art field can help set this development strategy as a mode of its praxis. The exigency here is that the current material and financial conditions of the supermajority in the art field—the low income from art and the requirement of space for material practice and exhibition—have to be reset. Actually existing conditions for art have to be grasped and mobilised as a transformative modular element in a chain of interests and valuation that extend well beyond the limited and experientially determined art field into finance, law and urban strategy. The practicalities of art require it.

This is in fact not much of a stretch: even now, art is cross-sectorial and transdisciplinary. And, significantly, it is part of a Global Urban Value Chain (GUVC) which can be manipulated. More exactly, because it is art, it ought to be manipulated—in ways that may be deemed inaccessible to those debilitated by the capitalisation set up by GUVCs. That manipulation includes working with legal and financial urban activists who have the technical skills to formulate developmental strategies supporting the interests of the urban poor. And such legal, contractual and municipal work is again anyway within the potential space of art as a cross-sectorial, trans-demographic and interdisciplinary practice.

It's a propitious time to follow through on this demand, because the neoliberal order of the past forty years is undergoing a global restructuring, affecting capital organisation at every scale and locality. The current political and legitimation crisis of neoliberalism means that the financially led accumulation familiar from (super)gentrification is now highly susceptible to delegitimation and revectoring by alternative models, revenue structures and interests of capitalisation. And just as contemporary art played an effective part in the hegemonisation and domination of neoliberal ordering, so art—which would have to be another art than contemporary art—can and should play its part in its undoing. ProDAG requires that art's manipulation of GUVCs strategises its own material prerequisites of low-provision workspace, cheap housing and access to transnational mobility as components in the medium-term alleviation of urban poverty. And that art's economy is revectored away from the increasingly plutocratic power of the urban rich and super-rich. What and who creatives instead appeal to for their own economies then has to shift from the one-sided extractive subservience to a neoliberal elite, requiring in turn a restructuring of art's economy, and the reorganisation of how its hierarchies are established.[8]

The essay 'Capitalising Antigentrification', was commissioned by the KW REALTY program, November 2018.

---

8   Summarising several of Richard Florida's correctives to creative-led urban renewal. See *The New Urban Crisis*, p. 10, and Chapter 10.

Die Vermarktung der Anti-Gentrifizierung

Stadtplanung auf der ganzen Welt hat jüngst die von Kreativen gelenkte Gentrifizierung als eine Entwicklungsstrategie angenommen, um den Wohlstand in den Städten zu steigern und zugleich Inklusion, Diversität und soziale Integration zu fördern, die für das Engagement dieser Städte in globalen Netzwerken sowie die Erhöhung des Kapitals bei minimalem politischen Widerspruch eine wichtige Rolle spielen. Ein Rundum-Gewinn. Mit wachsenden sozialökonomischen Ungleichheiten innerhalb großer Städte im gleichen Zeitraum – und zwischen globalen urbanen Hotspots, den sogenannten „Superstar-Städten" wie New York, London, Schanghai, Dubai und anderen – hat jedoch sogar Richard Florida, Chefmissionar für kreative Gentrifizierung als Weg zur städtischen „Erneuerung", seine früheren Verordnungen zurückgenommen:[1]

„[...] unsere Geografie zersplittert in kleine Bereiche des Wohlstands und geballter Überlegenheit sowie deutlich größere Gebiete von Armut und konzentrierter Benachteiligung. Es ist mir zunehmend klar geworden, dass die gleiche Bündelung von Talent und Wirtschaftsgütern ein einseitiges, ungleiches Städtewesen hervorbringt, in dem eine Handvoll Superstar-Städte und einige wenige Elite-Quartiere profitieren, während viele andere Gebiete nicht vorankommen oder in Rückstand geraten. Letztlich erzeugt dieselbe Kraft, die das Wachstum unserer Städte und Wirtschaft vorantreibt, weitestgehend auch die Kluften, die uns trennen und die Widersprüche, die uns bremsen."[2]

Die Gentrifizierung ist wesentlicher Bestandteil eines Prozesses, der zur sozialen Verankerung von Einkommens- und Vermögenskonzentration geführt hat, mit einer zunehmenden räumlichen Trennung von Arm und Reich *innerhalb* von Städten, *zwischen* Städten und zwischen Städten und den sie umgebenden Regionen. Neben diesem steigenden Gefälle der Ungleichheit sind Interaktionen zwischen unterschiedlichen demografischen Kategorien zunehmend kommerziell organisiert und erfolgen nicht mehr auf der Grundlage sozialer Gemeinsamkeiten oder gleicher Ansprüche an die Stadtnutzung.

Verdrängung, Mieterhöhungen, Privatisierung, Kommerzialisierung und kulturelle Homogenisierung durch eine transnationale Elite sind ebenso Teil dieses Prozesses wie die hegemoniale und kapitalwirtschaftliche Kontrolle durch diese Eliten. Wie Florida betont, bedeutet dies eine

---

1 „Superstar-Städte" ist ein Ausdruck, den Florida von Joseph Gyourko, Christopher Mayer und Todd Sinai übernimmt, „Superstar Cities", in: American Economic Journal: Economic Policy, 5:4, 2013, S. 167–199 [http://www.nber.org/papers/w12355.pdf].
2 Richard Florida: The New Urban Crisis: How Our Cities Are Increasing Inequality, Deepening Segregation, and Failing the Middle Class and What We Can Do About It. New York: Basic Books, 2017, S. XV.

Verringerung der sozialen Mobilität und eine Verstärkung von Armutsfallen.

Während Kreative einst die *spontane* Frontlinie der Gentrifizierung bildeten, ist der Kunstbereich heute vollständig in die Umwandlungsmechanismen der Stadt- und Kapitalentwicklung integriert. Im Gegensatz zu den Imperativen eines Kunstbereichs, der sich an linkskritische Imperative hält, wie es die zeitgenössische Kunst meist tut, ist die Kunst – und insbesondere die zeitgenössische Kunst – seit einiger Zeit ein Anziehungspunkt und keine Spielverderberin für Kapital- und kommunale Investitionen, formatiert durch Gentrifizierung.

Dies stellt ein großes Dilemma für den kritisch denkenden Kunstschaffenden dar. Doch Unterstützung ist bereits zur Stelle, um Abhilfe zu schaffen. Wie bereits erwähnt, wird Gentrifizierung mittlerweile als ein Kernproblem von städtischen Entscheidungsträger*innen erkannt, die darauf bestehen, dass die Städte Räume und Mieten für einkommensschwache Sektoren wie Kunstschaffende (und andere Unternehmer*innen des Kreativsektors) *schützen* müssen, um die urbane Vitalität zu erhalten und die Städte vor den schädlichen Auswirkungen einer ungehinderten Gentrifizierung zu bewahren. Die Änderung der politischen Agenda stellt jedoch nicht die Grundprämisse einer kreativ geleiteten Gentrifizierung infrage. Vielmehr ist die Überprüfung der Gentrifizierung ein gutes Ergebnis für die kreative Klasse einschließlich der Kunstschaffenden und könnte sogar optimal wirken: Kreative können so ihre Rolle bei der Umwandlung von Städten zu ihren eigenen Zwecken beibehalten – mit dem zusätzlichen Vorteil, dass die nachfolgende Entwicklung *um sie herum stattfindet*.

Es bleiben jedoch Fragen offen: Was ist mit denen, die auch Ansprüche – vielleicht pointiertere, historisch begründete – an städtische Standorte haben, aber keine Kreativen sind? Was passiert mit den Interessen und materiellen Bedingungen dieser Bevölkerung, wenn eine Kombination aus kreativ geleiteter Gentrifizierung und Anti-Gentrifizierung die Politik prägt? Diese Bedenken werden in der nachstehenden Schlussfolgerung aufgegriffen, erfordern aber zunächst eine Ausarbeitung der dynamischen Logik, die Gentrifizierung und Anti-Gentrifizierung miteinander verbindet, der Vor- und Nachteile, mit denen Kreative in dieser Umstrukturierungsdynamik konfrontiert sind, und der Schwierigkeit, die dies alles insbesondere für diejenigen in der politischen Linken darstellt. Die Ausarbeitung wird zu Anleitungen führen, wie das Kunstfeld dazu beitragen kann, einer tief sitzenden Armut Abhilfe zu schaffen und nicht den eigenen Interessen. Dies erscheint wichtig, denn, wie zu sehen sein wird, liegt das Interesse des Kunstfelds offensichtlich mehr in der Aufrechterhaltung der Armutsfalle.

Die Grundbegriffe für die vorliegende Diskussion lauten wie folgt:

Gentrifizierung: Ruth Glass definiert Gentrifizierung erstmals 1964 als Begriff; in Bezugnahme auf die sich verändernde soziale Zusammensetzung bestimmter Bereiche in London beschreibt Glass folgende Enwicklung:

„[...] *eines nach dem anderen wurden viele der Quartiere der Arbeiterklasse von der Mittelschicht erobert [...] Schäbige, bescheidene Stallungen und Hütten [...] wurden eingenommen [...] und sind zu eleganten, teuren Wohnhäusern geworden. Hat dieser Prozess der ‚Gentrifizierung' einmal in einer Gegend begonnen, schreitet er schnell voran."*

Die Hauptmerkmale der Gentrifizierung sind, dass „alle oder die meisten Bewohner der Arbeiterklasse vertrieben werden und sich der gesamte soziale Charakter des Stadtteils verändert". Gleichzeitig befinden sich diejenigen, die vertrieben wurden, in einer schlechteren Situation als zuvor, einschließlich weiterer Wege zu bestehenden Arbeitsplätzen und Schulen, daraus folgt aufgrund der größeren Entfernungen ein Verlust von Arbeitsplätzen und sinnvollen Unterstützungsstrukturen wie Familien – und auch der Verlust von Vertrautheit, durch die das tägliche Leben routinemäßig und sicher ist.

Mietlücke: Die wirtschaftliche Triebkraft für die Gentrifizierung wird in den 1980er Jahren durch Neil Smiths Stilisierung der Mietlücke theoretisiert. Smith schlägt vor, dass mit zunehmendem Alter und Verfall der Gebäude die Höhe der Miete, die aus ihnen gewonnen werden kann, abnimmt (Phase A des indikativen Diagramms unten). Steigt gleichzeitig die aus neuen Grundstücken und Gebäuden erzielbare Pacht weiter an (Diagrammlinie B), so machen Eigentümer*innen des Grundstücks/Gebäudes im Vergleich zum Einkommenspotenzial einen effektiven Verlust, dies ist die Mietlücke (schattiert).
 Wenn diese Eigentümerschaft kapitalistisch geprägt ist, wird sie die Einnahmen erhöhen, indem sie einen oder mehrere der folgenden Punkte umsetzt (Phase C): Erneuerung des Gebäudes oder der Bodennutzung, Erhöhung der Mieten oder Verkauf an eine andere Partei, die die Immobilie zu einem im Vergleich zum Marktwert reduzierten Preis erwerben kann – und sie dann renoviert, um den Rentgap-Zyklus neu zu starten (oder indem sie sie bei steigendem Marktwert weiterverkauft; „Flipping" oder „Land-Banking").
 Das Endergebnis der Schließung der Mietlücke in Richtung des höheren Marktpreises für potenzielle Mieten besteht in jedem Fall darin, diejenigen zu vertreiben, die sich die gestiegenen Preise nicht mehr leisten können, und diejenigen anzuziehen, die dies können – was deutlich macht, dass die Gentrifizierung eine dynamische soziale Neuordnung, eine Vermögensverbesserung, ist.

Neoliberalismus und Super-Gentrifizierung: Die im Sinne der Mietlücke verstandene Gentrifizierung wurde ab den 1920er Jahren auf die eine oder andere Weise theoretisiert, wenn nicht bereits vorher. Allerdings bemerkt Florida, dass sich die Gentrifizierung des frühen 21. Jahrhunderts von ihren Vorläufern durch drei Merkmale der Klassenneuordnung und der für den Neoliberalismus spezifischen Eigentumsstrukturen unterscheidet:

1. die zunehmende Bündelung von Kapitaleigentum und Vermögen durch eine Superminorität;
2. die Erosion einer Mittelschicht, die auch von Menschen aus historisch einkommensschwachen Verhältnissen erreicht werden kann;
3. die Erzielung von Einnahmen durch verschiedene Formen des Leasings und der Pacht *von* peripheren und

ärmeren Beteiligten eines jeden Sektors *an* den wohlhabenderen und damit zunehmend reicheren Kern, der Eigentümer von Schlüsselangeboten und Dienstleistungen ist.

Gentrifizierung als Kanal für neoliberale Akkumulation führt insbesondere zu sehr schnellen Miet- und Immobilienpreiserhöhungen, schnellerem Umsatz bei zunehmender Eigentumskonzentration, systematisierten Mietextraktionsprozessen und einer entsprechend beschleunigten sozialen Umstrukturierung. Es ist dies eine Gentrifizierung auf Steroiden, manchmal auch als Super-Gentrifizierung bezeichnet.

 Kreative mit den für das Kunstfeld typischen relativ niedrigen Einkommen haben ein Interesse an diesem Zusammenhang von Gentrifizierung und Super-Gentrifizierung: an Gentrifizierung, denn der Sektor nutzt die Mietlücke, um dichte Stadträume zu bewohnen, in denen sich Kunstszenen traditionell konzentrieren; und an Super-Gentrifizierung, weil das Kunstfeld heutzutage ökonomisch um die Konsummuster einer neoliberalen Elite wegen derer finanziellen Stärke organisiert ist. Beide Gegebenheiten kommen den Kreativen sehr entgegen: Kunstwerke, gestaltete Objekte und Erfahrungen, Ideen und Diskurse sowie allgemeine Innovationen – all das sind Schlüsselelemente für die Erweiterung der Erfahrung, die in einer kreativ geleiteten Gentrifizierung angestrebt wird und die wiederum auf kostengünstige Räume in städtischen Zentren angewiesen ist, die folglich als Servicestellen für elitäre Bereicherung dienen.

 Wie inzwischen weithin bekannt ist, führt die fortgesetzte Lobpreisung dessen, was Kreative tun, während gleichzeitig die materiellen Bedingungen beseitigt werden, die es ihnen ermöglichen, genau dies zu tun, zu einer Schließung der Mietlücke und damit zu Unmut und Frustrationen innerhalb des Kreativsektors. Es ist dementsprechend konsequent, dass sich Kreative dem Kampf gegen die Gentrifizierung anschließen. Doch dies erschließt einen dritten Vorteilsvektor: die Anti-Gentrifizierung.

 Nach der Anfangsphase der Gentrifizierung, von der sie noch profitiert, versucht die kreativ geleitete Anti-Gentrifizierung eine weitere Entwicklung derselben zu verhindern. Das bedeutet, dass gerade der einkommensschwache Kreativsektor ein zweifaches Problem für andere darstellt, die ebenfalls Opfer der Gentrifizierung sind.

 Erstens: Während Allianzen mit lokalen Gemeinschaften, die von Räumung, Obdachlosigkeit und Verdrängung bedroht sind, das gemeinsame Interesse an billiger Vermietung und Besitz von Immobilien bekräftigen – was als öffentliches Gut verstanden wird –, bedeutet diese Ausrichtung nicht den optimalen Zustand für den Kreativsektor. Stattdessen ist es für ihn am vorteilhaftesten, sich an einer Schnittstelle zwischen Super-Gentrifizierung (Produkte, Verkäufe), Gentrifizierung (urbane Existenz) und Anti-Gentrifizierung (Immobilienanforderungen) bequem einzurichten.

 Zweitens: In ihrer Solidarität mit der historisch bedingten armen Bevölkerung der Stadt, die stets von Vertreibung bedroht ist, erhalten und schreiben diejenigen Kreativen, die sich für die Anti-Gentrifizierung einsetzen, die Mietlücke fort, die auch eine stellvertretende Maßnahme für relative Verarmung und Investitionsabbau ist.

Die Vermarktung der Anti-Gentrifizierung
Suhail Malik

Zur Erläuterung: Jede Art von Entwicklung als Gentrifizierung identifizierend, schreibt eine solche Anti-Gentrifizierung die fortgesetzte Desinvestition in den ärmeren Stadtteilen fest, in denen eine ausreichend große Mietlücke zu verzeichnen ist. Im Namen einer solchen Solidarität kann die Anti-Gentrifizierung in Städten, die ansonsten ihre allgemeine Kapitalbasis und Produktivität erhöhen, damit bottom-up zu der durch die neoliberale Gentrifizierung gefestigten wirtschaftlichen Segregation beitragen. Noch alarmierender ist, dass – da die neoliberale Gentrifizierung die soziale Mobilität untergräbt und die urbane Segregation sowie die ungleiche Vermögensverteilung in Städten verstärkt – die Anti-Gentrifizierung die historisch festgefahrene Armutsfalle, in der die Armen über Generationen hinweg verharren, weiter manifestieren kann.

Kreative, die die Anti-Gentrifizierung unterstützen (unabsichtlich oder nicht), um ihren eigenen Bedarf an niedrigen Mieten und billigem Eigentum zu decken, können dadurch die Desinvestition aufrechterhalten und somit die Armut der Armen verstärken. Der direkte Nutzen der Anti-Gentrifizierung für Kreative verankert die auf Vermögen basierende soziale Hierarchie, die durch die städtische Raumordnung durchgesetzt wird. Diese fortgesetzte indirekte Ausbeutung der Armen und Festschreibung der ökonomisch-räumlichen Schichtung kann als „rechte Anti-Gentrifizierung" bezeichnet werden. Die rechte Anti-Gentrifizierung unterstützt die neoliberale Gentrifizierung.

Die Verschärfung der wirtschaftlichen und sozialen Segregation in den Städten stellt ein unüberwindbares Problem für die politische Linke dar, für die die gesellschaftliche Organisation einschließlich der Städte aufgrund zunehmender wirtschaftlicher und politischer Gleichstellung gerecht, soziokulturell expandierend, inklusiv, von kollektivem Interesse und sozial liberal sein sollte. Wirtschaftliche und erfahrene Armut werden durch die Verbesserung von Dienstleistungen, Versorgung und Infrastruktur gemildert, vom Grundbedarf an Wasser und Energie über erschwingliche Verkehrsverbindungen bis hin zu angemessenem Wohnen. Die Armutsfalle wird durch Investitionen in Infrastruktur und Menschen, durch die Veränderung ihrer Lebensbedingungen und materiellen Verhältnisse geöffnet. Dazu muss ein Weg aufgezeigt werden, der sich von den beiden Standardoptionen, Gentrifizierung und reaktive rechte Anti-Gentrifizierung, unterscheidet.

Ein solcher Weg ist nicht schwer zu formulieren: Nicht jede städtische Wirtschaftsentwicklung ist gentrifizierend, denn sie muss nicht von exogenen Interessen oder finanziell spekulativen Entwickelnden geleitet werden. Tatsächlich muss dieser letzte Begriff aus seinen inzwischen fast ausschließlichen Assoziationen mit der Kapitalkonzentration herausgeholt werden – Assoziationen, die in der neoliberalen Lehre verwurzelt sind. Entwicklung ist notwendig, um dem politischen Imperativ der sozialen Mobilität von einem ärmeren zu einem reicheren Teil der Bevölkerung gerecht zu werden. Und es ist diese Entwicklung, die durch die reaktive Bildung der rechten Anti-Gentrifizierung vereitelt wird. Doch eine linke Forderung nach Entwicklung übt nicht nur Druck auf die Gentrifizierung, sondern auch auf die Anti-Gentrifizierung aus. Obwohl die Linderung von Armut, Not und vor allem auch der zunehmende Zugang zu höheren Lebensstandards eine häufige Rechtfertigung für die Gentrifizierung darstellen, muss die politische Linke auch darauf bestehen, dass Verbesserungen des Einkommensniveaus, der Infrastruktur und der Dienstleistungen in armen Gebieten nicht zu Vertreibungen (direkt oder indirekt) führen. Vielmehr erhalten sie die Versorgung für ankommende Bedürftige aufrecht und verteidigen die Bestandsbewohnerschaft gegen Enteignung.

Im Großen und Ganzen ist eine Pro-Entwicklungs-Anti-Gentrifizierung (ProEAG) erforderlich. Die ProEAG kapitalisiert die Anti-Gentrifizierung: Sie erfordert die Bereitstellung von Kapital für die städtischen Armen, was alle sein können: Menschen jeglicher Hautfarbe, die über zwei Generationen deindustrialisierter Überschussbevölkerungen etablierten Armen, die neuen Armen (wie der wirtschaftliche oder politische Flüchtling) oder die ehemalige Mittelschicht. Anstatt nur die Interessen der vom Druck durch externe Preiserhöhungen und Landnahme bedrohten Gemeinden zu schützen, fördert die ProEAG die Forderungen der Wahlkreise, die verdrängt werden könnten, indem sie sich für die Entwicklung dieser Gebiete für diejenigen einsetzt, die in erster Linie dort leben. Diese Pro-Entwicklungs-Kapitalisierung zur Bekämpfung der Armut ist eine aktive linke Anti-Gentrifizierung.

Gegen die Bildung einer reaktiven rechten Anti-Gentrifizierung, die die Mietlücke aufrechterhalten will, sieht ein ProEAG-Ansatz auch vor, die Mietlücke durch folgende Modi von intensiv gelenkter Kapitalisierung zu schließen oder zumindest zu verkleinern:

1. Blockieren von Möglichkeiten zur Mieterhöhung oder zumindest Abschwächung ihrer Steigerungsraten, kurz: Mietpreisbeschränkungen;
2. Gewähren von Mietbeihilfen durch staatliche Unterstützung;
3. Senkung des marktüblichen Mietpreises für Immobilien durch Verzerrung des Preissystems, indem Marktkontrollen eingeführt werden.

Diese Maßnahmen reichen jedoch allein nicht aus, um eine ProEAG-Agenda zu erfüllen: Erstere ist eine abgeschwächte Form fortgesetzter Desinvestition und eine einfach zu handhabende, aber kurzfristige Variante der reaktiven Anti-Gentrifizierung. Der zweite Vorschlag verstärkt die Dynamiken der Mieterhöhungen, indem er die Einnahmen der Immobilieneigentümerschaft sichert und so das Kapital mit staatlicher Beihilfe weiter konzentriert – und gleichzeitig die Standardvorgänge der Gentrifizierung verzögert.

Wie die staatliche Wohnbauförderung kann auch die Mietpreisbindung nur dann zur ProEAG beitragen, wenn sie mit einer Umverteilung des Eigentums einhergeht. Das heißt, die ProEAG muss verbesserte Modelle und Praktiken der finanziellen, monetären und rechtlichen Mechanismen einführen, um die Verdrängung und weitere Herabsetzung der städtischen Armen zu verhindern.

Ein abschließender Vorschlag ist, dass ein überarbeitetes Kunstfeld dazu beitragen kann, diese Entwicklungsstrategie als einen Modus seiner Praxis zu etablieren. Die Forderung ist hier, dass die aktuellen materiellen und finanziellen Bedingungen einer großen Mehrheit im Kunstbereich – das geringe Einkommen aus der Kunst und der Bedarf an Raum für die materielle Praxis und

Ausstellung – zurückgesetzt werden müssen. Tatsächlich bestehende Bedingungen für die Kunst müssen als transformatives, modulares Element in einer Kette von Interessen und Bewertungen erfasst und mobilisiert werden, die weit über das begrenzte und empirisch bestimmte Kunstfeld hinausgehen und sich auf Finanzen, Recht und Stadtstrategie erstrecken. Die praktischen Aspekte der Kunst erfordern dies.

    Das ist in der Tat keine große Sache: Schon heute agiert Kunst branchenübergreifend und transdisziplinär. Und vor allem ist sie Teil einer globalen städtischen Wertschöpfungskette (GUVC = *Global Urban Value Chain*), die manipulierbar ist. Genauer gesagt, weil es sich um Kunst handelt, sollte sie manipuliert werden – auf eine Weise, die für diejenigen, die durch die von den GUVC geschaffene Kapitalisierung geschwächt sind, als unerreichbar erachtet werden kann. Diese Manipulation beinhaltet die Zusammenarbeit mit rechtlichen und finanziellen städtischen Agierenden, die über die technischen Fähigkeiten verfügen, Entwicklungsstrategien zu formulieren, die die Interessen der städtischen Armen unterstützen. Und solche rechtlichen, vertraglichen und kommunalen Arbeiten sind ohnehin wieder im Möglichkeitsraum der Kunst als eine branchenübergreifende, transdemografische und interdisziplinäre Praxis. Es ist ein günstiger Zeitpunkt, dieser Forderung nachzukommen, denn die neoliberale Ordnung der letzten 40 Jahre befindet sich in einer globalen Umstrukturierung, die sich auf die Kapitalorganisation jeder Größenordnung und Lokalität auswirkt. Die aktuelle politische und Legitimationskrise des Neoliberalismus bedeutet, dass die aus der (Super-)Gentrifizierung bekannte, finanziell gelenkte Akkumulation heute sehr anfällig für Delegitimierung und Re-Vektorisierung durch alternative Modelle, Einkommensstrukturen und Kapitalisierungsinteressen ist. Und so, wie die zeitgenössische Kunst eine wirksame Rolle für die Hegemonialisierung und Dominanz der neoliberalen Ordnung gespielt hat, so kann und sollte die Kunst – die eine andere Kunst als die zeitgenössische Kunst sein müsste – ihren Teil zu deren Auflösung beitragen. Die ProEAG verlangt, dass die Manipulation von GUVC durch die Kunst ihre eigenen materiellen Grundanforderungen an schlichten Arbeitsraum, preiswertes Wohnen und Zugang zu transnationaler Mobilität als Komponenten zur mittelfristigen Linderung der städtischen Armut strategisiert. Und diese Kunstwirtschaft wird von der zunehmend plutokratischen Macht der städtischen Reichen und Superreichen gleichsam weggesteuert.

    Was und wen die Kreativen stattdessen für ihre eigenen Ökonomien ansprechen, muss sich dann von der einseitigen extraktiven Unterwerfung gegenüber einer neoliberalen Elite verlagern, was wiederum eine Umstrukturierung der Kunstwirtschaft und die Reorganisation ihrer Hierarchiebildung erfordert.

Übersetzt von Jana Thormählen

Berlin and the Blockchain

The Berlin of the 1990s still brings tears to the eyes of artists and investors alike. It was a legendary era of unregulated freedom – in which legendary Berlin club life began, as did the investments of large real estate companies, which until the mid-2000s would acquire state-owned properties at ridiculous prices and achieve astronomical returns.
The Berlin of the 1990s made social and cultural innovation possible, was low-threshold, imaginative, unregulated, adventurous and free. It was also the starting point of the current Berlin housing crisis – based on the unregulated and unsustainable sale of state-owned real estate of that decade.

Since its mythical introduction and the generation of the so-called Genesis block – the first Bitcoin block – ten years ago, the development of blockchain has fascinated artists and investors alike. In many ways, it resembles the ambivalent relationship between artistic freedom and the economic Wild West, as offered by Berlin in the 1990s.

Using blockchain, artists conceived social utopias and illustrated these ideas by programming and testing them in practice. To name but a few, in 2014 the artists Pedro Victor Brandao and Maira das Neves developed a Bitcoin 'mining farm' in the coal-mining area of Oer Erkenschwick, based on coal mining in the Ruhr area, and handed the cryptos they produced to the neighbourhood, so they could take the fate of their city into their own hands.

Terra0 developed a blockchain-based system that allows natural resources such as forests, flowers and mushrooms to manage themselves, and in 2015, the MAK Vienna museum acquired a blockchain-based work – Harm van den Dorpel's Event Listeners (2015), a limited edition 'screensaver'. In 2017, Ruth Cathlow, co-founder of Furtherfield, a London-based platform for art and digital technologies, stated: 'We know that the blockchain is an important and powerful new technology but we don't know what a blockchain can do yet.'

By 2020, blockchain technologies seem to have outgrown their infancy, and many parallels to the financial-historical developments of the city of Berlin are becoming apparent. Only a few economic adventurers relied on Berlin real estate in the 1990s, just as only a few of them used their computer graphics cards to mine Bitcoin. With minimal economic investment, they were able to reap the returns of a lifetime only a few years later. In the meantime, the global financial market has arrived in both worlds – Berlin real estate is the standard in the portfolios of global hedge funds, and blockchain is no longer the sole playground of artists and creative tech nerds: governments have published the first blockchain strategies. Germany relies on blockchain strategies for the technological development of the energy sector; India, Australia and the United Arab Emirates announce their own strategies in turn; and Belarus exempts crypto investors from tax burdens and invests in a Special Economic Zone, a crypto park, and a 'mining hotel'. Global companies are announcing sustainable investments,

Berlin and the Blockchain
Matthias Einhoff

or even their own decentralized blockchain-based payment systems.

The starting point for the turbulent developments in Berlin and the digital financial world were each major paradigm shifts: the fall of the Berlin Wall, with the subsequent spatial, economic and administrative merging of the city of Berlin on the one hand, and the publication of the white paper by Satoshi Nakamoto (a pseudonym used by the still-unknown developer(s), on the other.)

But why should blockchain be more than just another technological step in the history of digital innovation? Why should it be a miracle of social and economic innovation? Why did the white paper become a source of inspiration even for artistic work? Ben Vickers, technical director of the Serpentine Galleries in London, makes the connection in the following terms: 'Artists who were previously thinking through almost utopian ideas or different organizing structures as part of their practice have got mixed up in the blockchain space, and then suddenly, they've found themselves migrating away from the art world. They're now participating in this emerging blockchain economy and are producing companies but working with an artistic toolset.' Vickers sees the city of Berlin at the centre of this development.

To understand why the blockchain is a contender for the greatest digital renewal since the introduction of the internet itself, it helps to understand what problems it can solve: It rid the digital world of the so-called 'double spending' problem. 'Multiple spending' means a transaction of a value from person A) to person B), in which person A) keeps a copy of the value for himself and thus spends the value twice. In cash terms, imagine that person A) makes a perfect colour copy of a banknote before giving it to person B). This would be highly problematic for the integrity of

Blockchain mining rig the þit, Brandao/das Neves, 2014

its value, and making the banknote as counterfeit-proof as possible is costly and time-consuming.

In the digital world, it is much more difficult to prevent the illegal creation of copies. The associated cryptographic and legal effort can only be provided by large companies and governments, and even then, the data is not 100 per cent secured against illegal access and distribution. Similar to the analogue world, strong central control systems are needed.

The blockchain is a form of encryption that makes it impossible to produce illegal copies without the users' system being made aware of it. The form of encryption incorporates the history of all previously made transactions into each individual value. Think of it as a banking book (or 'ledger'), which is managed not only by a central bank but also by all users who trade in these values. The bank ledger is written directly into the value. Each time a value is to be transferred from person A) to person B), all those trading in the network are informed, and the transaction is transferred to every bankbook, that is, every value. Only if the counterfeiter controls a majority of all computers and values involved in the calculation process, could this new majority of computers claim that the fake is the correct version of the value in question. However, the forgers would need enormous computing power, since the complete accounting history on all computers would have to be recalculated from the beginning. This high hurdle is both the strength and weakness of blockchains or decentralized banking books (distributed ledger). The enormous computational effort required from all users involved makes the system sluggish, and requires an enormous amount of energy. Although more efficient further developments of blockchain applications are on the way, discussions about the ecological sense of the technology have flared up.

For some simple areas of global trade, the classic blockchain is, despite its shortcomings, a suitable tool. It is capable of generating trust between trading partners without the regulatory intervention of nation states and trade organizations. More complex social systems dependent on human interaction reach their limits in the blockchain: Flexibility and adaptation to changes in creative processes can only be inadequately captured by the classic blockchain. In decentralized autonomous organizations – DAOs for short – these deficits are overcome by combining social interaction possibilities and blockchain-based 'smart contracts'.

The influence of blockchain applications in the global transaction market is still small. After an initial phase of consolidation, crypto-currencies are still in their adolescence – subject to capricious fluctuations, not yet localized socially, but brimming with great hopes and revolutionary ideas. And here may lie the unique strength of blockchain: as a trigger and renewer of social discourses. Paul Cocksworth, as a Marxist thinker, sees in blockchain the potential for the working class to take charge of its own destiny without becoming an oppressive hegemonic class in their own right. David Colombia is of the opinion that blockchain cements neoliberal structures, since the precondition of a blockchain – physical network infrastructure and computing power – is still in the hands of global companies and nation states protecting their interests. Cyberlibertarians view the ultimate networking of information and integrated communication channels as a chance to eliminate the burden of human error, and the Chinese state is likely to see this similarly. Conservative, humanist economists see blockchaining as a loss of human sovereignty. Traditional neo liberal thinkers fear the takeover of market mechanisms by a planned economy run by artificial intelligence. The cards of economic theory have been reshuffled since the birth of Bitcoin, which coincided in turn with the deep crisis of the 21st century banking system. This wake-up call is visualized, criticized and accelerated by artistic prototypes. The above economic questions are the very subject matter of these works, they are at the centre of their considerations and are not merely discursive accessories. Art shows the way out of adolescent fantasy, into the speculative world of new models of society.

Berlin und die Blockchain

Warum hat Blockchain das Potenzial, eine Wundertüte für gesellschaftliche und ökonomische Innovation zu sein? Warum wurde das Bitcoin-Whitepaper zu einer Inspirationsquelle künstlerischer Arbeiten? Ben Vickers, technischer Direktor der Serpentine Galleries in London, stellt den Zusammenhang über die Potenziale der Blockchain für gesellschaftliche Veränderungen her: „Artists who were previously thinking through almost utopian ideas or different organising structures as part of their practice have got mixed up in the blockchain space, and then suddenly, they've found themselves migrating away from the art world. They're now participating in this emergent blockchain economy and are producing companies but working with an artistic toolset." Vickers sieht die Stadt Berlin im Zentrum dieser Entwicklung.

  Das Berlin der 1990er Jahre treibt noch heute Kunstschaffenden und Investor*innen gleichermaßen Tränen in die Augen. Eine sagenumwobene Ära der unregulierten Freiräume – in denen das legendäre Berliner Clubleben genauso seinen Ausgang nahm wie die Investitionen großer Immobilienkonzerne, die bis in die Mitte der 2000er Jahre landeseigene Immobilien zu Spottpreisen erwerben und mit ihnen Renditen in astronomischen Höhen erzielen konnten. Das Berlin der 1990er Jahre ermöglichte gesellschaftlich-kulturelle Innovation, war niedrigschwellig, ideenreich, unreguliert, abenteuerlich und frei. Es war gleichzeitig der Ausgangspunkt der aktuellen Berliner Wohnungskrise – die auf dem unregulierten und unnachhaltigen Verkauf landeseigener Immobilien jener Dekade basiert.

  Die Entwicklung von Blockchain übt seit seiner zum Mythos gereiften Einführung und der Generierung des sogenannten Genesis-Block – dem ersten Bitcoin-Block – vor nunmehr zehn Jahren eine Faszination auf Kunstschaffende und Investor*innen aus, die dem ambivalenten Verhältnis von künstlerischen Freiheiten und wirtschaftlichem Wild West, wie es das Berlin der 1990er Jahre bot, in Vielem gleicht: Anhand von Blockchain erdachten Kunstschaffende gesellschaftliche Utopien und entwickelten repräsentative Werke dieser Ideen, indem sie sie programmierten und praktisch erprobten. Ich nenne an dieser Stelle vier Beispiele.

  2014 entwickelte das Kunstduo Pedro Victor Brandao und Maira das Neves in Anlehnung an das Schürfen von Kohle im Ruhrgebiet einen Bitcoin – Mining-Farm – im Kohlestandort Oer Erkenschwick und verschenkte die produzierten Kryptos an die Nachbarschaft, sodass diese die Geschicke ihrer Stadt selbst in die Hand nehmen könne.[1] Das Kollektiv Terra0 entwickelte ein blockchainbasiertes System, das es natürlichen Ressourcen wie Wäldern, Blumen, Pilzen ermöglichen soll, sich selbst zu verwalten.[2] 2015 erwirbt erstmals ein Museum eine blockchainbasierte Arbeit: Harm van den Dorpels *Event Listeners* (2015), einen

---

1 http://thebpit.org/
2 https://terra0.org/

Berlin und die Blockchain
Matthias Einhoff

Screensaver in limitierter Auflage.[3] Und 2017 konstatiert Ruth Cathlow, Mitgründerin von Furtherfield, einer Plattform für Kunst und digitale Technologien aus London: „We know that the blockchain is an important and powerful new technology but we don't know what a blockchain can do yet."

Keine zwei Jahre später scheinen Blockchain-Technologien den Kinderschuhen entwachsen und es zeigen sich viele Parallelen zu den finanzgeschichtlichen Entwicklungen der Stadt Berlin. Nur wenige wirtschaftliche Glücksritter setzen in den 1990ern auf Berliner Immobilien, genauso, wie nur wenige ihre Computer-Grafikkarten zum Schürfen von Bitcoin nutzen. Bei minimalem ökonomischen Mitteleinsatz können sie jeweils nur wenige Jahre später die Rendite ihres Lebens einfahren. Inzwischen ist in beiden Welten der globale Finanzmarkt angekommen: Berliner Immobilien sind Standards in den Portfolios globaler Hedgefonds und auch die Blockchain ist nicht länger die alleinige Spielwiese von Kunstschaffenden und kreativen Tech-Nerds: Regierungen haben erste Blockchain-Strategien publiziert. Deutschland setzt auf Blockchain zur technologischen Entwicklung des Energiesektors,[4] Indien, Australien, die Emirate kündigen eigene Blockchain-Strategien an,[5] Weißrussland befreit Krypto-Investoren von Steuerlasten[6] und investiert in eine Sonderwirtschaftszone, einen Krypto-Park und ein Mining-Hotel.[7] Global agierende Firmen kündigen nachhaltige Investitionen oder gleich eigene dezentrale blockchainbasierte Zahlungssysteme an.[8]

Ausgangspunkt der turbulenten Entwicklungen in Berlin und der digitalen Finanzwelt waren jeweils große Paradigmenwechsel: der Fall der Berliner Mauer mit der räumlichen, wirtschaftlichen und verwalterischen Zusammenführung der Stadt Berlin auf der einen Seite; und die Veröffentlichung des Whitepapers von Satoshi Nakamoto[9] (ein von den bis heute unbekannten Entwickler*innen genutztes Pseudonym) auf der anderen Seite. Doch warum sollte Blockchain mehr sein als ein weiterer technologischer Schritt in der Geschichte digitaler Innovationen?

Um zu verstehen, warum die Blockchain eine Anwärterin auf die größte digitale Erneuerung seit der Einführung des Internets selbst ist, hilft es zu verstehen, welche Probleme die Blockchain lösen kann: Sie entledigt die digitale Welt des sogenannten Double-spending-Problems. Übersetzt bedeutet der Begriff Mehrfachausgaben und meint eine Transaktion eines Wertes von Person A auf Person B, in der Person A eine Kopie des Wertes für sich behält und den Wert damit zweimal ausgibt. Übertragen

---

3   https://www.artnews.com/art-news/market/mak-vienna-becomes-first-museum-to-acquire-art-using-bitcoin-a-harm-van-den-dorpel-3995/
4   https://www.bmwi.de/Redaktion/DE/Pressemitteilungen/2019/20190918-bundesregierung-verabschiedet-blockchain-strategie.html
5   https://de.cointelegraph.com/news/indian-government-to-issue-national-blockchain-strategy
6   https://www.handelsblatt.com/finanzen/maerkte/devisen-rohstoffe/alexander-lukaschenko-europas-letzter-diktator-will-blockchain-koenig-werden/20785872.html?ticket=ST-46128358-7y39Ezm7nxVdFXyLJE1o-ap6
7   https://www.coinkurier.de/weissrussland-ist-ein-unentdecktes-krypto-paradies-und-hat-ein-mining-hotel/
8   https://www.forbes.com/sites/biserdimitrov/2019/08/13/large-enterprises-are-betting-on-blockchain-in-2019/#12c6284a1bff
9   https://bitcoin.org/en/bitcoin-paper

Berlin und die Blockchain
Matthias Einhoff

auf analoges Geld stelle man sich vor, dass Person A eine perfekte Farbkopie eines Geldscheins macht, bevor sie ihn Person B übergibt. Dies wäre für die Integrität des Wertes hochgradig problematisch – und wird daher aufwendig durch möglichst fälschungssichere Geldscheine und vor allem durch einen Staat, der den Akt des *double spending* kontrolliert und stark sanktioniert, unterbunden.

In der digitalen Welt ist es deutlich schwieriger, das illegale Erstellen von Kopien zu unterbinden. Der damit verbundene kryptografische und juristische Aufwand kann lediglich durch große Firmen und Staaten erbracht werden, und auch dann sind die Daten nicht 100-prozentig sicher vor Zugriff und illegaler Verbreitung. Ähnlich wie in der analogen Welt bedarf es starker zentraler Kontrollsysteme, die verhindern, dass der grundsätzlich einfache Akt des Kopierens illegal vollzogen wird.

Die Blockchain ist eine Form der Verschlüsselung, die es unmöglich macht, illegale Kopien eines Wertes zu erstellen, ohne dass das System der Nutzenden es bemerkt. Die Form der Verschlüsselung zieht die Historie aller vorher gemachten Transaktionen in jeden einzelnen Wert mit ein. Vorstellen kann man sich dies wie ein Bankenbuch (oder *Ledger*), das nicht nur von einer zentralen Bank geführt wird, sondern von allen Nutzenden, die mit den Werten handeln. Das Bankenbuch ist direkt in den Wert eingeschrieben. Jedes Mal, wenn ein Wert von Person A auf Person B übertragen werden soll, werden alle im Netzwerk mit dem Wert Handelnden darüber informiert und der Vorgang wird in jedes Bankenbuch, also jeden Wert, übertragen. Sollte also der Versuch unternommen werden, einen Wert mehrfach auszugeben, oder illegal zu übertragen, würden dies die anderen Nutzenden bemerken, da sie alle „Buch führen" und diese unzulässige Übertragung als falsch unterbinden können.

Einzig wenn die Fälschenden über eine Mehrheit aller am Rechenprozess beteiligten Computer und Werte verfügen, könnte diese neue Mehrheit der Rechner behaupten, die gemachte Fälschung sei die korrekte Generierung des Wertes und die eigentlich richtige Generierung die Fälschung. Hierfür müssten die Fälschenden jedoch neben der Mehrheit der Rechner über eine enorme Rechenpower verfügen, da die komplette Buchungshistorie auf allen Rechnern von Anfang an neu berechnet werden müsste. Diese hohe Hürde ist einerseits die Stärke, andererseits die Schwäche von Blockchain beziehungsweise dem dezentralen Bankenbuch (Distributed Ledger). Der enorme rechnerische Aufwand bei allen Beteiligten macht das System träge und kommt mit einem enormen Energieaufwand daher. Obwohl effizientere Weiterentwicklungen von Blockchain-Anwendungen auf dem Weg sind, ist die Diskussion um die ökologische Sinnhaftigkeit der Technik entbrannt.

Für einige einfache Bereiche des globalen Handels ist die klassische Blockchain trotz ihrer Defizite ein geeignetes Werkzeug. Sie ist in der Lage, ohne das regulierende Eingreifen von Nationalstaaten und Handelsorganisationen, Vertrauen zwischen Handelspartner*innen zu generieren. Komplexere und von menschlicher Interaktion abhängige soziale Systeme stoßen bei der Blockchain an ihre Grenzen: Flexibilität und Anpassung an Veränderungen in kreativen Prozessen können von der klassischen Blockchain nur unzureichend erfasst werden. In dezentralen autonomen Organisationen – kurz DAOs – werden diese Defizite durch die Verbindung von sozialen Interaktionsmöglichkeiten und blockchainbasierten *Smart Contracts* überwunden.

Der Einfluss von Blockchain-Anwendungen auf den weltweiten Transaktionsmarkt ist noch gering. Nach einer ersten Phase der Konsolidierung befinden sich Kryptowährungen immer noch im gesellschaftlichen Jugendzimmer – großen launischen Schwankungen unterworfen, gesellschaftlich noch nicht lokalisiert, aber mit großen Hoffnungen und revolutionären Ideen verbunden.

ALLESANDERSPLATZ
KUNSTrePUBLIK

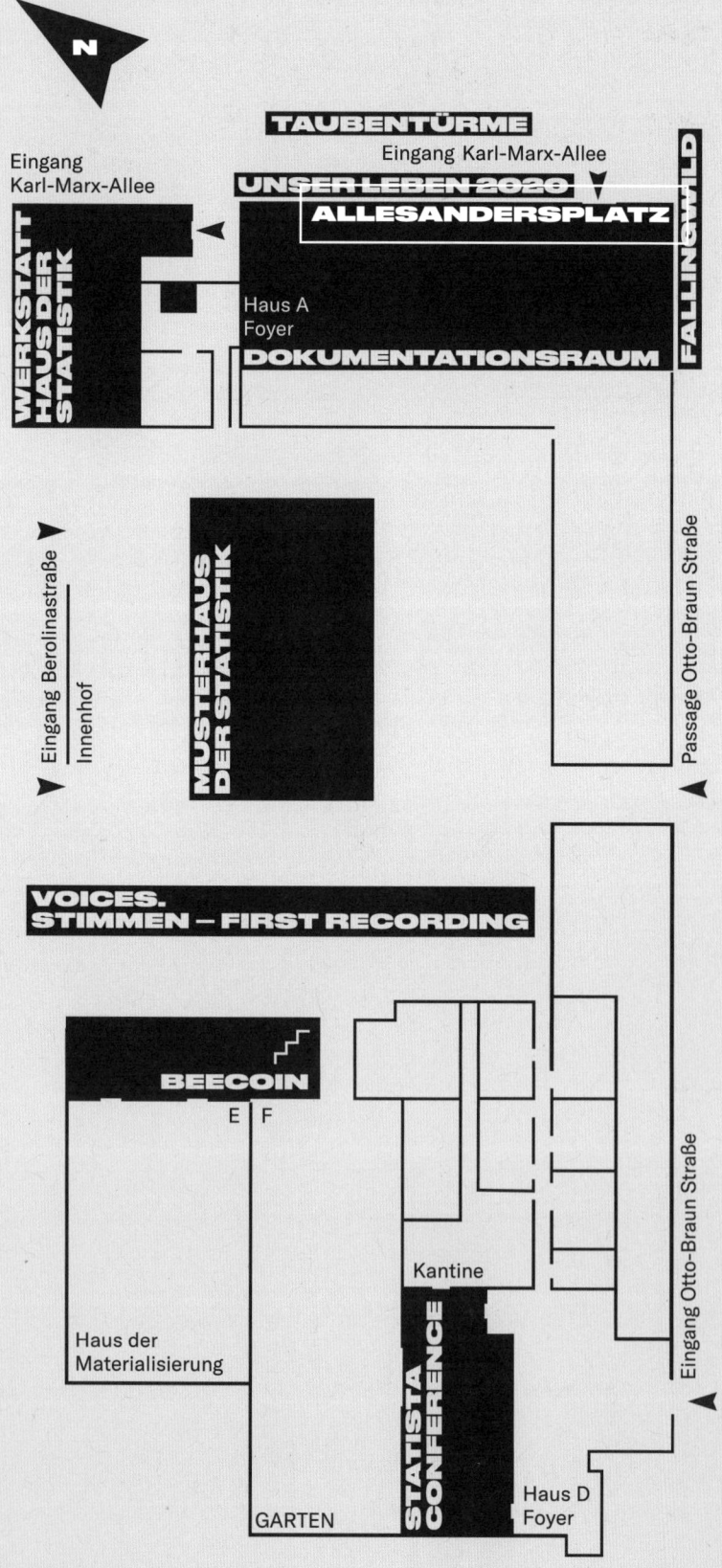

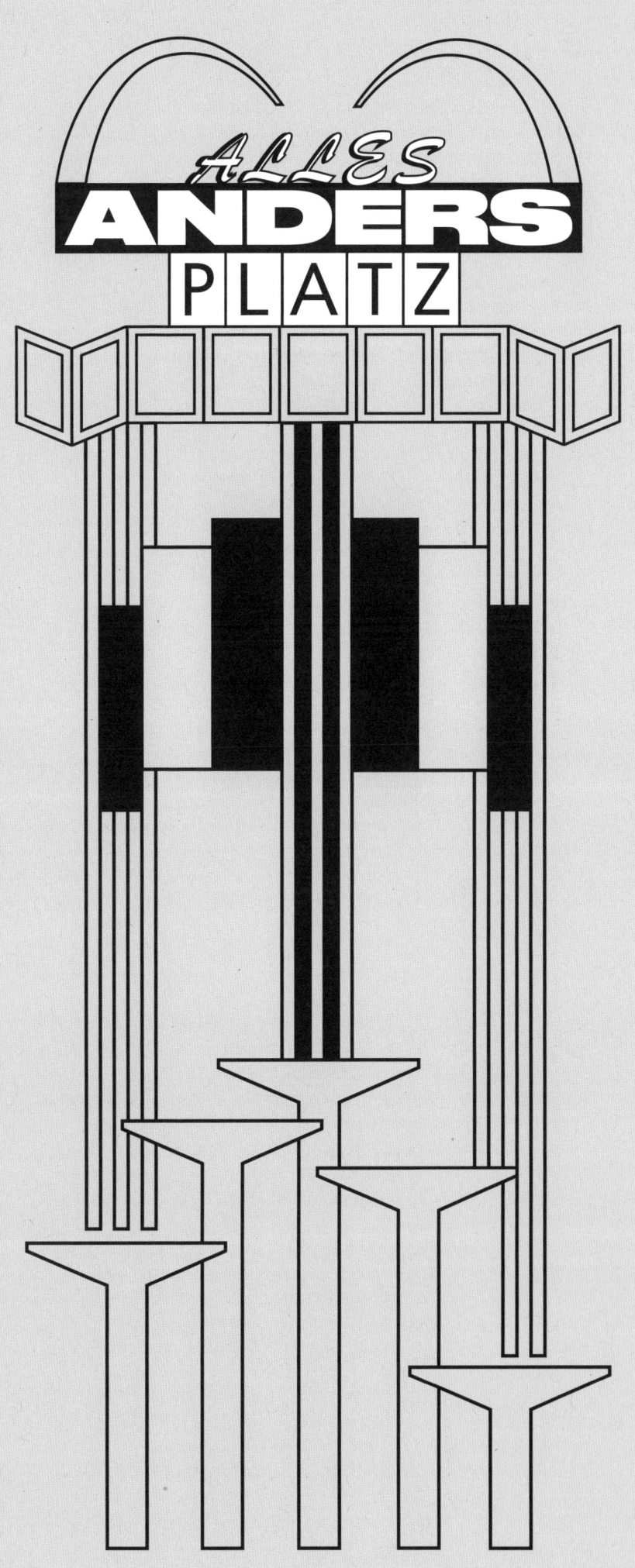

Allesandersplatz

Since May 2019, white signage on the roof of the Haus der Statistik (HdS) has been beaming its message far and wide, lending a new face to the vacant building with its rows of missing window panes, and proclaiming the power of change with nothing more than a shift in three letters: ALLESANDERSPLATZ (Altogether Different Square) is a clear nod to the adjacent city square, 'The Alex,' which was named after Czar Alexander I in 1805, to signal Prussia's close bond with Russia at that time. Though interrupted by the First and Second World Wars, this friendship (between states meanwhile transmuted into the GDR and the USSR) persisted also after 1945. In fact, the first phase of reconstruction in the socialist capital Berlin was launched in the early 1950s with an urban planning homage to the sister city Moscow. The tree-lined, stately boulevard Karl-Marx-Allee (originally: Stalinallee) was designed to host military parades and to house distinguished GDR citizens. The HdS was added in 1969: a modern overture at Karl-Marx-Allee no. 1.

'*Zielgerichtet werben*' (targeted advertising) was the original signage on the HdS building, along with an arrow pointing skywards. Advertising in the GDR was a tool of urban design, referring not so much to consumer products as to a broader ideology. The Central Office of Statistics, based at HdS, was concerned not so much with diversity, say, as with keeping tabs, statistics, on ALL and ALLES, in order then to forecast trends that in turn would serve the Politburo as a basis for the planned economy.

The term ALLESANDERS aptly describes the situation of many East Berliners in the years after the fall of the Berlin Wall, for the political shift turned their world order on its head overnight. Yet many of those who were privileged members of East German society live in the nearby apartments to this day: they are still the majority in the HdS neighborhood.

Following its integration into the administrative structures of the Federal Republic of Germany in the early 1990s, the Central Office of Statistics was turned into the Office of Statistics for the reconfigured territory of the former GDR. Also, a newly founded institution moved into the building: the Federal Commission for the Records of the State Security Service of the former German Democratic Republic (Bundesbeauftragte für die Stasi Unterlagen). Citizens could now apply to view any files compiled on them by the East German secret police and its informants. Many files contained intimate details disclosed by family and friends.

ALLESANDERSPLATZ is keeping a watchful eye on The Alex, not least on the master plan drawn up by Kollhoff in 1994, and the urban development plan of 2000. The HdS was earmarked for replacement by a new tower block— but things took an ALTOGETHER DIFFERENT turn. Berlin needs meeting places that serve the common good. And the oft-cited capitalist determinism that swears by financial dividends to be squeezed from city space could become something ALTOGETHER DIFFERENT here too.

ALLESANDERSPLATZ stands for the continual and unusual process of urban development now underway in and around the HdS—and, above all, for better proposals made for its future use. The very thing Alexanderplatz and

other inner-city spaces currently fail to offer is being hammered out here. It's a space where a broad variety of groups can live and work; where inclusive access and community-oriented programs take priority; where people come together to discuss issues of relevance to the city they want to live in; and, above all, a space where they can put their ideas into practice.

[1]
Demonstration 4.11.89, HdS Alexanderplatz

Allesandersplatz

Seit Mai 2019 strahlt auf dem Dach des Hauses der Statistik (HdS) dezent ein weißer Schriftzug. Er gibt dem leer stehenden, weitgehend fensterlosen Haus einen neuen Namen und proklamiert Alternativen: Mit einer Veränderung von drei Buchstaben verweist ALLESANDERSPLATZ klar auf den angrenzenden Alexanderplatz. Namensgeber war ab 1805 Zar Alexander I., diese Geste unterstrich die enge Bindung Preußens an Russland. Diese Freundschaft – unterbrochen durch zwei Weltkriege – zweier im Laufe der Zeit zur Sowjetunion und DDR gewandelten Staaten setzte sich nach dem Ende des Zweiten Weltkriegs fort. In städtebaulicher Referenz zur Bruderstadt Moskau entstand in den 1950er Jahren im ersten Bauabschnitt des neuen sozialistischen Berliner Hauptstadtzentrum die Karl-Marx-Allee als Pracht- und Paradestraße. An deren Anfang befindet sich mit der Hausnummer 1 seit 1969 das Haus der Statistik.

[1]

Auf dessen Dach wurde der Schriftzug „Zielgerichtet werben" mit einem Pfeil in den Himmel installiert. Werbung in der DDR war stadträumliches Gestaltungselement und verwies weniger auf ein Konsumprodukt, als vielmehr auf eine Ideologie: den gewünschten gesellschaftlichen Mehrwert. In der im HdS ansässigen Staatlichen Zentralverwaltung für Statistik ging es weniger darum ANDERES, sondern ALLES in Zahlen zu erfassen, um daraus Prognosen zu errechnen, die als Grundlage für die Zielvorgaben des Politbüros dienten.

Mit dem Mauerfall beschreibt der Begriff ALLESANDERS die Lebenssituation für viele Ostberliner*innen in den Wendejahren treffend, wurde doch quasi über Nacht die alte Ordnung auf den Kopf gestellt. In den angrenzenden Wohnungen verblieben viel der in der DDR Privilegierten und formen so einen großen Teil der Nachbarschaft.

Die Staatliche Zentralverwaltung für Statistik wurde mit der Eingliederung in die BRD-Struktur Anfang der 1990er Jahre zum Statistischen Amt der fünf neuen Bundesländer transfomiert. Ein neugegründetes Amt zog in das Gebäude ein: jenes der Bundesbeauftragten für die Stasi-Unterlagen. Die Bürgerschaft kann hier Antrag auf Akteneinsicht in ihre von der Staatssicherheit gesammelte Statik und deren Informant*innen stellen. Bei einigen gaben Freundinnen und Freunde sowie Familienmitglieder intime Daten weiter.

Der ALLESANDERSPLATZ schaut wach auf den Alexanderplatz und seine im Masterplan von Kollhoff 1994 vorgeschlagenen und im Jahre 2000 im Bebauungsplan festgehaltenen baulichen Vorstellungen. Das HdS sollte laut Plan einem Hochausbau weichen, aber es kam ANDERS. Berlin braucht gemeinwohlorientierte Begegnungsräume und der viel beschworene kapitalistische Determinismus nach der Finanzrendite von Raum kann auch hier ANDERS sein.

Heute verweist ALLESANDERSPLATZ auf den laufenden ungewöhnlichen städtebaulichen Prozess bei der Entwicklung des Hauses und des Quartiers (vgl. Koop 5), aber vor allem auf den Anspruch für die späteren Nutzungen. Hier soll entstehen, was am Alexanderplatz und auch in anderen Teilen der Innenstadt fehlt: ein Haus, in dem unterschiedliche Gruppen arbeiten und leben. Es sollen über Programmierungen Gemeinschaftsangebote und -flächen entstehen, in denen diese in direkten Kontakt kommen, gesellschaftlich relevante Fragen diskutieren und vor allem in die Praxis überführen.

Installing *ALLESANDERSPLATZ* / *Installation des ALLESANDERSPLATZ*

fallingwild
Labor k3000

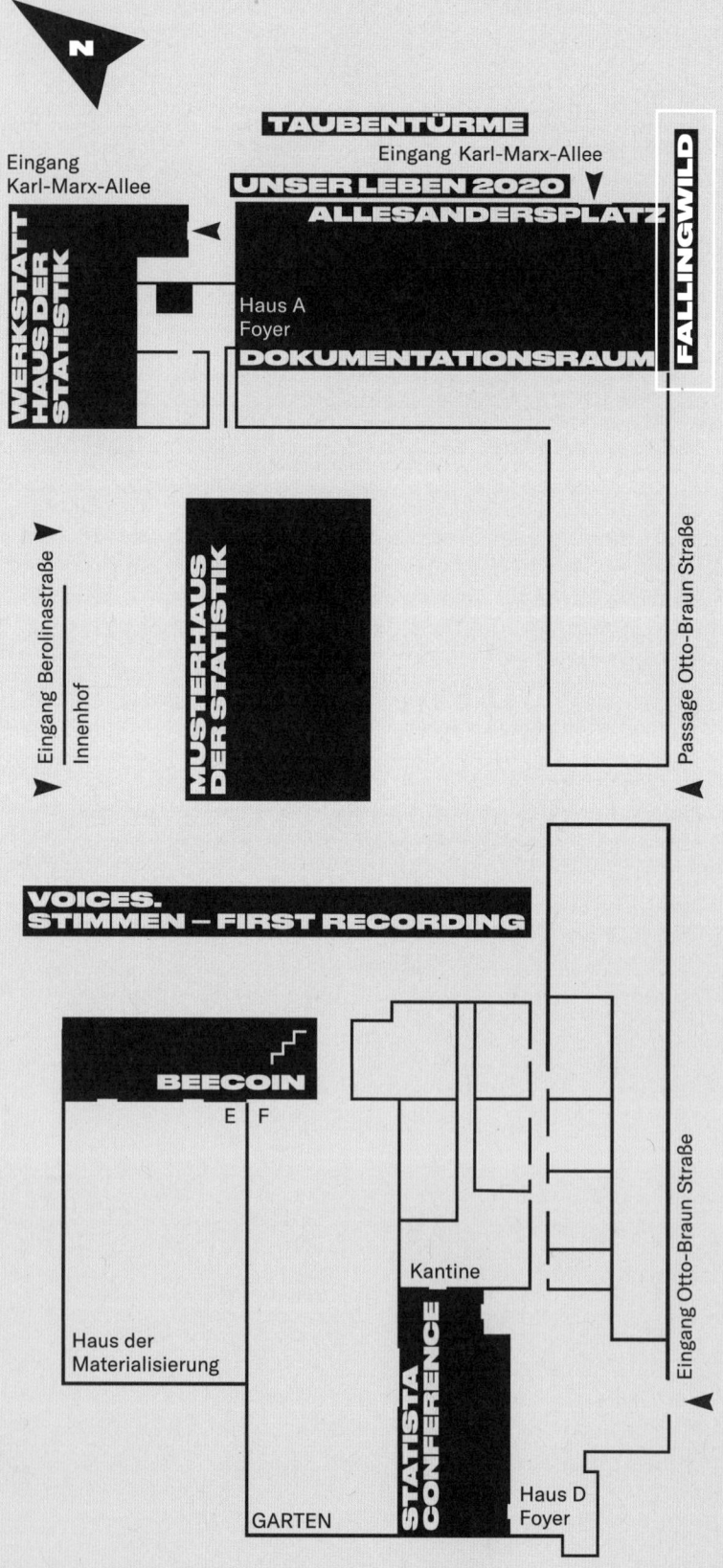

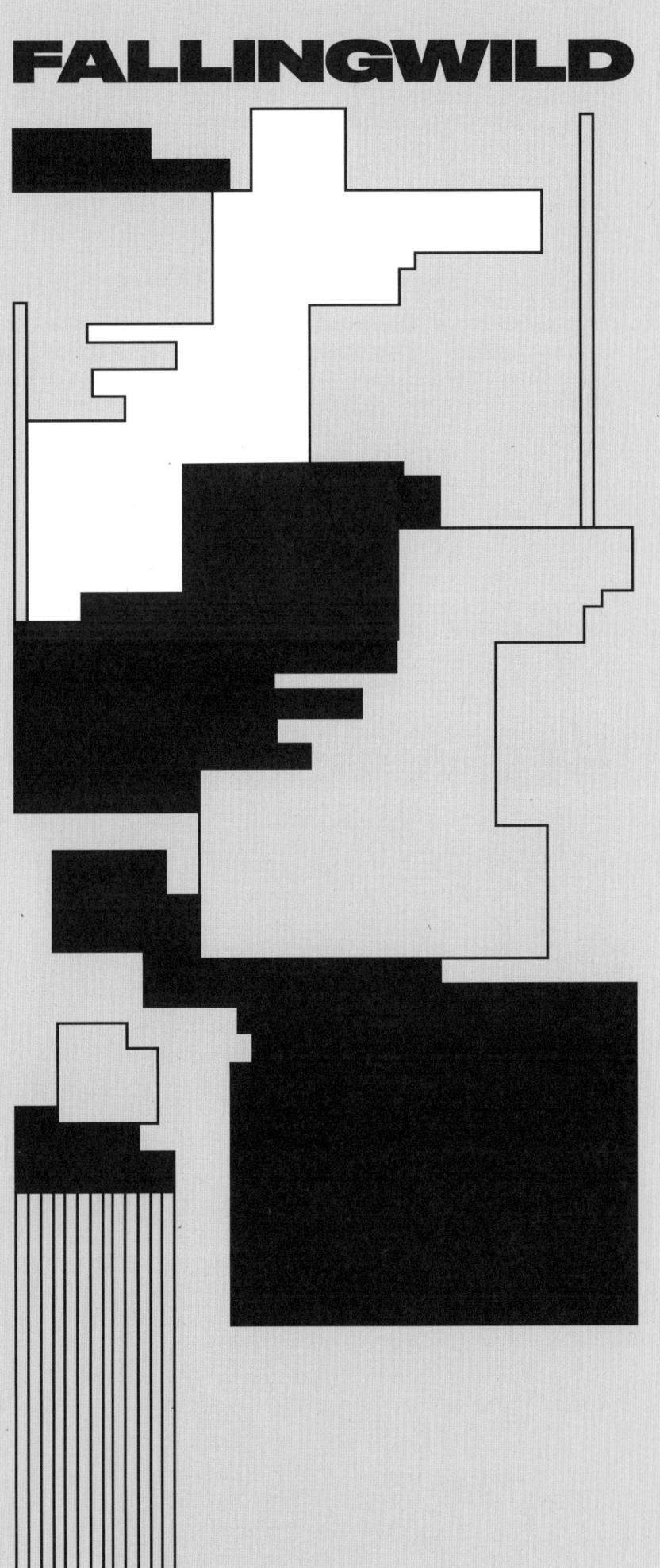

fallingwild

Animals as spatial producers and urban actors are the topic of Labor k3000's conversations with experts in nature conservation, biology, architecture, construction, and urban development, featured in a new documentary film. The diverse needs of various species also inform the test façade developed by Labor k3000, an architectural proposal for the Haus A façade of HdS, currently under sweeping renovation. The 1:1 model aims to create substitute habitats for swifts, redtails and bats – already nesting in the building in large numbers – and proposes a future façade for Haus A, populated and overgrown by various life forms. The design by Labor k3000 reinterprets the modern modular system of the prefabricated building façade: from industrialised concrete component production to a typified wood architecture, created in an environmentally friendly craft process. The title is a reference to Frank Lloyd Wright's famous house Fallingwater, which, while designed to make the most of its dramatic natural setting, actually preferred to ignore interspecies relationships. *fallingwild* thus marks an engagement not only with latter-day building practices, but with the modernist heritage at large – of which the HdS complex is a spectacular example, in all its blatant shortcomings and discreet potentials.

[1]

fallingwild

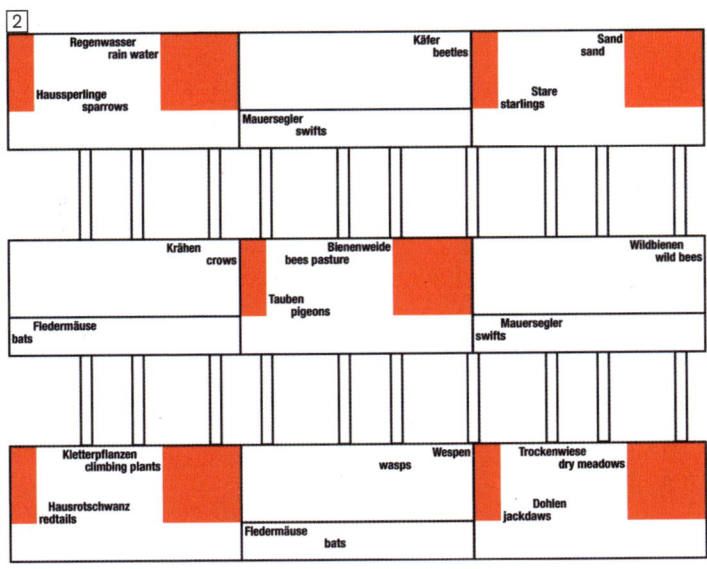

Zur Frage von Tieren als Raumproduzenten und Stadtakteuren führte Labor k3000 Gespräche mit Akteur*innen aus den Bereichen Naturschutz, Biologie, Architektur, Bauindustrie und Stadtentwicklung. Diese Gespräche wurden als filmisches Dokument im September 2019 erstmalig vorgestellt. Dazu wurden an einer Testfassade gestalterische Lösungen für Haus A des Hauses der Statistik (HdS) entwickelt und erprobt, die vielfältige Nutzungen für unterschiedliche Spezies berücksichtigen. Das entstandene 1:1-Modell zielt darauf ab, Ersatzhabitate zu erzeugen für Mauersegler, Fledermäuse und Rotschwänze – die ja bereits in großer Zahl am Gebäude nisten – und schlägt eine künftige Fassade für Haus A vor, von unterschiedlichsten Lebensformen bewohnt und überwachsen. Der Entwurf von Labor k3000 interpretiert das moderne modulare System der vorgefertigten Gebäudefassade neu: von einem industriellen Betonkomponenten hin zu einer Holzarchitektur, in einem umweltfreundlichen Arbeitsprozess hergestellt. Der Titel bezieht sich auf Frank Loyd Wrights berühmtes Haus Fallingwater, das sich mit der umgebenden Natur zu einer dramatischen Kulisse verbindet, aber keine Inter-Spezies-Beziehungen berücksichtigte. *fallingwild* ist nicht nur eine Auseinandersetzung mit heutigen Baupraktiken, sondern auch mit unserem modernistischen Erbe als Ganzes. Der eigentliche Gebäudekomplex des HdS stellt ein spektakuläres Beispiel dieses Erbes dar, mit all seinen Mängeln und potenziellen Stärken.

[1]
Labor k3000, *fallingwild*, 2019-ongoing, filmed interviews & functional design proposal for HdS facade / Labor k3000, *fallingwild*, seit 2019, gefilmte Interviews & funktionaler Gestaltungsvorschlag für die HdS-Fassade

[2]
Diagrammatic sketch for *fallingwild* / Diagramm zu *fallingwild*

Pigeon Towers / Taubentürme
KUNSTrePUBLIK

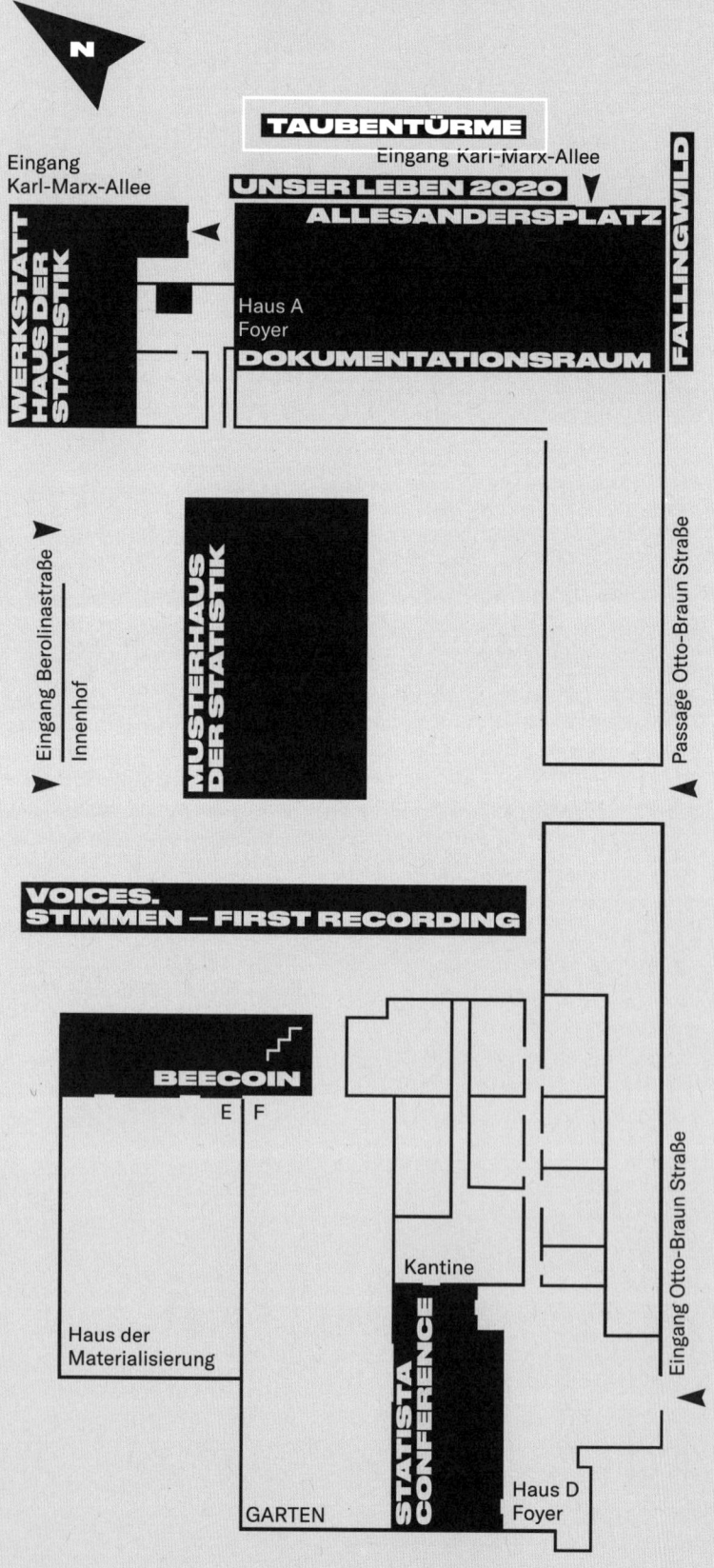

Pigeon Towers

And behold, the dove returned to him in the evening with a freshly plucked olive leaf in her beak. So Noah knew that the waters had receded from the earth. (Genesis 8,11)

What waves of investment flooded East Berlin, following its incorporation into the Federal Republic of Germany, did so gradually at first, then ever more ruthlessly, swamping people's homes. On Alexanderplatz, pigeons moved into what is probably the largest dovecote or, less euphemistically, the largest pigeon tower in Europe: a building earmarked for demolition at the time, with gaps where its many window panes had once been. Pigeons are cavity-nesting birds, and soon settled in the spaces between the floors of the HdS; and they greatly multiplied in there.

Stripped to its skeleton when refurbishment began, the HdS lost all its interior fittings and the pigeons lost their habitat. Out they flocked, in search of one of the rare nesting places left among the bird-control wirings and other barricades on the neighboring buildings.

The pigeon is related to the dove, which is a potent symbol of fertility and peace and, according to the Christian Trinity, of the Holy Ghost. The dove represents the energy of connectivity and solidarity inasmuch as it inspires common values among the faithful.

In modern times, the dove lost its powerful unifying symbolism. It had enjoyed a bond with human beings since the end of the Biblical flood, nourished and cherished as messenger, dung supplier, drone, and choice tidbit. Yet in recent decades, its status dramatically

Pigeon Towers
KUNSTrePUBLIK

declined—much as its lowly cousin, the common pigeon, which now flies unfettered across the city, as that proverbial airborne rat. The pigeon does not enjoy the measure of protection afforded other wild species, such as the swift. Responsibility for its welfare lies with Berlin's Bezirksämter (district administrations), but they interpret this duty very broadly, and eschew cooperation with the general public. For example, the Bezirksamt Mitte has actually charged pigeon protection associations around Alexanderplatz with illegally feeding the birds.

Under the aegis of the Commissioner for Animal Rights in Berlin (a member of the Senate Department of Justice) a regional pigeon plan is currently under development. In addition to providing suitable habitats, the focus is on strategic measures to limit breeding. In close conversation with the authorities, KUNSTrePUBLIK is building multi-storied structures on stilts where pigeons can rest, nest, and feed. Their exterior is painted with red and white stripes, not unlike the traffic signage that surrounds them. Moreover, by means of motion sensors in their nesting boxes, the pigeons direct the lighting of architectural elements on the HdS façade.

Ultimately, the hope is that the pigeons return to the renovated house as permanent residents, and that, by virtue of their symbolic power, they help strengthen and preserve the spirit of the Common Good at HdS.

[1]
KUNSTrePUBLIK, Pigeon Towers, 2019-ongoing, functional bird shelters / KUNSTrePUBLIK, Taubentürme, seit 2019, funktionale Vogelhäuser

Taubentürme

Gegen Abend kam die Taube zurück und siehe: In ihrem Schnabel hatte sie einen frischen Ölzweig. Da wusste Noach, dass das Wasser auf der Erde abgenommen hatte. (1. Mose 8,11)

Welch Sintflut von Investitionen brach nach der Eingliederung Ostberlins in die Bundesrepublik Deutschland herein und umspülte erst langsam und dann immer deutlicher die Häuser der Bewohnerschaft dieser Stadt. In einem fensterlos gemachten, zum Abriss bestimmten Haus am Alexanderplatz zogen die Tauben in den wohl voluminösesten „Taubenschlag" Europas ein. Als Höhlenbrüterinnen nisteten sie in den Zwischendecken der ehemaligen Statistik-Büros und mehrten sich in großer Zahl. Mit der einsetzenden Sanierung wurde das Gebäude auf sein Grundskelett zurückgebaut, mit seinen Einbauten verloren die Tauben ihr Habitat. Sie schwärmten aus, auf der Suche nach den wenigen Nistnischen in den mit Stacheln und Sperren wehrhaften Architekturen der Umgebung.

Die Taube gilt als Zeichen der Fruchtbarkeit, ist Symbol für den Weltfrieden und in der christlichen Dreifaltigkeit Symbol des Heiligen Geistes. Die Taube repräsentiert die Energie der Verbundenheit, indem sie die Inspiration, das Gemeinschaftliche, Vereinende der durch sie Glaubenden möglich macht.

In der Moderne verlor die Taube ihre verbindende Symbolkraft. Einst gehegt und gepflegt, ist sie als Überbringerin von Botschaften, Düngerlieferantin, Drohne und begehrte Speise seit dem Ende der biblischen Sintflut seit Jahrhunderten mit dem Mensch verbunden. Ihr Wert und Ansehen fiel in den letzten Jahrzehnten drastisch und

die Taube lebt nun als „Ratte der Lüfte" verwildert in den Städten. Die Tauben genießen daher nicht den Artenschutz eines Wildtieres wie der Mauersegler. Verantwortlich für deren Fürsorge sind die Bezirksämter, die ihren Aufsichtspflichten sehr unterschiedlich nachkommen und Koopertionen mit der Zivilgesellschaft auch ablehnen: Um den Alexanderplatz gibt es Taubenschutzvereine, deren Aktive unter dem Vorwurf der Fütterung vom Bezirksamt Mitte verklagt wurden.

Unter der Leitung der Tierschutzbeauftragten von Berlin wird aktuell ein Taubenkonzept entwickelt. Dieses fokussiert – neben der Schaffung von geeigneten Unterbringungen – auf eine Strategie der Geburtenkontrolle. KUNSTrePUBLIK baut die neuen Aufenthalts-, Futter- und Nisthäuser im Stil mehrstöckiger Pfahlbauten. Deren Oberfläche ist, analog zu Verkehrssystemen, rot-weiß gestreift. Durch Bewegungsmelder in ihren Nistkästen werden zudem beleuchtete Architekturfragmente am HdS gesteuert.

Ziel ist, dass die Tauben als dauerhafte Bewohnerinnen in das renovierte Haus zurückkehren und Kraft ihrer Symbolik das Gemeinwohl des Hauses verstärken und bewahren.

1 Modular light display on HdS façade steered by pigeons / Die modulare Lichtinstallation an der Fassade des HdS wird von den Tauben „gesteuert"

Voices. Stimmen – first recording
raumlabor & Bernadette La Hengst

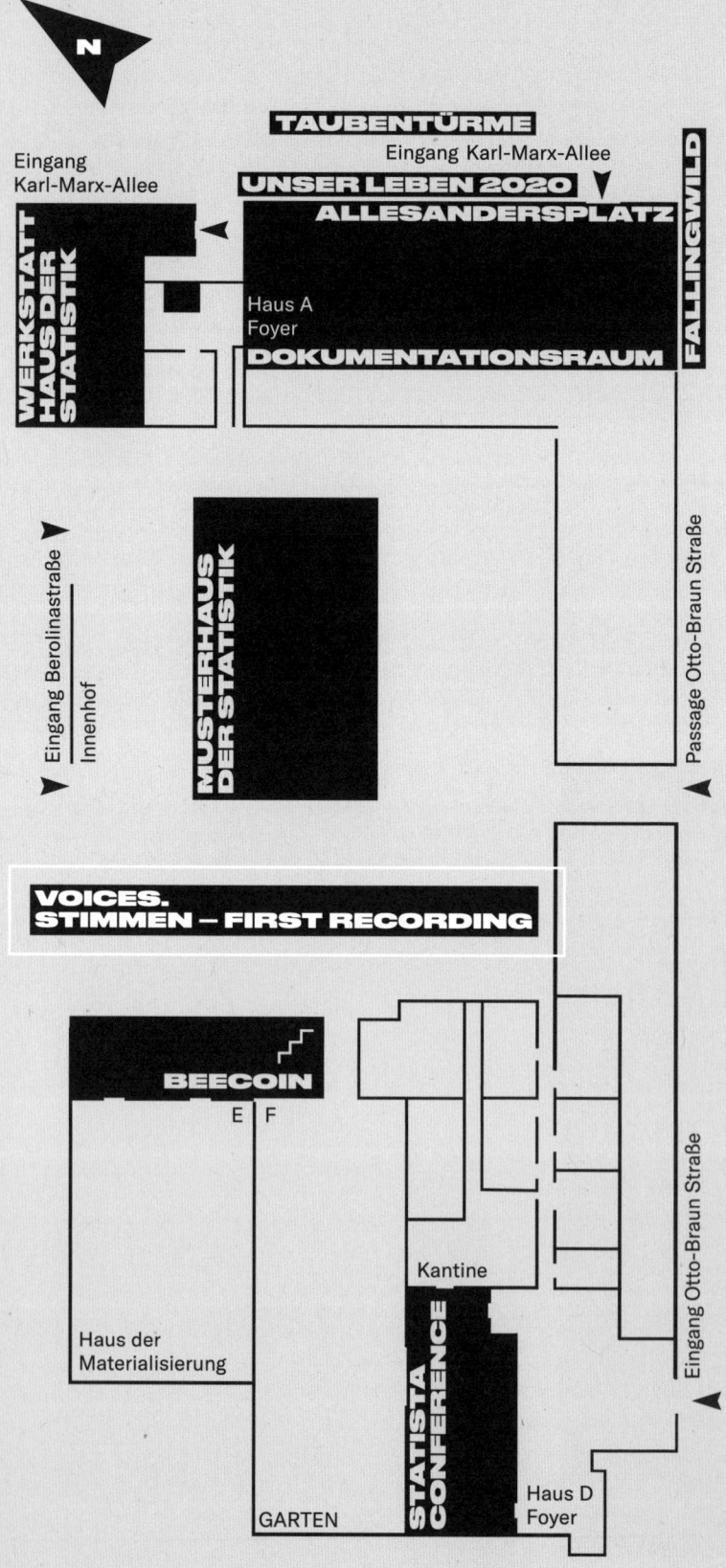

Voices – first recording

raumlabor & Bernadette La Hengst

The Berlin Haus der Statistik (HdS) is the outcome of civic engagement and cooperative urban development. Opening it up to potential synergies with its surroundings can have a collective space-making impact that is far greater than the sum of its individual parts. Currently, the building itself is undergoing a radical transformation. Its former role is over and done with. Over a decade of vacancy, wind and weather have taken a great toll on the building, and the fleeting visitors, urban adventurers and treasure hunters have all sought shelter here, with many of them leaving their mark.

The collective process currently underway, envisioning a future for this architectural ensemble, is in itself choral in character. The said future is not set in stone, it can still be shaped and steered cooperatively. The distinctive qualities of this process emerge from the hopes, insecurities, and the urge to create collectively, side by side; the HdS complex as melting pot for a myriad of projections.

By the time new tenants move in the building will be completely converted, gutted of all but foundational steel and concrete remains. New fixtures and fittings will follow. Until the proposed long-term uses take hold, the vacant shell leaves plenty of scope for potential readings of its current state, and for reflection on the contemporary production of urban space at large. *Anything goes* is the motto, at least for now. Pilot projects, experiments, test phases and other pioneer usages are already being launched. This preliminary stage of examining the potential of the space allows us to explore, and possibly find answers to the question of how we wish to live together in the future.

Our own task was to coordinate various polarities in and around the HdS (acoustics, sound, on-site performances, etc.), and to bring together, as a choir, the many different voices that constitute an urban community. We aimed to render visible a multitude of voices within a given spatial context, to lend it form, to invite it to take the stage—this, for us, is what really counts. In tentatively appropriating the space, in permeating it with sound, we literally give a voice to a collective sense of place, and raise questions regarding the future of this particular building, and the city in general, not to mention the role that people can play within it.

For STATISTA, a choral performance was choreographed to mark the opening event in September 2019. The point of departure was Haus A, with its view of Alexanderplatz and the TV tower. Voices rang out from the building, amplified by wooden megaphones. They called out current statistics on Berlin, provoking a dialogue between the choir, the vernissage audience, and passers-by gathered on the sidewalk. Statistics were presented on living conditions in Berlin 2019, reflecting dramatic shifts in the cost of living. Rent levels have increased substantially in recent years; at best, our choir members live in the hope of some kind of inheritance, otherwise their prospects of living long-term in the city center are practically zero.

Gradually, the choir dissimulated among the general public, its members humming, hissing, and making

Voices – first recording
raumlabor & Bernadette La Hengst

odd popping noises, while moving as one towards a designated meeting point. Their first song was 'The Brain'—a nod to the HdS as computer center. The choir kept moving as it sang, pulling the crowd in its wake as it headed around the building, toward Haus D. We pursued our choreography, our specific positions, to a staggered rhythm, turning the choral performance into a Gesamtkunstwerk. The HdS courtyards were our specially designed backdrop; they became amphitheater and stage set to further underscore and dramatize our very own group performance.

[1]
raumlabor & Bernadette La Hengst, Voices – first recording, 2019-ongoing, neighborhood choir & handmade megaphones of various sizes /
raumlabor & Bernadette La Hengst, Voices. Stimmen – first recording, Nachbarschaftschor & Megaphone variabler Größe

Voices. Stimmen – first recording

Das Gesamtprojekt Haus der Statistik (HdS) ist ein Produkt zivilgesellschaftlichen Engagements und kooperativer Stadtentwicklung. Im Zusammenwirken werden aus Einzelnen gemeinsam produktiv wirkende Raumproduzierende. Zurzeit befindet sich das Gebäudeensemble in einer Transformation. Seine ehemalige Nutzung ist verblichen.

Über zehn Jahre Leerstand haben das Gebäude stark gezeichnet: Wind und Wetter, eine fluktuierende Besucherschaft, urbane Abenteuer- und Schutzsuchende hat es behaust. Viele haben Spuren hinterlassen. Der Prozess der gemeinsamen Erfindung der Zukunft dieses Ensembles hat ebenfalls eine vielstimmige Qualität. Dass die Zukunft dieses Ortes nicht schon determiniert ist, sondern in vielen Feldern gemeinsam und im Hinblick auf das Gemeinwohl erst entwickelt wird, ist eine besondere Qualität dieses Prozesses. Es existieren Hoffnungen, Schaffenslust und Unsicherheit gleichzeitig. Der Komplex ist im Zentrum einer Vielzahl von Projektionen.

Das Gebäude wird umgebaut und neu besiedelt. Es wird entkernt und als Skelettbau stehenbleiben. Neue Ausbauten werden folgen. Bevor sich neue Nutzungen ansiedeln, den Raum in Gebrauch nehmen, bietet der Leerraum Platz für mögliche Lesarten und eine Reflexion der gegenwärtigen Stadtproduktion. Noch ist alles möglich. Im Umbauprozess erfolgen wegbereitende Testnutzungen, Experimente und erste Ingebrauchnahmen. Dieses vorfühlende Handeln vor Ort erlaubt es uns, die Frage, wie wir in Zukunft zusammenleben wollen, gemeinsam zu bearbeiten.

Kern der Arbeit ist eine Orchestrierung (Stimme, Akustik, Sound, Raumbespielung) der Spannungsfelder um das HdS durch einen gemeinsamen Chor mit verschiedenen Stimmen der Stadtgesellschaft. Vielstimmigkeit in einem räumlichen Kontext sichtbar machen, ihr eine Form geben, sie auf die Bühne bitten – das ist uns wichtig. Die spekulative Ingebrauchnahme und Durchdringung des Ortes mit den Stimmen deutet auf Zusammenhänge hin und bietet Raum, Fragen zur Zukunft des Ortes und der Stadt sowie dem Platz der Menschen in diesen Prozessen und Räumen zu stellen.

Im Rahmen von STATISTA folgten die Chorauftritte einer Choreografie. Der Ausgangspunkt liegt in Haus A mit dem Alexanderplatz und dem Fernsehturm im Blick. Aus hölzernen Megaphonen dringen Stimmen aus dem Gebäude. Sie rufen Statistiken des heutigen Berlins auf, beginnen einen Dialog mit den Stimmen des Chores, der sich ins Publikum auf dem breiten Fußweg mischt. Die Lebenssituation in Berlin 2019 mit den steigenden Preisen für Wohnen und Leben wird in Statistiken präsentiert. Die Mietpreise sind um 78 Prozent gestiegen. So und so viele Chormitglieder dürfen dank einer Erbschaft oder vorhandenem Vermögen darauf hoffen, dauerhaft in der Innenstadt wohnen bleiben zu können.

Der im Publikum verteilte Chor beginnt sich zu formieren. Die Sänger*innen summen, zischen, ploppen und bewegen sich auf eine gemeinsame Mitte zu. Das erste Lied ist *the brain* – der Chor wird zur Stimme des Rechenzent-

Voices stimmen – first recording
raumlabor & Bernadette La Hengst

rums im HdS. Er singt im Gehen, zieht das Publikum mit sich um das Gebäude herum zum zweiten Eingang im Haus D. Wir entwickeln eine Choreografie, Platzierungen, eine zeitliche Staffelung, die den Chorauftritt zu einer Gesamtinszenierung werden lassen, die das als Amphitheater interpretierte Hofvolumen bespielt. Diese Inszenierung wird von speziell entworfenen und hergestellten Raumfragmenten unterstützt – angelehnt an die Idee eines Bühnenbildes im Theater.

1 2
raumlabor & Bernadette La Hengst, *Voices – first recording*, 2019-ongoing, neighborhood choir & handmade megaphones of various sizes / raumlabor & Bernadette La Hengst, *Voices. Stimmen – first recording*, seit 2019: Nachbarschaftschor und selbstgemachte Megaphone variabler Größe

Musterhaus der Statistik
openBerlin & KUNSTrePUBLIK

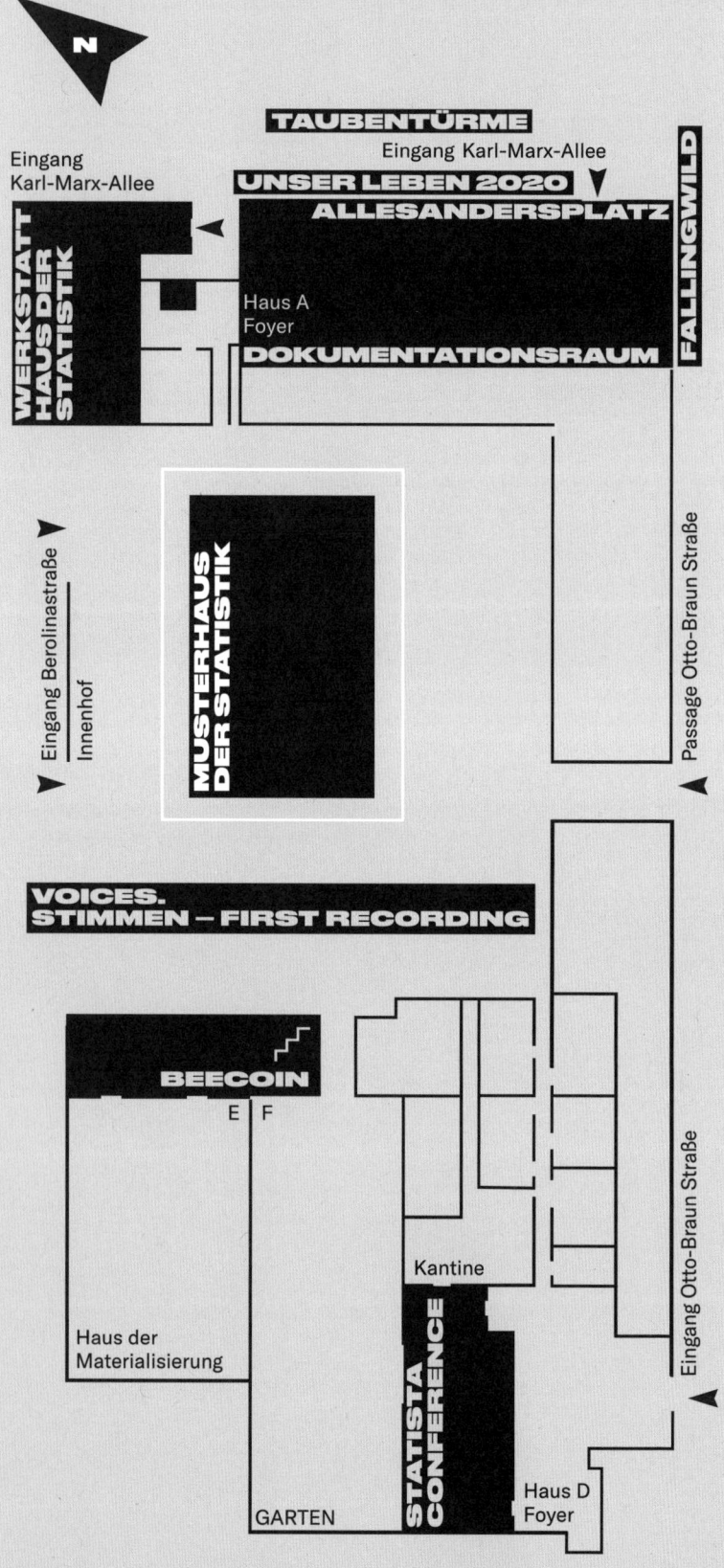

MUSTERHAUS DER STATISTIK

Musterhaus der Statistik

Longstanding residents of the Karl-Marx-Allee, whose East German biographies have largely sunk into oblivion, view recent developments at the HdS with great scepticism. A major turning point in the lives of those Party faithful, for whom the Karl-Marx-Allee housing was originally built, was the protest rally of November 4, 1989, which was the first ever rally in the vicinity to be authorized without being stage-managed by the government. But it was the 'financial crisis' of 2008 which truly took the wind out of the sails of this flagship architectural ensemble. Demolition plans, and the systematic removal of all window panes, seemed to have sealed the fate of the massive HdS complex once and for all. The decade of vacancy that followed marked an all-time historical low for this gateway to the showcase Karl Marx boulevard.

However, a new urban movement is now laying claim to spaces in and around the HdS, in ways that build on the socialist GDR's erstwhile utopian foundations: issues such as the public ownership of land and property, self-determination, and the common good. These efforts to collectively forge the venue's future identity have been met with a surprising degree of approbation.

It is in this context that the artist collective openBerlin, in collaboration with KUNSTrePUBLIK and STATISTA, set up a temporary structure in the courtyard, a defunct bumper car facility, now a prototype of the HdS in miniature that serves the neighborhood and broader public as a meeting place, and encourages research into future modes of housing, work, and leisure. The very historical context raises a number of questions: How can collective authorship shape public space? How best to foster a sense of collective responsibility for the identity and usage of public spaces? And how can such activities take shape for and with a neighborhood?

Thanks to a rapid series of events, this mobile structure became an independently managed polyfunctional space; an expanded urban living room of sorts, and a living experiment in self-management and personal responsibility. Hosting everything from electro-tango evenings, to

1

yoga classes, to open meetings, to discussions with groups such as 'Extinction Rebellion' and the referendum initiative 'Deutsche Wohnen & Co enteignen'. The Musterhaus infrastructure offered free access to power supply, hi-fi equipment, a daylight projector, modular furniture, a kitchen, WCs, running water, garbage disposal and more.

Contrary to other courtyards, this one was reclaimed by and for the community, after years of stagnation. The neighbors' initial skepticism gave way, at times, to frank and lively exchanges with both the HdS initiative and the broader urban movements it attracted. No one had ever dreamed that the HdS would remain within the public eye so persistently, nor that an old asphalt parking lot would ever come to life. And it is vital, now, to ensure that these developments don't lose their momentum, that the local residents' past and present struggles are made known, and that our crafting of inner-city spaces—which we like to call our own mode of statecraft—is passed on to future generations.

1 2
openBerlin & KUNSTrePUBLIK, Musterhaus, 2019-ongoing, bumper car facility as discursive platform / openBerlin & KUNSTrePUBLIK, Musterhaus, seit 2019: ein Autoscooter avanciert zur Diskussionsplattform

Musterhaus der Statistik

Ein großer Teil der Bewohnerschaft der Karl-Marx-Allee, deren Geschichte und Biografie in der DDR heute in Vergessenheit geraten ist, betrachtet das Geschehen im Haus der Statistik (HdS) mit skeptischem Blick. Mit der Alexanderplatz-Demonstration am 4. November 1989, die als erste nicht staatlich gelenkte Kundgebung vor dem HdS auf eindrückliche Weise die bevorstehende Veränderung des politischen, wirtschaftlichen und gesellschaftlichen Systems andeutete, entstand zugleich auch ein biografischer Wendepunkt für die sogenannten Erstbeziehenden der Karl-Marx-Allee. Im Zuge der Finanzkrise 2008 hauchte der Gebäudekomplex den letzten Funken Leben aus. Der großmaßstäbliche Leerstand, dessen Schicksal durch die Abrissvorstellungen im Planwerk Innenstadt und der Demontage der Fenster scheinbar besiegelt war, stellt in der gesamten Entwicklung einen Tiefpunkt und eine historische Zäsur für den Eingang der Karl-Marx-Allee dar.

  Nach zehn Jahren des gähnenden Leerstands eignete sich eine neue städtische Bewegung die Räume im HdS an, die an die Grundlagen der vergangenen sozialistischen Utopien der DDR anknüpft. Themen wie gemeinschaftliches Eigentum, Selbstverwaltung, Gemeinwohl oder Mitgestaltung fanden im Mitwirkungsprozess hier nun eine unerwartete Wertschätzung.

  Aus dieser Situation heraus errichteten KUNSTrePUBLIK und openBerlin einen überdachten fliegenden Bau im Innenhof, der als Musterhaus zukünftige Wohn-, Arbeits- und Freizeitwelten in Zusammenarbeit mit der Nachbarschaft und der Stadtgesellschaft erforscht. Aus dem historischen Kontext heraus stellte sich eine Reihe von Fragen: Wie gestaltet eine kollektive Autorschaft öffentlichen Raum? Wie lässt sich das Gefühl einer gemeinschaftlichen Verantwortung gegenüber der Mitgestaltung öffentlicher Räume erzeugen? Und wie entfaltet sich ein praxisbezogenes Wirkungsfeld für die Nachbarschaft?

  Mit einer Reihe von Veranstaltungen, die über einen gemeinschaftlich geführten Kalender den „fliegenden Bau" zu einem selbstgebauten, selbstverwalteten und multifunktionalen Raum formten, entstand eine Art erweitertes Stadtwohnzimmer für die Nachbarschaft. Vom Elektrotangoabend über eine regelmäßig stattfindende Jogaklasse bis hin zu Plena und politischen Diskussionsveranstaltungen mit der Gruppe „Extinction Rebellion" und dem Bündnis „Deutsche Wohnen und Co enteignen" wurde das Musterhaus in Eigenregie und Eigenverantwortung genutzt. Im Gegenzug erhielten die Beteiligten kostenlos Zugang zu einer umfangreichen Infrastruktur: Stromanschluss, Musikanlage, Tageslichtbeamer, Stühle, Tische und Zugang zu Küche, WC, Wasser und Müllcontainern usw.

  Zum ersten Mal nach langer Stagnation fand wieder eine Aneignung des Hinterhofs für gemeinschaftliche Aktivitäten statt. Aus der anfänglich skeptischen Haltung der Nachbarschaft entwickelte sich ein zum Teil offener und lebhafter Austausch mit den Agierenden der Initiative HdS und der erweiterten Stadtgesellschaft. Niemand hätte eine Belebung der versiegelten Parkplatzfläche

Musterhaus der Statistik
openBerlin & KUNSTrePUBLIK

und ein solches Ausmaß an Aufmerksamkeit der Öffentlichkeit für möglich gehalten. Nun gilt es, die Dynamik dieser Entwicklung weiterzuführen, die Geschichten und die Biografien der Anwohnerschaft zu erzählen und an kommende Generationen weiterzugeben.

[1] openBerlin & KUNSTrePUBLIK, *Musterhaus*, 2019-ongoing, bumper car facility as discursive platform / openBerlin & KUNSTrePUBLIK, *Musterhaus*, seit 2019: ein Autoscooter avanciert zur Diskussionsplattform

STATISTA Coin
Economic Space Agency (ECSA)

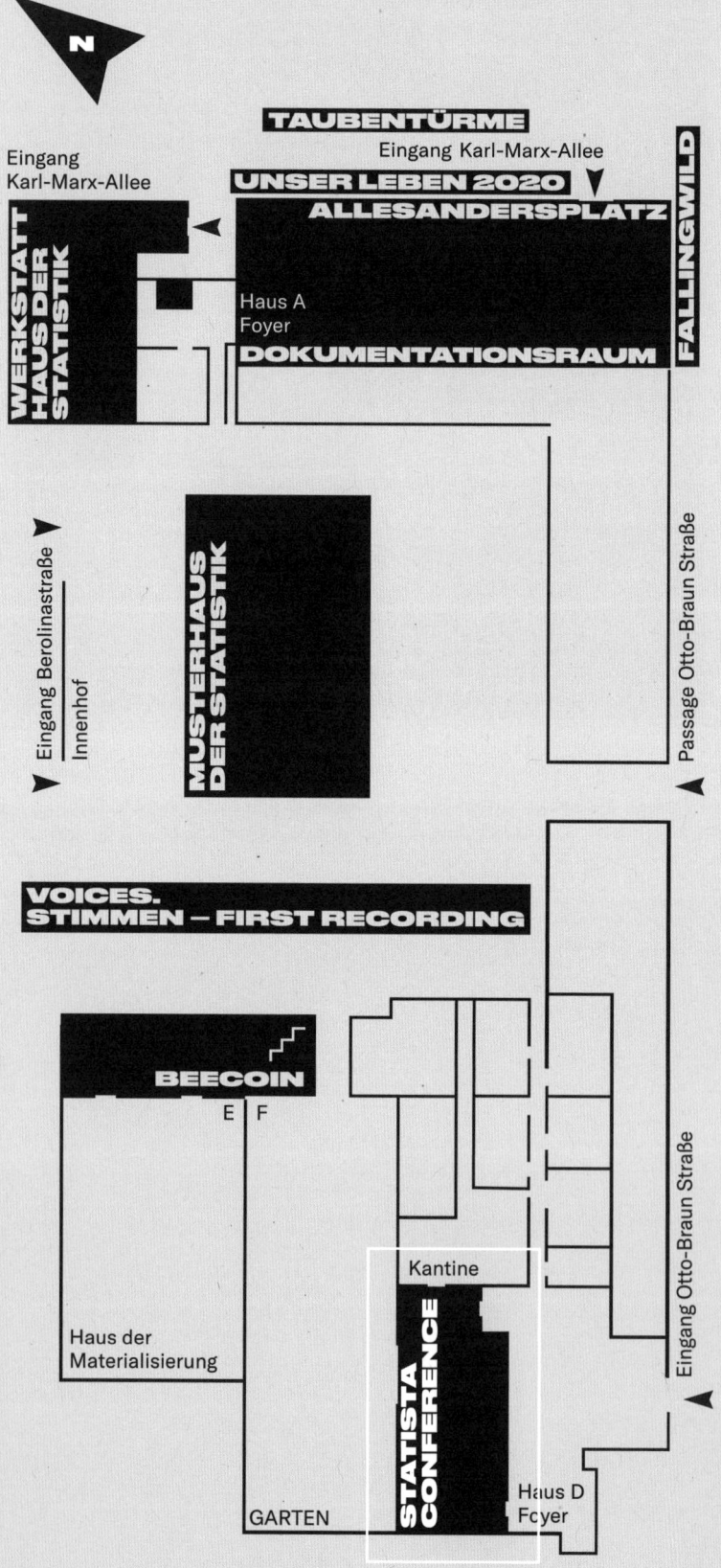

Statista coin – is not a coin
Economic Space Agency (ECSA)

Statista coin – is not a coin

ARGUMENT: Cryptocurrencies present themselves as a proclamation of a new economy. But this promise veils a mimicry of the old economy, reaffirming the existing distribution of wealth as the dominant economic power.

PRELUDE: Economy is a social machine. As with all social machines, it forms a provenance of rights. Thus, economy can be translated into rights and the networks of their interrelations: ownership is a composite of rights towards a car, for example, or an amount of some given currency. Rights can also represent an allotment of a wage or an ability to initiate an economic organization, such as a corporation. In essence, rights provide a comprehensive analytic that correlates between economy and governance.

But what does this tell us of cryptocurrencies?

ALLEGORY: Think of a complex machine, its internal workings cryptic to its users. They can only understand this machine by means of the buttons it offers for interaction. The users learn of the machine by pressing these buttons, and observing the consequences. To explain the machine they tell stories of the buttons and the things they 'do' – the machine itself remains hidden from their stories.

Coins and currencies reflect a nature similar to these buttons. They present a surface layer, appearing as a concrete economy, but the role of such direct structures is mostly servile, tracing the machinery underneath.

Similarly, cryptocurrencies provide us with new buttons. As long as their focus remains upon coins, they imply new interfaces to the old economic machinery. In practice, they're realized as new instruments of investment, increasing the flexibility of wealth. This will only expand the capabilities of wealth-based speculation, to the detriment of other forms of economy.

Thus, with cryptocurrencies, the unwealthy are ultimately playing a losing game. They can only profit when the existing wealth profits. Therefore, while cryptocurrencies might win some local battles, in the long term, they're helping us to lose the war over economic inequality.

But within such technologies lie other possibilities. These require a shift of perspective, from cryptocurrencies to cryptoeconomies. A focus not upon new coins, playing with old value, but upon the reconception of economic rights and the modular redesign of economies.

Even at a small scale, such organizations provide reflections upon the economy itself, as actionable speculations. If they grow, they can expand our rights, offering us alternatives as a matter of choice. Such possibilities are critical for challenging the ceremonial corpse of our democracy.

But to approach these directions, we have to engage the very actions that express economy, to ourselves and others. For these reasons, 'Statista Coin' is not a coin, conventionally speaking. The focus of its development lies elsewhere: Toward the expressibility of economic rights, and

Statista coin – is not a coin
Economic Space Agency (ECSA)

the organizations of such rights. The communities utilizing it can formulate their own structures of value, and offer them to others.

And the coin? Well, that is an interface, a button. A way to interact with the machinery of your economy. Nothing less, nothing more.

EPIGRAM: An economy should not play itself for the sake of losing, or winning. At its heart, an economy is a game of enablement, a play being born between possibilities.

[1] View of HdS courtyard / Innenhof des HdS

Statistacoin – ist kein Coin

EINWAND: Kryptowährungen geben sich als Vorboten einer neuen Wirtschaftsordnung aus. Dieses Versprechen jedoch verschleiert das Nachahmen der alten Wirtschaftsordnung, die die bestehende Wohlstandsverteilung als vorherrschendes ökonomisches Machtmittel festigt.

PRÄAMBEL: Die Wirtschaft ist eine soziale Maschine. Wie bei allen sozialen Maschinen handelt es sich um eine Rechteprovenienz. Daher lässt sich die Wirtschaft über Rechte und deren Beziehungsnetzwerke definieren: Eigentum beispielsweise kann gleichermaßen der Rechteverbund an einem Auto oder an einem gewissen Betrag einer Währung sein. Rechte können auch den Anteil an einem Lohn oder die Fähigkeit, eine Wirtschaftsorganisation wie ein Unternehmen zu gründen, repräsentieren. Im Kern geben uns Rechte eine umfassende analytische Methodik an die Hand, die mit der Wirtschaft und der *Governance* korreliert.

Was aber sagt das über Kryptowährungen aus?

ALLEGORIE: Man stelle sich eine komplexe Maschine vor, deren Einbauten und Funktionsweise für ihre Benutzerschaft kryptisch sind. Diese können sich die Funktionsweise der Maschine nur erschließen, indem sie über die Tasten mit ihr interagieren. Indem die Nutzenden also beobachten, welchen Effekt das Drücken der Tasten hat, machen sie sich mit der Maschine vertraut. Um die Funktion der Maschine zu erklären, erzählen sie Geschichten von den Tasten und den Dingen, die diese „tun" – die Maschine selbst findet in ihren Geschichten keine Erwähnung.

Coins – die Einheit der meisten Kryptowährungen – und gewöhnliche Währungen weisen ähnliche Eigenschaften wie diese Tasten auf. Sie repräsentieren eine Oberflächenschicht, muten wie eine konkrete Wirtschaftsordnung an. Dabei haben solch direkte Strukturen meist eine untergeordnete Funktion, die von der darunterliegenden Maschinerie gesteuert wird.
    Gleichermaßen stellen uns auch Kryptowährungen neue Tasten zur Verfügung. Solange ihr Schwerpunkt allerdings weiterhin auf Coins liegt, generieren sie lediglich neue Interfaces für die alte Wirtschaftsmaschinerie. In der Praxis werden sie in Form von Anlageinstrumenten eingesetzt, die die Wohlstandsflexibilität vergrößern. Dies wiederum wird die Kapazitäten der reichtumsbasierten Spekulation weiter ausweiten, zum Schaden anderer Wirtschaftsformen.
    Somit werden die Mittellosen das Spiel mit den Kryptowährungen letztendlich verlieren. Sie können nur profitieren, wenn der bereits akkumulierte Wohlstand profitiert. Während Kryptowährungen also die ein oder andere Schlacht für sich entscheiden mögen, lassen sie uns im Kampf gegen wirtschaftliche Ungleichheit ins Hintertreffen geraten. Doch solche Technologien bergen auch andere Möglichkeiten. Wiederum setzt deren Umsetzung einen Perspektivwechsel voraus: von Kryptowährungen zu Krypto-

Statistacoin – ist kein Coin
Economic Space Agency (ECSA)

wirtschaften. Hier liegt der Fokus nicht auf neuen Coins, die mit alten Werten gedeckt sind, sondern auf der Neukonzeption des Wirtschaftsrechts und der modularen Neugestaltung der Wirtschaftssysteme.

In Form von praktikablen Spekulationen geben solche Organisationen im kleinen Maßstab Einblick in die Funktionsweisen der Wirtschaft selbst. Wachsen sie, können sie unsere Rechte ausweiten und uns Alternativen aufzeigen, aus denen wir frei wählen können. Solche Möglichkeiten sind entscheidend für die Infragestellung des zu Zeremonienzwecken aufgebahrten Leichnams unserer Demokratie. Doch um einen Schritt in diese Richtung zu tun, müssen wir uns mit ebenjenen Aktivitäten auseinandersetzen, durch die sich diese Wirtschaft in unserem eigenen Leben und dem anderer manifestiert.

Aus diesen Gründen sind Statistacoins keine Coins im herkömmlichen Sinne. Ihre Entwicklung zielt im Wesentlichen auf etwas anderes ab: die Ausdrückbarkeit von wirtschaftlichen Rechten und die Organisation solcher Rechte. Statistacoin ist ein Interface, eine Taste, eine Art und Weise, mit der Wirtschaftsmaschinerie zu interagieren – nicht weniger und nicht mehr.

EPIGRAMM: Eine Wirtschaft sollte beim eigenen Spiel nicht die Absicht verfolgen, zu verlieren oder zu gewinnen. Im Grunde handelt es sich bei einer Wirtschaft um ein Ermöglichungsspiel, ein Schauspiel, das zwischen den Möglichkeiten entsteht.

[1] View of HdS Studio 'Werkstatt – Haus der Statistik' / Ansicht der Werkstatt – Haus der Statistik

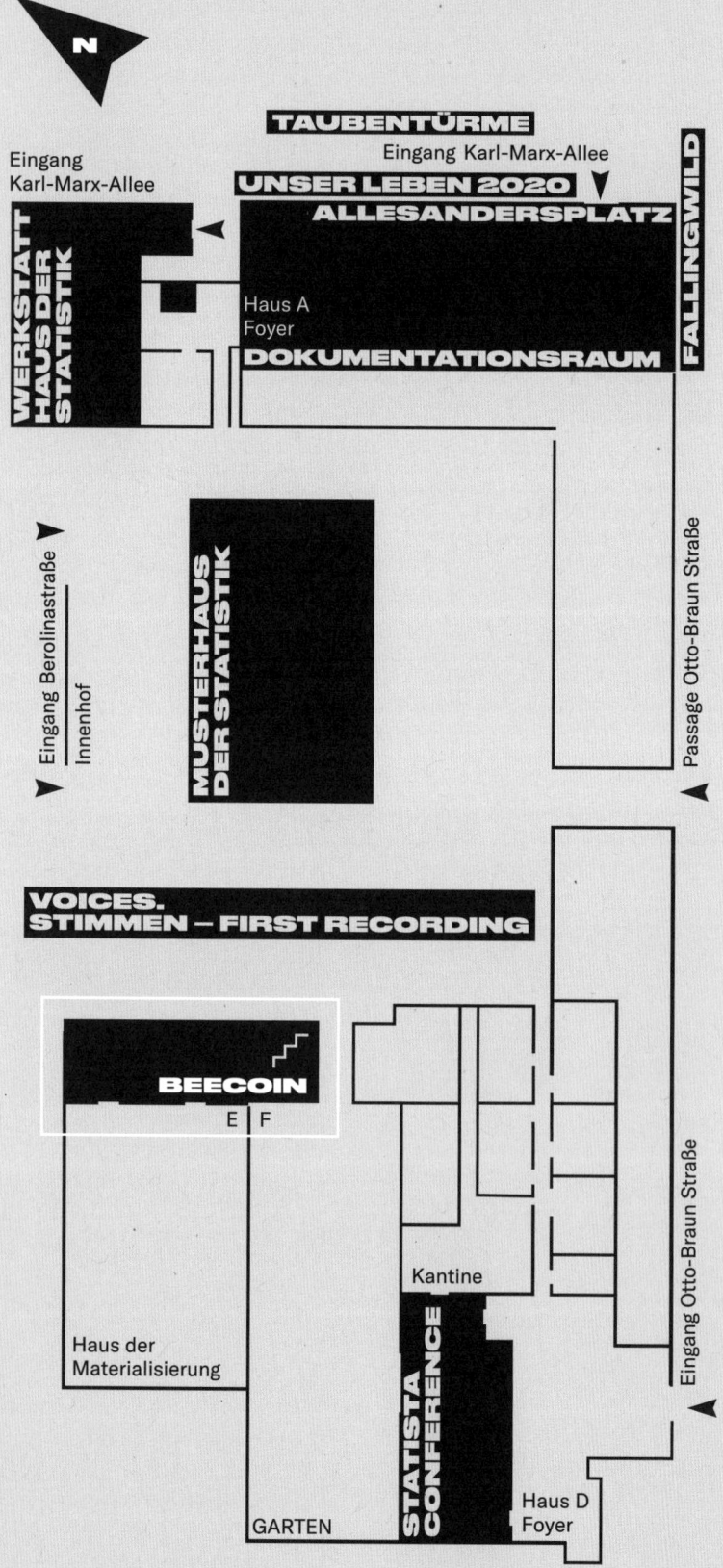

Beecoin/Bee-DAO – the human out of focus

Beecoin has long pursued the desire for an alternative currency that would run against the current of the fiat systems, to create an economic sphere of autonomous exchange. A coin linked to the value of honey, or a coin produced by the constant reproduction of the beehive. But over the course of the project, the hive became a shell from which a decentralized autonomous organization – DAO for short – emerged.

With the help of 'smart contracts' to automate administrative tasks and simplify coordination processes, the first prototype of the Bee-DAO was launched. The DAO can be understood as a club treasury, in which all members are treasurers and board members at the same time, without the administrative hassle, but with the same powers. Similar to an association statute, the Bee-DAO defines a common goal: the improvement of living conditions for bees. The Bee-DAO sees itself as an organization that generates, finances and constantly redefines its own capacity to act.

The only reference point which cannot be renegotiated is data generated by sensors in the beehive, which feed real-time information on the well-being of the bees into the DAO.

Measurements include the total weight of a bee population, temperature, humidity and environmental data such as outside temperature, cloud cover and fine dust. Differential values – such as weight differences – are essential to understand the input or consumption of pollen and nectar. In the Beecoin project, the temperature in the nest room was used as a particularly sensitive indicator of well-being, as it must always remain 35°C ± 1 degree.

In order to better understand the possible activities in the DAO – i.e. the association activities – it is useful to describe three forms of interaction here:

1. **Beekeepers as trustees of the bees:** The sensors in the beehive allow us to draw conclusions about the bees' well-being. They also allow the beekeeper to propose that the DAO reward his work with shares. Shares have a value, which is measured in ETH, a crypto-currency which the beekeeper can convert into EURO; always provided the bees are doing well. Other members can also make suggestions, without doing any beekeeping work (see below).

2. **Activists on behalf of the bees:** To name one example, a member wants to organize a demonstration against the unregulated use of pesticides in agriculture. For this purpose, she demands a certain number of DAO shares, which in turn contribute to the financing of her demo once converted into ETH.

3. **Donations:** Anyone aiming to increase the value of shares in the DAO can request a small number of shares which they underlay with a large amount of ETH. This corrresponds to the principle of 'donations' in the analogous world of associations.

Beecoin
KUNSTrePUBLIK

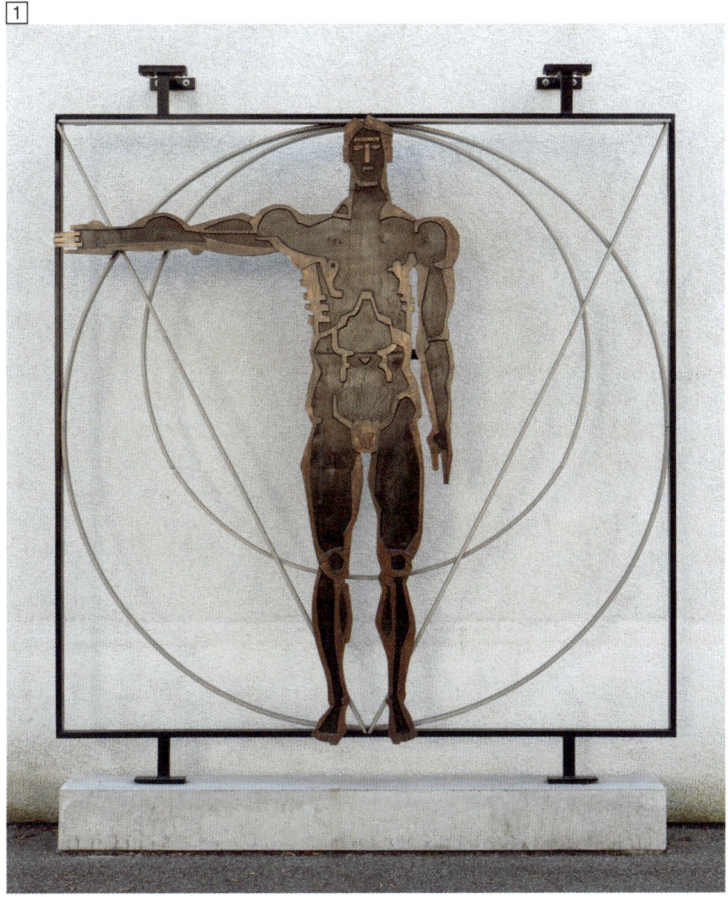

A vote on proposals is based on the majority principle. After a pre-defined period of time, a proposal is accepted and the corresponding 'shares' are given or withheld.

The Beecoin project extends the concept of the common good to the reproduction of a species we depend on every day and that maintains our ecosystems: bees. It reviews social utopias of modernity, discusses them further and tests them in immediate practical applications.

It bears mentioning that HdS was the place where data on the demographic and economic development of the GDR was collected. What is now known as 'Big Data' was developed, practised and backed up by computer power at the time. The artist Karl Hillert (1927–2004) was commissioned in 1970 to design the sculpture '*The History of Mathematics*'. In the centre of the five-part sculpture is – as the measure of all things – the human being. Around fifty years later, questions of statecraft are being asked again, under very different circumstances. The computing power of the HdS at the time is equivalent to that of a laptop today. The 'man at the centre' is facing difficult ecological and social challenges. In fact, social decisions being replaced by hyper-intelligent machines was already a socialist

[1]
Karl Hillert, *The History of Mathematics*, 1970, glass & various metals, one of five square configurations 260 x 260 cm / Karl Hillert, Die Geschichte der Mathematik, Glas und diverse Metalle, eines von fünf quadratischen Elementen, 260 x 260 cm

vision underlying the creation of the sculpture, a vision which now seems more technically feasible than ever.

The most vivid example of computer-controlled socialism was the Cybersyn project developed under Salvador Allende. The data from all state-owned companies was transferred by teletext to a control centre where it was analysed. The project was terminated before its completion, with the fall of Allende at the hands of Pinochet's military junta. Cybersyn always remained a promise of an unfulfilled digital socialism. Other attempts to realize the vision of a socialist planned economy on the basis of 'Big Data' also failed, due to a simple hurdle: the amount of data. Not only were countless actors needed to collect and transmit it, countless others were needed to structure and classify the data, and countless decisions needed to be based on the resulting classifications. The complexity of an economic system that could do better than the 'invisible hand' of the free market was too much for the level of data processing at that time.

Thirty years after the fall of the Berlin Wall, we can confidently speak of a paradigm shift in data processing. Complex geographical, demographic and economic developments are captured by sensors and processed by databases that lead to decisions and actions through algorithms without the slightest human interference. The dream of an efficient, superior planned economy, pursued at the House of Statistics over forty years ago, appears feasible. The one problem is the 'human being at the centre'. A human that has overcome many challenges anthropocentrically, has domesticated useful animals, has exterminated others, reshaped the planet with infrastructure and tamed the dangers of wilderness – but despite his resulting knowledge of complex global interrelationships, he is not able to make sustainable systemic changes that allow for a peaceful future.

The Beecoin project addresses this existential flaw – human self-centredness – and attempts to create a prototypical platform that does not follow the interests of humans, but those of another creature central to the survival of mankind: the bees.

Bees pollinate around 71 out of 100 crops, which cover 90 per cent of the world's food requirements. No bees means fewer plants. Or to put it in euros: the value of pollination is 500 billion euros annually.

The loss of bees is a phenomenon that is making itself felt worldwide, especially in North America and Europe. In North America, the loss amounts to 30–40 per cent of commercial honey bee colonies, while in Europe, the loss is estimated at 25 per cent since 1985. These statistics represent only the tip of the iceberg. (Honeybees are the best documented species, in stark contrast to wild bee populations. However, scientific studies show that a diversity of wild bee species is of utmost importance for sustainable plant production.) The complexity of these issues is difficult to tackle unless addressed together. Only collective consideration of the complex ecological interactions between bees, humans, plants, climate and other factors can provide us with answers. A different, non-anthropocentric way of thinking and systemic action is needed. Beecoin is a project of the KUNSTrePUBLIK artist collective, in cooperation with Hiveeyes and Nascent. The project was

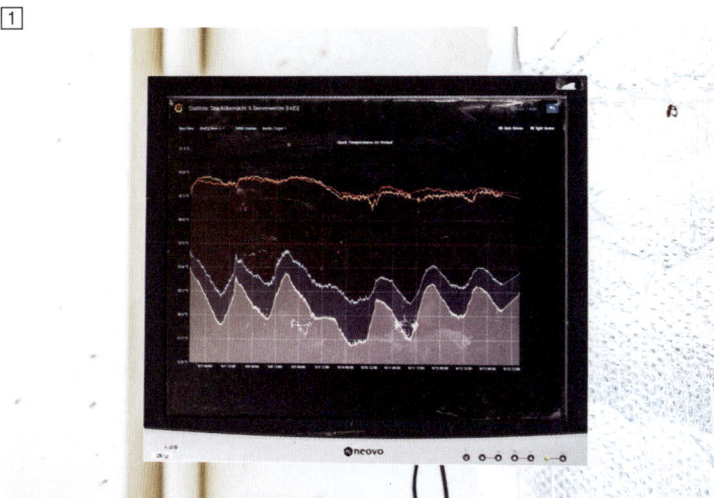

coordinated and co-designed by Stephanie Holl-Trieu, and accompanied by Moabees.

The Beecoin project builds on the research of Hiveeyes, a Berlin-based project that develops surveillance infrastructure and DIY toolkits based on open source software, affordable hardware and wireless telemetry. The project was supervised and accompanied by beekeeper Clemens Gruber.

The Bee-DAO was digitally developed by the production studio Nascent (nascent.energy) and Terra0 (https://terra0.org). Nascent is a production studio founded by Paul Seidler and Max Hampshire that develops Minimal Viable Tech (MVT) solutions for institutional or private infrastructures. Building on their research on network resilience, counter-economies, eco-technology and crypto-currencies, Nascent also develops tactics and strategies for building P2P economies.

As part of the Beecoin project, the artist and beekeeping collective Moabees organizes visits to the beehives in the HdS, planning various interventions along the way. Sensors within the beehives were examined which contrasted human perception with that of bees. Audience members were portrayed with the help of a bee camera. Thanks to the photochemical process of cyanotypes, artefacts from the HdS and its courtyards were collected and assessed. Ultraviolet (sun)light – invisible to the human eye – was used for exposing the cyanotypes. Bees, however, do use UV-rays to recognize blossoms.

[1]
Beecoin installation in the former data management center of HdS /
Beecoin Installation im ehemaligen Rechenzentrum des HdS

Beecoin/Bee-DAO – der Mensch nicht im Mittelpunkt

Beecoin verfolgte lange den Wunsch nach einer alternativen Währung, die gegen den Strom der FIAT-Systeme laufen sollte, um eine Wirtschaftssphäre mit autonomem Austausch zu schaffen: eine Münze, die an den Wert des Honigs gebunden ist, oder eine Münze, die durch die ständige Reproduktion des Bienenstocks erzeugt wird. Doch im Laufe des Projekts wurde der Bienenstock zur Hülle, aus der eine dezentralisierte autonome Organisation – kurz: DAO – hervorging.

Mithilfe von *Smart Contracts*, die dazu dienen, Verwaltungsaufgaben zu automatisieren und Abstimmungsprozesse zu vereinfachen, wurde der erste Prototyp des Bee-DAO auf den Weg gebracht. Verstanden werden kann der DAO wie eine Vereinskasse, in der alle Mitglieder gleichzeitig Schatzmeister*innen und Vorstände sind, ohne den damit verbundenen verwalterischen Aufwand, jedoch mit den gleichen Befugnissen. Ähnlich einer Vereinssatzung definiert der Bee-DAO ein gemeinsames Ziel: die Verbesserung der Bedingungen für Bienen. Der Bee-DAO versteht sich als ein Verein, der Handlungsfähigkeit erzeugt, finanziert und immer wieder neu definiert.

Die einzigen, nicht redefinierbaren Referenzpunkte sind Daten, erzeugt durch Sensoren in den Bienenbehausungen, die in Echtzeit Information zum Wohlergehen der Bienen in den DAO einspeisen. Gemessen werden Gesamtgewicht einer Bienenpopulation, Temperaturwerte, Luftfeuchtigkeit und Umgebungsdaten, wie Außentemperatur, Bewölkung und Feinstaub. Entscheidend, um das Wohlergehen zu erfassen, sind Differenzwerte – wie Gewichtsunterschiede, um den Eintrag oder Verbrauch von Pollen und Nektar zu verstehen. Im *Beecoin*-Projekt wurde vor allem die Temperatur im Brutnestraum zu Rate gezogen, da diese stets bei 35 Grad Celsius (± 1 Grad) liegen muss und somit ein besonders sensibler Indikator des Wohlergehens ist. Um die möglichen Aktivitäten im DAO – also die Vereinsaktivitäten – besser zu verstehen, ist es nützlich, drei Formen der Interaktionen prototypisch zu beschreiben:

1. **Imker*innen als Treuhänder*innen der Bienen:** Die Sensoren im Bienenstock und die daraus resultierenden Daten lassen Schlüsse auf das Wohlergehen zu. Sie erlauben es den Imker*innen, dem DAO vorzuschlagen, seine Arbeit mit Anteilen (*Shares*) am DAO zu belohnen. *Shares* haben einen Wert, der in ETH, einer Kryptowährung, gemessen wird und den die Imker*innen in Euro umwandeln können, um die Bienenpflege zu leisten. Immer vorausgesetzt, den Bienen geht es gut. Andere Mitglieder des DAO können auch, ohne bienenpflegerische Arbeit zu leisten, Vorschläge machen, die dem Wohlergehen von Bienen zugute kommen.

2. **Aktivist*innen im Interesse der Bienen:** Ein Mitglied des DAO (also ein Vereinsmitglied) möchte beispiels-

weise eine Demonstration gegen den unregulierten Einsatz von Pestiziden in der Landwirtschaft organisieren. Es fordert hierfür eine bestimmte Anzahl von *Shares* am DAO ein, die wiederum über die Umwandlung in ETH zur Finanzierung der Aktion beitragen.

3. **Spenden für das Wohlergehen:** Menschen mit dem Anliegen, den Wert der *Shares* im DAO zu steigern, können vorschlagen, eine geringe Anzahl von *Shares* zu erhalten und diese mit einer großen Menge an ETH zu unterlegen. Dies entspricht in Analogie zur Vereinswelt dem Prinzip der Spende.

Die Abstimmung über die jeweiligen Vorschläge erfolgt nach dem Mehrheitsprinzip. Nach einem vordefinierten Zeitraum wird ein Vorschlag angenommen, und entsprechende *Shares* werden abgegeben oder abgelehnt.

Das Projekt *Beecoin* erweitert den Begriff des Gemeinguts auf die Reproduktion einer Art, auf die wir täglich angewiesen sind, um unsere Ökosysteme zu erhalten: die Bienen. Es greift die gesellschaftlichen Utopien der Moderne auf, kritisiert sie, denkt sie weiter und bringt sie in unmittelbare praktische Anwendungen, die nur dann dem Wohlergehen des Menschen dienen, wenn dieser aus dem Mittelpunkt gerückt ist.

Das Haus der Statistik (HdS) war jener Ort, an dem Daten über die demografische und wirtschaftliche Entwicklung der DDR gesammelt wurden. Was heute unter dem Begriff Big Data firmiert, wurde hier entwickelt, praktiziert und mit Rechenpower unterlegt. Der Künstler Karl Hillert (1927–2004) wurde 1970 beauftragt, die Bauplastik Die Geschichte der Mathematik zu gestalten. Sie befand sich ebenerdig vor dem Bauwerk, in dem Teile des STATISTA-Projekts umgesetzt wurden. Im Mittelpunkt der fünfteiligen Plastik befindet sich – als Maß aller Dinge – der Mensch. Rund 50 Jahre später werden unter anderen Vorzeichen die Fragen nach einer Staatskunst erneut gestellt. Die Rechenpower der damaligen im HdS befindlichen Anlage entspricht der eines Laptops. Der Mensch im Mittelpunkt steht vor schwierigen ökologischen und gesellschaftlichen Herausforderungen. Dass gesellschaftliche Entscheidungen durch hyperintelligente Maschinen ersetzt werden könnten, war bereits in der Entstehungszeit der Plastik eine Vision des Sozialismus, die nun, 50 Jahre später, technisch umsetzbarer denn je erscheint.

Das anschaulichste Beispiel eines computergesteuerten Sozialismus war das unter Salvador Allende entwickelte Projekt Cybersyn.[1] Die Daten aller staatseigenen Betriebe wurden per Teletext in eine Steuerungszentrale übertragen und dort ausgewertet. Das Projekt wurde vor seiner Vollendung mit dem Sturz Allendes durch Pinochets Militär-Junta beendet, sodass Cybersyn stets das Versprechen eines unerfüllten Digitalsozialismus blieb. Auch andere Versuche, die Vision einer sozialistischen Planwirtschaft anhand von Big Data zu realisieren, scheiterten an einer schlichten Hürde: der Menge der Daten. Man brauchte nicht nur unzählige Akteur*innen, die die Daten erfassen und übermitteln, sondern wiederum unzählige, die die Daten

---

[1] https://www.newstatesman.com/world/2018/08/project-cybersyn-afterlife-chile-s-socialist-internet

strukturieren, einordnen; und schließlich unzählige Instanzen, die aus den Zuordnungen Entscheidungen treffen. Die Komplexität eines Wirtschaftssystems, das gerade nicht der „unsichtbaren Hand" des freien Marktes überlassen sein sollte, überforderte den damaligen Stand der Datenverarbeitung.

30 Jahre nach dem Fall der Berliner Mauer kann getrost von einem Paradigmenwechsel im Verarbeiten von Daten gesprochen werden. Komplexe geografische, demografische und ökonomische Entwicklungen werden durch Sensoren erfasst, in Datenbanken verarbeitet, die durch Algorithmen zu Entscheidungen und Handlungen führen, ohne die geringste Einmischung durch Menschen.[2] Der technologische Stand, um den im HdS vor über 40 Jahren verfolgten Traum einer effizienten, überlegenen Planwirtschaft zu realisieren, erscheint erreicht. Das Problem ist der Mensch im Mittelpunkt. Er konnte viele Herausforderungen und Plagen anthropozentrisch überwinden; er hat Tiere, die ihm nützlich sind, domestiziert, andere ausgerottet; er hat den Planeten mit Infrastruktur überformt und die Gefahren der Wildnis gebändigt; aber er ist trotz seines Wissens über die komplexen globalen Zusammenhänge nicht in der Lage, nachhaltige systemische Veränderungen vorzunehmen, die eine friedvolle Zukunft wahrscheinlicher machen.

Das *Beecoin*-Projekt setzt an diesem existenziellen Makel – der menschlichen Selbstbezogenheit – an und versucht prototypisch eine ökonomische und soziale Plattform zu schaffen, die nicht den Interessen von Menschen, sondern denen eines anderen für das Überleben der Menschheit zentralen Lebewesens folgt: denen der Bienen.

Bienen bestäuben rund 71 von 100 Nutzpflanzen, die 90 Prozent des weltweiten Bedarfs an Nahrung decken. Keine Bienen, weniger Pflanzen. Oder um es in Euro auszudrücken: Der Wert der Bestäubungsleistung liegt bei 500 Milliarden Euro jährlich. Der Verlust von Bienen ist ein Phänomen, das sich weltweit, insbesondere in Nordamerika und Europa, bemerkbar macht. In Nordamerika liegt der Verlust bei 30–40 Prozent der kommerziellen Honigbienenvölker, während in Europa der Verlust von Honigbienenvölkern seit 1985 auf 25 Prozent geschätzt wird. Diese Statistiken stellen nur die Spitze des Eisbergs dar. Die Honigbienen sind die am besten dokumentierte Art, was in krassem Gegensatz zu den Wildbienenpopulationen steht. Wissenschaftliche Untersuchungen zeigen jedoch, dass eine Vielfalt von Wildbienenarten für eine nachhaltige Pflanzenproduktion von größter Bedeutung ist. Die Komplexität der Fragen rund um die Lebensgrundlagen der Bienen ist schwer zu durchdringen, wenn sie nicht gemeinsam bewältigt wird. Nur in der kollektiven Betrachtung der komplexen ökologischen Wechselwirkungen von Bienen, Mensch, Pflanzen, Klima und vielen Faktoren mehr können Antworten gefunden werden, die die schwierige Situation, in der wir uns untrennbar mit den Bienen befinden, verbessern

---

[2] Amazon sicherte sich unlängst ein Patent für *Anticipatory Shipping*, einen Versandalgorithmus, der anhand von eingehenden Daten ohne eine vorherige Einsicht durch einen Menschen und – das ist das Novum – ohne eine Bestellung Waren versendet. Die Algorithmen verarbeiten eingehende Daten zum Wetter, bezüglich gesellschaftlicher Konflikte, Feiertage etc., um die Verteilung der Ware zu optimieren und eine schnellstmögliche Verfügbarkeit – als Marktvorteil – zu ermöglichen.

Beecoin
KUNSTrePUBLIK

können. Es braucht ein anderes, ein nicht anthropozentrisches Denken und systemisches Handeln.

Beecoin ist ein Projekt von KUNSTrePUBLIK in Zusammenarbeit mit Hiveeyes und Nascent. Koordiniert und co-designed wurde das Projekt durch Stephanie Holl-Trieu. Auch Moabees begleitet *Beecoin*. Das Projekt *Beecoin* baut auf der Forschung von Hiveeyes auf, einem in Berlin ansässigen Projekt, das Überwachungsinfrastruktur und DIY-Toolkits entwickelt, die auf Open-Source-Software, erschwinglicher Hardware und drahtloser Telemetrie basieren. Imkerisch betreut und begleitet wurde das Projekt durch Clemens Gruber.

Digital entwickelt wurde der Bee-DAO durch das Produktionsstudio Nascent und Terra0. Nascent ist ein von Paul Seidler und Max Hampshire gegründetes Produktionsstudio, das Minimal-Viable-Tech-Lösungen für institutionelle oder private Infrastrukturen entwickelt. Aufbauend auf ihren Forschungen zu Netzwerk-Resilienz, *Counter-Economies*, Öko-Technologie und Kryptowährungen entwickelt Nascent auch Taktiken und Strategien für den Aufbau von P2P-Ökonomien.

[1]
Karl Hillert, The History of Mathematics, 1970, glass & various metals, one of five square configurations 260 x 260 cm / Karl Hillert, Die Geschichte der Mathematik, Glas und diverse Metalle, eines von fünf quadratischen Elementen, 260 x 260 cm

Im Rahmen des *Beecoin*-Projekts arrangiert das Künstler- und Imkerkollektiv Moabees Besuche bei den Bienen und Interventionen im HdS. Es erfolgen Untersuchungen der in den Bienenstöcken installierten Sensoren, der menschlichen Wahrnehmungsorgane und des Facettenauges der Bienen. Mit einer Bienenkamera entstehen Porträtaufnahmen der Besucher*innen. Durch den fotochemischen Prozess der Cyanotypie werden Artefakte aus dem Haus und dem Hof gesammelt und erfasst. Zur Belichtung der Cyanotypien wird ultraviolettes (Sonnen-)Licht – für das menschliche Auge meist unsichtbar – verwendet. Bienen können UV-Licht sehen und nutzen es, um Blüten zu erkennen.

[1]
Beehive, made out of the original window frames of HdS / Bienenstock, erstellt aus den urprünglichen Fensterrahmen des HdS

Following pages: / Folgende Seiten:

[1]
1970s view of HdS from Alexander-platz / Blick vom Alexanderplatz aus dem HdS, 1970er Jahre.

[2] [3] [4]
openBerlin & KUNSTrePUBLIK, Musterhaus, 2019-ongoing, bumper car facility as discursive platform / openBerlin & KUNSTrePUBLIK, Musterhaus, seit 2019: ein Autoscooter avanciert zur Diskussionsplattform

5

HdS courtyard during Berlin Art Week opening, 11.9.19 / Innenhof des HdS während der Eröffnung der Berlin Art Week, 11.09.2019

6

anschlaege.de & Image-Shift, Unser Leben 2020, 2020, 7 PVC tarps, 10.5 x 8 m each / anschlaege.de & Image-Shift, Unser Leben 2020, 2020, 7 PVC-Planen, je 10,5 x 8 m

7
KUNSTrePUBLIK, Pigeon Towers, 2019-ongoing, functional bird shelters / KUNSTrePUBLIK, Taubentürme, seit 2019, funktionale Vogelhäuser

8
Pigeon Towers and modular light display by night, with lights flashing in concert with bird movements / Taubentürme und die modulare Lichtinstallation bei Nacht, gesteuert von der Bewegung der Vögel

9
Labor k3000, *fallingwild*, 2019-ongoing, filmed interviews & functional design proposal for HdS facade (detail) / Labor k3000, *fallingwild*, seit 2019, gefilmte Interviews & funktionaler Gestaltungsvorschlag für die HdS-Fassade (Detail)

10
KUNSTrePUBLIK & various collaborators, *Beecoin*, 2019-ongoing, beehives as DAO (closeup of hive) / KUNSTrePUBLIK & diverse Kooperationspartner, *Beecoin*, seit 2019, Bienenstöcke als DAO (Nahaufnahme des Stocks)

11
Beecoin audience on *Berlin Art Week* opening night, 11.9.19 / *Beecoin*-Besichtigung im Zuge der *Berlin Art Week* Eröffnungsnacht, 11.09.2019

12
raumlabor & Bernadette La Hengst, *Voices – first recording*, 2019-ongoing, neighborhood choir & handmade megaphones of various sizes / raumlabor & Bernadette La Hengst, *Voices. Stimmen – first recording*, seit 2019, Nachbarschaftschor & Megaphone variabler Größe

[13] [14]
raumlabor & Bernadette La Hengst, *Voices: first recording*, 2019-ongoing, neighborhood choir & handmade megaphones of various sizes / raumlabor & Bernadette La Hengst, *Voices. Stimmen – first recording*, Nachbarschaftschor & Megaphone variabler Größe

[15]
ZK/U, *ALLESANDERSPLATZ*, 2019, site specific rooftop signage /
ZK/U, *ALLESANDERSPLATZ*, 2019, orstbezogene Leuchtschrift auf dem Dach

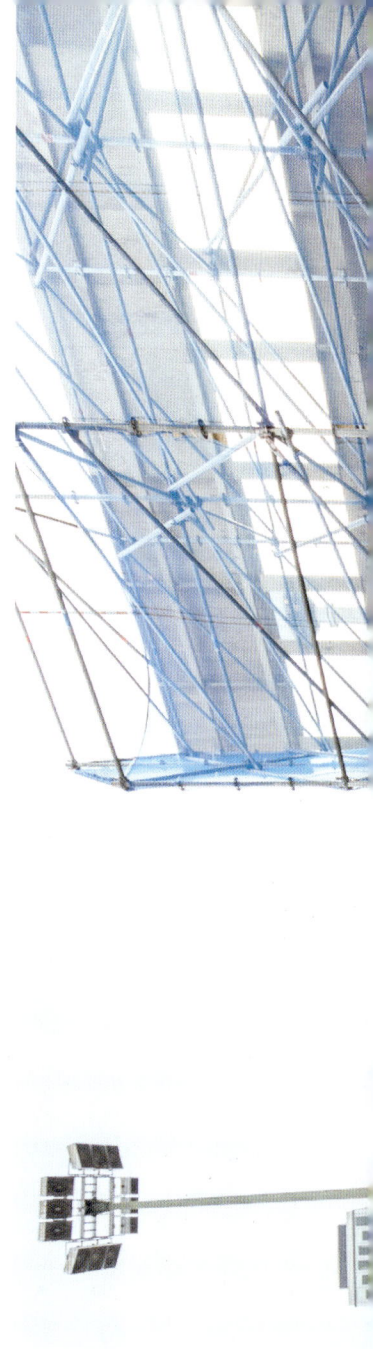

Unser Leben 2020
Image-Shift & anschlaege.de

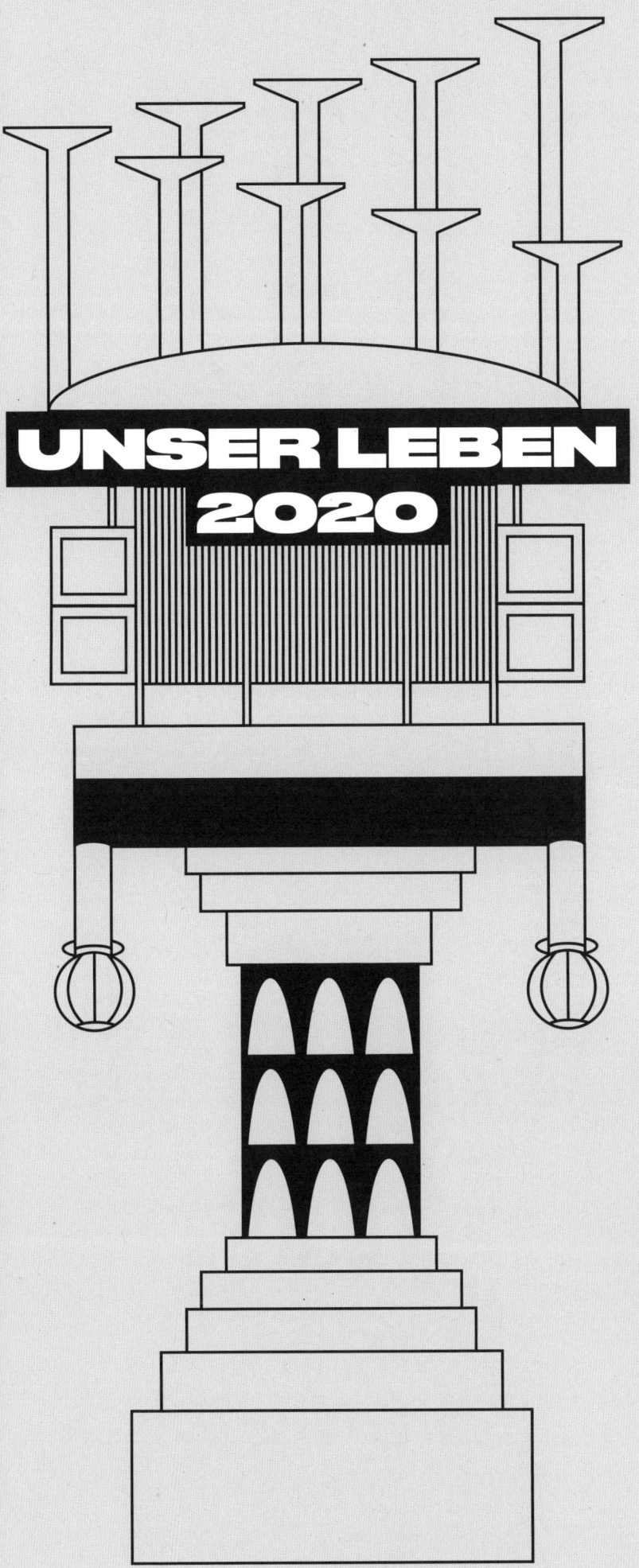

Unser Leben 2020

Ever since the 1960s, Walter Womacka has marked Alexanderplatz like no other artist. Womacka authored the *Brunnen der Völkerfreundschaft* ('Fountain of Friendship', 1970) and the copper relief *Mensch und Raum* ('Man and Space', 1971), as well as *Unser Leben* ('Our Life', 1964), a gigantic frieze marking the Haus des Lehrers ('House of the Teacher'), facing the HdS—still the largest artwork in Europe. *Unser Leben 2020* is a reference to Womacka's GDR frieze.

When Womacka designed his frieze, he claimed with confidence: 'What lies behind us was infernal. Not that things are easy now, but we are making progress. Our children's children will live in Communism.' We are those children. Yet—not least in view of Womacka's frieze—we have more questions than answers. One thing is for sure, however: We do not live in Communism.

We live in a city where the great majority of people are unable to find a suitable and affordable apartment to rent, which is why we are fighting back. We mobilize resistance through open meetings, campaigns, and protest marches. Alexanderplatz is a great place for that sort of thing. But it's seen better days. In the photos from November 4, 1989, the square is packed solid, chockablock with protesters—also between the *Weltzeituhr* (world clock) and the Haus des Lehrers, where a consumer electronics store now hides Womacka's optimistic Socialists from view. Would there be room enough on Alexanderplatz still, to protest again, one million strong, for the renationalization of housing, say? Probably. But unless Kollhoff's plans to 'Manhattan-ize' the Alex are scrapped it would be a bit of a squeeze—demonstrations big enough to rock the state's foundations would have to go elsewhere. Urban planning can be a super means of suppressing revolution, as Haussmann showed in Paris. Who is so afraid of the Imminent Uprising as to block its path with a phalanx of skyscrapers? Who is afraid of cyclists, school kid protests, and tenants' rights initiatives? Whose parade do we rain on when we open our mouths?

For our part, we're keeping our eyes peeled, and will never stop asking whether we're on the right track. All of which fed into our artwork: a mural as a mosaic, but as a printed PVC tarp, made not for all eternity but for the here and now. That's the difference between Womacka and us. That said, his moxie and optimism are infectious. He did teach us a thing or two.

p. 155
Unser Leben 2020
Image-Shift & anschlaege.de

1

2

1
Haus des Lehrers, 1971

2
anschlaege & Image-Shift, Unser Leben 2020, 7 PVC tarps,
73 x 8 m (10.5 x 8 m each) / Image-Shift & anschlaege.de, Unser Leben 2020,
2020, 7 PVC-Planen, 73 x 8 m (je 10,5 x 8 m)

Unser Leben 2020

Ab 1964 prägte Künstler Walter Womacka die Gestaltung des Alexanderplatzes. Der *Brunnen der Völkerfreundschaft* (1970) und das Kupferrelief *Mensch und Raum* (1971) gehen auf ihn zurück. Der dem Haus der Statistik zugewandte Bildfries *Unser Leben* (1964) am Haus des Lehrers gilt flächenmäßig als das größte Kunstwerk Europas. *Unser Leben 2020* bezieht sich auf diese Arbeit.

Als Womacka sein Wandbild entwarf, war er sich sicher: „Was hinter uns liegt, war fürchterlich. Auch jetzt ist nicht leicht, aber es geht vorwärts. Die Enkel werden im Kommunismus leben." Wir sind diese Enkel. Wir haben mehr Fragen als Antworten. Aber eines wissen wir sicher: Wir leben nicht im Kommunismus.

Wir leben in einer Stadt, in der es für den größten Teil der Bevölkerung unmöglich ist, eine passende und bezahlbare Wohnung zu finden. Dagegen begehren wir auf. Wir organisieren uns, halten Plena ab, protestieren, demonstrieren. Der Alexanderplatz eignet sich gut dafür. Aber er eignete sich schon mal besser. Auf den Fotos vom 4. November 1989 ist der Platz schwarz vor Menschen. Sie stehen überall. Auch zwischen Weltzeituhr und Haus des Lehrers, wo heute ein Heimelektronikmarkt den Blick auf Womackas Bild mit den optimistischen Sozialisten versperrt. Wäre auf dem Alex dennoch genug Raum, um hier wieder mit einer Million Menschen zu demonstrieren, zum Beispiel für die Vergesellschaftung von Wohnraum? Wahrscheinlich. Aber wenn Kollhoffs Pläne, den Alex mit Hochhäusern zuzupflastern, nicht platzen, wird es eng: kein Platz mehr für Demonstrationen, die so groß sind, eine staatliche Ordnung zu erschüttern. Stadtplanung kann Aufstandsbekämpfung sein – Haussmann hat es in Paris vorgemacht. Wer fürchtet den kommenden Aufstand so sehr, dass er ihm eine Hochhausphalanx in den Weg bauen möchte? Wem machen Radfahrer*innen, Schülerdemos und Mieterinitiativen Angst? In wessen Suppe spucken wir, wenn wir den Mund aufmachen?

Wir fahren auf Sicht und fragen uns immer wieder, ob wir noch auf dem richtigen Weg sind. So ist unser Wandbild entstanden – nicht als Mosaik, sondern als Plane; nicht für die Ewigkeit, sondern für den Augenblick. Das unterscheidet uns von Womacka. Aber von seiner Heiterkeit und seinem Optimismus können wir uns eine Scheibe abschneiden.

Best of Ishtar

Ishtar Gate was an in-house critical model for STATISTA, publishing an ongoing series of critical commentary surrounding the project, beginning May 2019. This running commentary was primarily catalysed by cultural theorist Penny Rafferty, and the following section offers a series of extracts from her texts. Rafferty's passages aside, Ishtar Gate featured an open function allowing the STATISTA team and the public to add to Rafferty's thoughts; an interactive mode of collective authorship.

This was not the only function of the platform: Ishtar Gate also rewarded its users with *Ishtar*, a token that will eventually be exchanged for goods and services in the real world, be it a coffee or a studio space, within a network of participating local institutions. This localized/in-house currency offered the transactional foundation for a 'passivity oriented' microeconomy. The project was conceptually borne of a collaboration between Rafferty and Nascent, a production studio based in Berlin, which focuses on decentralized P2P technology.

    The art world is not a success. It is not progressive, it is not beautiful, it is not just, it is not virtuous, it is not unbiased and it frequently misses opportunities to perform better. The art world we all live in everyone loathes. At first, we dislike it, and, in the long term, we despise it. This machine of accelerated aesthetics, burnouts, precarious living, 24/7 availability and galvanized gossip is motivated by survival, and decisions are based on illusionary gain, rather than a common good.

    This does not mean that all cultural workers are inherently filled with the prerequisite greed and selfish motivations, quite the opposite. I'm encouraged by the thought that many perform their duties because they have good intentions – but that the art world has been subsumed by something not entirely human. Something which in some circles we call Capitalism. Capitalism is authoritarian, as well as ineffective. It is also racist, sexist, and rewards those who monopolize empowering positions. Sound familiar? Yet another common denominator between Capitalism and today's art world is a shared interest in economic crisis.

    There is one difference here, however: the art world has always declared itself to be in crisis, and the starving artist is an age-old archetype that some say is still a rite of passage into this field. (Ironically, those who like to highlight these rites and rituals enjoy ample free dinners and VIP cocktail invites.)

    Given that art genres, vogues, and hypes have been changing as easily as catwalk seasons, perhaps the very foundations could change too? Many have been asking themselves what might happen if the users actually owned this machine, rather than being forced to pump their liquid guts into some extra-statecraft monstrosity? What would happen to art? Would the art world fade out of existence if it started working for its patrons, its producers, its believers, as opposed to juicing them?

    Meaningful change must start as a societal concept – not as a legal bill or a statistic – if it is to flourish and become the new status quo. How to platform these concepts? How to gain enough of the population's attention to be considered a public intermediary? Can art really perform this task? STATISTA has found itself in exactly that role of both facilitator and creator. Under the guise of art, STATISTA aims to address multiple imbalances that make up the city infrastructure. In order to do that, it must first sell its primary mode of communication: art. If it fails to sell art, it fails to sell any radical concepts that stand behind the work, and it will also fall short of the debate on why transformational politics are needed in Berlin right now. Sometimes, according to a much-quoted phrase by Brian Eno, 'the strongest single importance of a work of art is the celebration of some kind of temporary community.' One could liken the STATISTA exhibition to precisely such a temporary community. But how to translate the temporary into the local, and, from there, into the city's long-term infrastructure. Art has always argued for its ability to be publicly relevant, yet few projects actually test themselves the way STATISTA did. On that note: will STATISTA be granted space and legitimacy even if it fails? Should it be granted all these things, merely because it tried where others did not?

  Wandering around the STATISTA opening, many of my peers asked me, 'Where is the Art? What should I see?' This very puzzlement (and the increasing anxiety around 'cancel culture') makes STATISTA's lack of visibility look oddly fragile. Like a frail sheath of skin over a broken building, crawling with people laying track lines everywhere, to the point where one could barely see its surface, let alone sense its muscle memory. The skin I did see was invisible to most, even in the strangely surreal fairground setting of the Berlin Art Week opening party. With speeches given, a DJ playing, *Sekt* being poured and bunting flying, the setting was closer to a summer fête than your typical White Cube regalia. Yet the usual suspects still clinked champagne glasses and crunched over the tarmac to embrace one another. On the one hand, not being able to see the art is more telling about the art world at large than it is about STATISTA. We've become so formulaic, in our reading of art, that when a piece is invisible or inconspicuous we consider it hidden or absent. FOMO and the viewers' time economy are of course not helpful here.

  On the other hand, does the viewer still validate a work of art? Can the people's choice defy the market's choice – and if nobody looks at a given work of art, is it still art? Well, the freeports in Geneva would argue that their dividends rely on that premise. (Those freeport artworks, encased in Swiss steel cubes, did attract ample attention, and wrenched many eyes wide open, but whose eyes are we talking about here? Public ones, or the professional retinas of the art world?) And if the viewer is merely autonomous garnish, what is the role of the artist or curator: do we believe they owe the viewer anything?

  Perhaps STATISTA did fail in this task of caring for its audience when it simply gathered its viewers in a vacant lot, only to pontificate on pet ideas. Such as the labour of bees as a '*Verein*', or the gift of multi-functional city facades, or even the shy questions: Where and What has become of Contemporary Art? In a sense, STATISTA exhibited the social nuances of both the art world and the city it inhabits. Unwittingly, the viewers became a work in themselves. They added to the prevalent memetic discourse, what with their art-viewing attire accentuating the surreal landscape of Prada bags amidst the rubble piles, and with

Best of Ishtar
Penny Rafferty

their flailing mental efforts completing the cultural economy of the event. Yet the sense of something lost was still palpable. It was emanating from the all-male line-up during the ceremonious thank-yous, from the lack of press releases (which left many viewers in the dark), to the 'documentation room' filled with faraway projects from other faraway cities. All methods have their pros and cons, but the key question is whether they access the viewers in the ways they intended. Can we board up a window that offers a view, and still expect people to look out? Will they strain to peep through the cracks, pressing their cheeks against the splintered wood, just to, say, experience something or other, rather than accept and contemplate the void? Transparency, freedom of speech, pay per view, social views, likes, viewer statistics, augmented reality, queuing on Everest and risking one's life for a selfie: the world we live in today is built to be viewed. Its viewers demand to be able to see.

Ishtar Gate

Ishtar Gate ist eine Kooperation zwischen Autorin Penny Rafferty und dem Berliner IT-Büro Nascent, das auf dezentralisierte Peer-to-Peer-Systeme spezialisiert ist. Zu Ishtar Gate gehört ein internes Kritikverfahren: Rafferty hat zu STATISTA fortlaufend kritische Kommentare veröffentlicht, die über eine offene Funktion verfügen, mit der externe sowie kollektive Beiträge möglich sind. Ishtar Gate belohnt seine Nutzerschaft mit einem Gutschein, der bei den teilnehmenden lokalen Institutionen (einschließlich KW und ZK/U) gegen reale Dinge eingelöst werden kann. Diese Eigenwährung bildet mit ihrem Tauschprinzip die Grundlage einer Mikroökonomie, die sich am „Prinzip der Passivität" orientiert. Allein durch Lesen, das Verlinken von Beiträgen und Kommentaren sowie auch das Kommentieren und Erstellen eigener Inhalte können Nutzende sogenannte Ishtar verdienen. Im folgenden Abschnitt finden Sie eine Reihe von Auszügen aus Penny Raffertys Texten zum Thema.

Die Kunstwelt ist keine Erfolgsgeschichte. Sie ist nicht progressiv, sie ist nicht schön, sie ist nicht gerecht, sie ist nicht tugendhaft, sie ist nicht unvoreingenommen, und sie verpasst regelmäßig die Chance, sich zu bessern. Die Kunstwelt, der wir alle angehören, ist allen zuwider. Anfangs entwickeln wir eine Abneigung, langfristig fangen wir an, sie zu hassen. Diese Maschine der akzelerierten Ästhetik, der Burnouts, des prekären Lebens, der ständigen Verfügbarkeit und des himmelschreienden *Gossip* wird angetrieben vom Überlebenstrieb, während die Entscheidungen mit Blick auf einen trügerischen Gewinn statt im Interesse des Gemeinwohls getroffen werden.

Das bedeutet nicht, dass alle Kulturschaffenden von einem lebensnotwendigen Neid erfüllt und eigennützig motiviert sind – ganz im Gegenteil. Mich ermuntert der Gedanke, dass viele ihre Pflicht mit guten Absichten erfüllen, die Kunstwelt aber von etwas befallen ist, dass nicht vollständig menschlich ist – von etwas, das wir in bestimmten Kreisen als Kapitalismus bezeichnen. Der Kapitalismus ist so autoritär wie ineffektiv. Zudem ist er rassistisch und sexistisch und spielt denjenigen in die Hände, die die Machtpositionen an sich reißen. Kommt Ihnen das bekannt vor? Ein weiterer gemeinsamer Nenner von Kapitalismus und der heutigen Kunstwelt ist ein geteiltes Interesse an Wirtschaftskrisen.

Allerdings gibt es einen entscheidenden Unterschied: Die Kunstwelt hat immer behauptet, in einer Krise zu stecken, und der oder die darbende Kunstschaffende ist ein jahrhundertealter Archetyp, dessen Zustand manchen noch immer als Übergangsritus zum Künstlerdasein gilt. (Ironischerweise kommen jene, die besonders laut auf diese Riten und Rituale pochen, ständig in den Genuss von Gratis-Dinners und Einladungen zu VIP-Cocktailpartys.)

Wenn Kunstgenres, Moden und Hypes inzwischen im Rhythmus der Laufstegsaisons wechseln, sollte dann nicht auch ein tief greifender Wandel möglich sein? Viele haben sich die Frage gestellt, was geschehe, wenn die Nutzer*innen der Maschine tatsächlich im Besitz der Maschine wären, statt gezwungen zu sein, ihre Eingeweide in ein außerstaatliches Monstrum zu pumpen. Was würde dann aus der Kunst? Würde die Kunstwelt aufhören zu existieren, wenn sie im Interesse ihres Mäzenatentums, ihrer Produzent*innen und ihrer treuen Anhängerschaft arbeitete, statt sie zu melken?

      Tief greifender Wandel muss als gesellschaftliches Konzept beginnen – nicht als Gesetzesentwurf oder als Statistik –, wenn er sich durchsetzen und zum neuen Status quo werden soll. Auf welche Weise kann eine Plattform für diese Konzepte geschaffen werden? Wie lässt sich genügend Aufmerksamkeit in der Bevölkerung generieren, um als öffentliche Vermittlungsinstanz anerkannt zu werden? Ist Kunst dieser Aufgabe wirklich gewachsen? STATISTA fand sich sowohl in der Rolle als Vermittlerin wie auch als Produzentin wieder. Unter dem Deckmantel der Kunst thematisiert STATISTA die vielzähligen Ungleichheiten, die die Infrastruktur der Stadt ausmachen. Um dies zu tun, muss sie zunächst ihren primären Kommunikationsmodus vermarkten: die Kunst selbst. Scheitert sie daran, Kunst zu vermarkten, dann wird es ihr erstens auch nicht gelingen, die radikalen Konzepte, die hinter diesen Arbeiten stehen, zu vermarkten. Zweitens wird sie sich nicht an der dringenden Debatte um die Notwendigkeit einer transformatorischen Politik in Berlin beteiligen können. Laut einem vielzitierten Satz von Brian Eno ist es die „bei Weitem wichtigste Aufgabe eines Kunstwerks, irgendeine Art temporäre Gemeinschaft zu feiern". Die STATISTA-Ausstellung ließe sich mit genau einer solchen temporären Gemeinschaft vergleichen. Aber wie lässt sich das Temporäre auf das Lokale und von dort – auf lange Sicht – auf die Infrastruktur der Stadt übertragen? Während Kunst immer von sich behauptet hat, öffentliche Relevanz zu haben, nehmen sich nur wenige Projekte derart gewissenhaft unter die Lupe, wie STATISTA es getan hat. In diesem Sinne stellt sich die Frage, ob STATISTA in Zukunft auch dann Raum und Legitimität zuerkannt werden wird, wenn das Projekt scheitert. Steht ihm diese Legitimation zu, nur weil es nichts unversucht gelassen hat, was andere nicht anzurühren wagten?

      Während ich durch die STATISTA-Eröffnung schlenderte, fragten mich viele meiner Kolleg*innen: „Wo ist die Kunst?" Diese Verwirrung (und die wachsende Angst vor *cancel culture*) lässt STATISTAs mangelnde Sichtbarkeit seltsam fragil wirken. Die Ausstellung gleicht einer über ein verfallenes Gebäude gespannten, porösen Haut, auf der die wimmelnden Menschen derart viele Spuren hinterlassen, dass die Oberfläche kaum noch sichtbar ist. Die von mir gesehene Haut war für die meisten unsichtbar, selbst im Kontext der eigentümlich surrealen Szenerie, die die Eröffnungsfeier der *Berlin Art Week* darstellt. Mit den gehaltenen Reden, einem DJ, dem ausgeschenkten Sekt und den wehenden Fahnen ähnelte das Setting eher einem Sommerfest, denn der typischen Inszenierung des *White Cube*. Dennoch ließen die üblichen Verdächtigen ihre Sektgläser klingen und knirschten lautstark über den Asphalt, um einander um den Hals zu fallen. Einerseits sagt die unsichtbare Kunst in diesem Fall mehr über die Kunstwelt aus, als über STATISTA: Unsere Auffassung von Kunst ist derart formelhaft geworden, dass wir eine unsichtbare oder subtile Arbeit als verborgen oder gar abwesend erachten. FOMO (*fear of missing out*) und die Zeitökonomie des Publikums tun ihr Übriges.
Andererseits: Wertschätzen die Betrachtenden das Kunstwerk überhaupt noch? Kann die Wahl der Menschen der

Ishtar Gate
Penny Rafferty

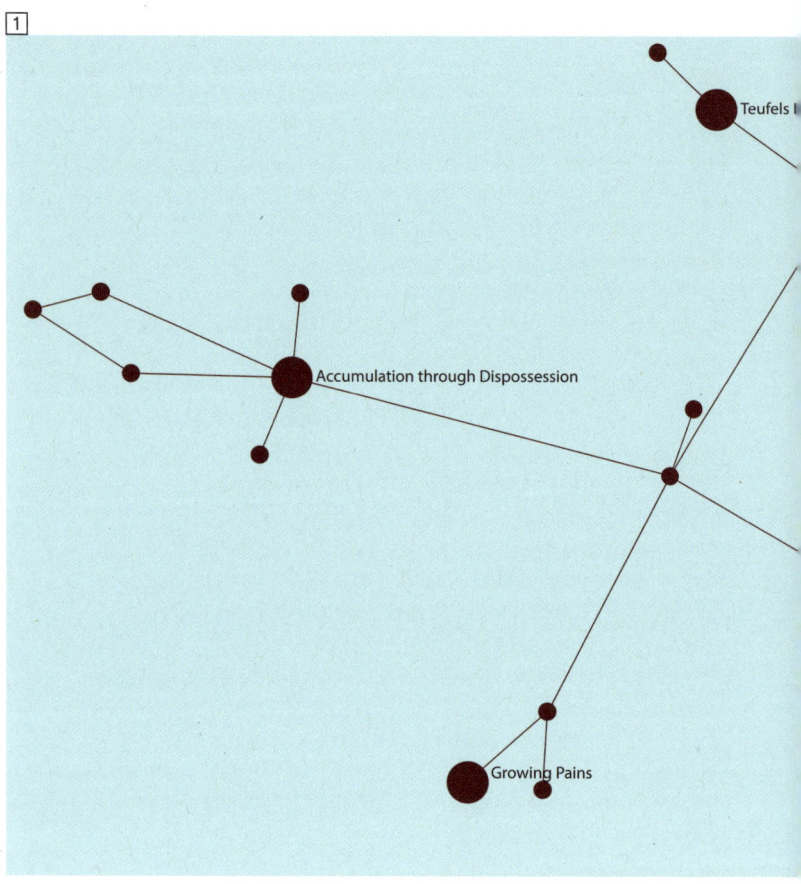

Wahl des Marktes die Stirn bieten? Und handelt es sich noch um Kunst, wenn niemand das Kunstwerk betrachtet?

Nun, der Freihafen von Genf zumindest würde argumentieren, dass seine Dividenden sich auf diese Prämisse stützen. (Jene Kunstwerke im Freihafen, die eingeschlossen sind in Schweizer Stahlwürfel, haben große Aufmerksamkeit erregt und viele Augen weit geöffnet. Doch von wessen Augen ist hier die Rede – von den Augen der Öffentlichkeit oder den professionellen Retinas der Kunstwelt?) Wenn das Publikum bloß als eigenverantwortliche Deko fungiert, welche Rolle kommt dann den Kunstschaffenden und Kuratierenden zu? Glauben wir, dass sie dem Publikum etwas schulden?

Vielleicht konnte STATISTA der Aufgabe nicht gerecht werden, für ihr Publikum zu sorgen, als sie ihre Besucherschaft einfach auf einem unbebauten Grundstück versammelte, nur um über die eigenen Lieblingstheorien zu pontifizieren. Um eine Reihe von Beispielen der vorgebrachten Theorien zu nennen: fleißige Bienen als Metapher für die Arbeit im Verein; der Segen multifunktionaler Häuserfassaden oder gar die scheuen Fragen: „Was ist aus der zeitgenössischen Kunst geworden und wo ist sie geblieben?" In gewissem Sinne hat STATISTA die sozialen Charakteristika sowohl der Kunstwelt als auch der von ihr eingenommenen Stadt an den Tag gelegt. Ohne sich dessen bewusst zu sein, sind die Betrachtenden selbst Teil einer Arbeit geworden. Sie trugen zum vorherrschenden Diskurs bei, akzentuierten mit ihrem kunstaffinen Habitus die surreale Landschaft aus Prada-Taschen inmitten der Schutthaufen, und komplettierten mit ihren ausschweifenden Denkanstrengungen die Kulturökonomie des Events. Das ausschließlich männliche Line-up der feierlichen Danksagungen, der Mangel an Pressetexten (der einen großen Teil der Besucherschaft im Unklaren ließ) und der mit ent-

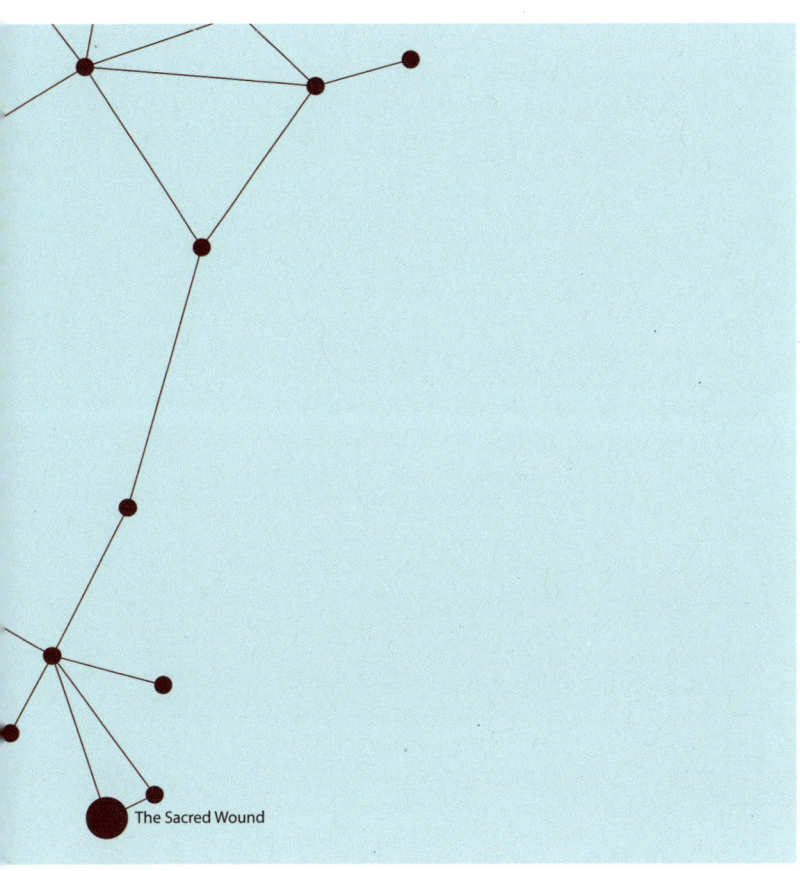

legenen Projekten von anderen, ebenfalls entlegenen Städten gefüllte „Dokumentationsraum" vermittelten das eindeutige Gefühl, dass etwas verloren gegangen war.

Alle Methoden haben ihre Vor- und Nachteile, aber die Kernfrage besteht darin, ob sie das Publikum in der vorgesehenen Weise erreichen. Können wir ein Fenster, das eine gute Aussicht bietet, mit Brettern vernageln und trotzdem von Leuten erwarten, dass sie hinaussehen? Werden sie sich die Mühe machen, ihre Wangen gegen das splittrige Holz zu pressen und durch die Ritzen zu lugen, nur um etwas, dieses oder jenes, sagen wir mal, zu erfahren, statt sich mit der Leere abzufinden und darüber zu kontemplieren? Transparenz, Redefreiheit, *pay per view*, gesellschaftliche Sichtweisen, Likes, Zuschauerstatistiken, *augmented reality*, Schlangestehen am Mount Everest und Sich-für-ein-Selfie-in-Lebensgefahr-Begeben: Die Welt, in der wir heute leben, ist geschaffen, um betrachtet zu werden. Ihre Betrachter*innen verlangen danach, sehen zu können.

[1]
Screenshot of Penny Rafferty & Nascent, *Ishtar Gate*, 2019, online experiment in collective authorship / Screenshot von Penny Rafferty & Nascent: *Ishtar Gate*, 2019, Online-Experiment zu kollektiver Autorenschaft

STATISTA Conference at Haus der Statistik
Campus in Camps, CATPC (Cercle d'Art des Travailleurs de Plantation Congolaise), Chto Delat, ExRotaprint, Khalil Sakakini Cultural Center, MACAO, Nachbarschaftsakademie Prinzessinnengärten, PlanBude, ruangrupa

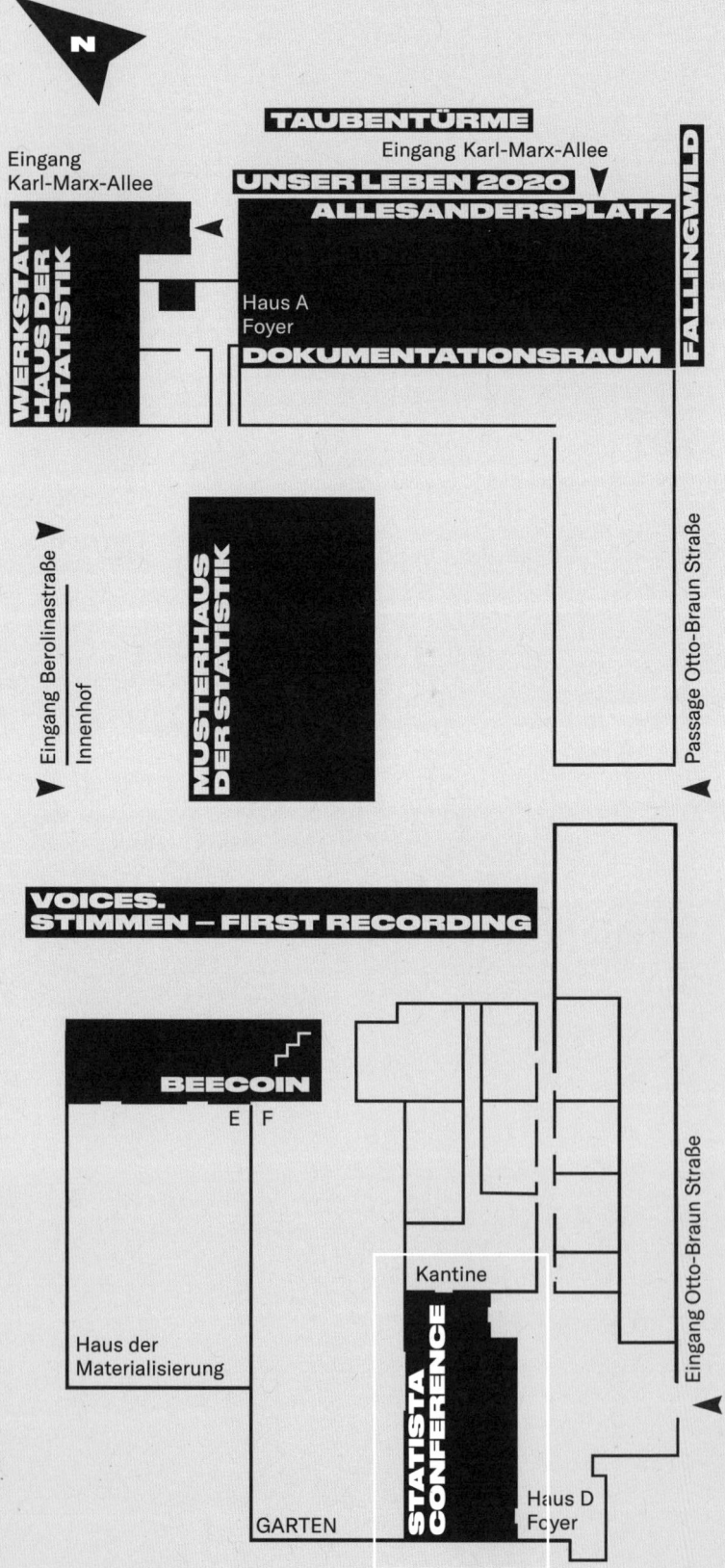

Conference Introduction

The STATISTA conference offered a collective snapshot of a possible future as proposed by nine collectives. To be sure, the invited organizations all contend with wildly different settings, in radically distinct locations. But they came together as a medley of deeply comparable approaches, all of them embodied by collectively owned structures with long-term agendas of redistribution. A tenth collective was the HdS itself, offering a historical backdrop and a conceptual touchstone, to measure ourselves by, and to help consolidate the common ground between us.

Smaller workshop settings allowed for in-depth engagements, while the lectures were broadcasted by sub_text, an itinerant platform for sonic knowledge production ranging from investigative reporting to experimental sound and music, in partnership with Threads Radio in Tottenham, London. All participants equally contributed materials to the STATISTA Documentation Room.

The following pages feature contributions that are diagrammatic, experimental materials. They reflect the practices of the nine invited collectives in ways that are more haptic, didactic and suggestive than what conventional self-portraits usually allow for. To name but a few, ruangrupa designed a game for two that whets your appetite for proactive spatial strategies. The Sakakini Cultural Center based the newest rendition of their poster series on the STATISTA workshop in Berlin. Campus in Camps devised a proposal for the HdS, drawing on their longstanding effort to register refugee camps in the West Bank as UNESCO World Heritage sites.

The actual, material setting for our conference event was a sprawling infrastructure designed and built by Making Futures, a Summer Academy under the auspices of the Berlin University of the Arts. A protagonist of this initiative was architect Markus Bader, also a member of STATISTA participant raumlabor. The itinerary, the canteen and the seating arrangements devised by Making Futures students were an excellent example of synergies of use at HdS. During the ongoing, interim phase of renovation, as countless cultural initiatives scramble to use the space – and to implant it firmly in the public eye – you can get in each other's way, in exasperating fashion, but you also build on each other's input to impressive effect.

Images on the following pages / Bilder auf den folgende Seiten:

[1]
Tsaplya Olga Egorova & Dmitry Vilensky, Rosa's House of Culture

[2]
Renée Tribble, PlanBude

[3]
View of presentation by ExRotaprint / Vortrag von ExRotaprint

[4]
Traces left by Making Futures students prior to STATISTA conference / Spuren der Making Futures Veranstaltung, die STATISTA vorausging

Einleitung zur Konferenz

Die STATISTA-Konferenz bot die kollektive Momentaufnahme einer von neun Kollektiven entworfenen Zukunftsvision dar. Natürlich engagieren sich die eingeladenen Organisationen in höchst unterschiedlichen Umfeldern, und an äußerst unterschiedlichen Standorten. Doch kommen sie als Verbund durchaus vergleichbarer Ansätze zusammen: Alle neun verkörpern Gemeinschaftsstrukturen, die sich langfristig der Umverteilung von kulturellem und sogar finanziellem Kapital verschrieben haben. Als zehntes Kollektiv lieferte der Kontext des Hauses der Statistik (HdS) sowohl einen geschichtlichen Hintergrund wie auch einen konzeptuellen Prüfstein, an dem wir uns messen und unsere gemeinsame Basis konsolidieren konnten.

Kleinere Workshop-Settings ließen tiefer gehende Annäherungen an bestimmte Themen zu. Die Vorträge wurden via Threads Radio gesendet (Tottenham, London), in Kooperation mit sub_ʇxǝʇ, einer Plattform für akustische Wissensproduktion, deren Schwerpunkte von Reportage bis hin zu experimenteller Musik reichen. Darüber hinaus steuerten alle Teilnehmenden gleichermaßen Materialien zum STATISTA-Dokumentationsraum bei.

Die nachfolgenden Seiten enthalten Beiträge mit schematischen, spielerischen, experimentellen Materialien. Diese stellen die Praktiken der neun eingeladenen Kollektive auf haptische, didaktische, suggestive Weise dar. Um nur einige der Beiträge zu nennen: ruangrupa entwickelte ein Spiel für zwei, das Lust auf proaktive Raumstrategien macht. Das Sakakini Cultural Center widmete die neueste Ausgabe seiner Posterserie dem STATISTA-Workshop in Berlin. Campus in Camps entwickelte einen Entwurf für das HdS, der auf dessen langjährigem Engagement für die Ernennung eines Flüchtlingslagers im Westjordanland zum UNESCO-Weltkulturerbe beruht.

Das eigentliche, materielle Setting unserer Konferenz bildete eine weitläufige Infrastruktur wurde entworfen und umgesetzt von Making Futures, einer Sommerakademie unter der Schirmherrschaft der Universität der Künste. Ein Protagonist dieser Initiative ist Architekt Markus Bader, Mitglied von raumlabor.

Das Inventar, die Kantine und das Arrangement der Sitzgelegenheiten, entwickelt von Making Futures Studierenden, waren beispielhaft für die Raumnutzungssynergien des HdS. Während der anhaltenden Interimsphase der Renovierungen, in der unzählige kulturelle Initiativen den Raum nutzen – und ihn dadurch auch in den Fokus der Öffentlichkeit rücken – tritt man sich auf die Füße, aber man baut dennoch auf den gegenseitigen Input, oft mit verblüffenden Ergebnissen.

5
Audience view, STATISTA conference / Publikum, STATISTA Konferenz

6
Emanuele Braga & Maddalena Fragnito, MACAO

7
Mathieu Kilapi Kasiama & Ced'Art Tamasala, CATPC, Janke Brands, IHA

8
Farid Rakun, ruangrupa

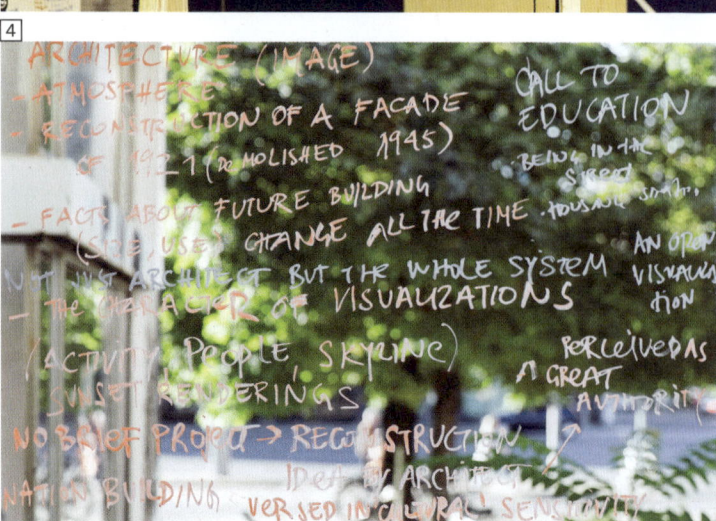

CATPC

First of all, I would like to thank the whole team in Berlin for your attention to our project.

We, le Cercle d'Art de Travailleurs Plantation Congolaise (CATPC), now have the real pleasure of contributing to this beautiful teamwork accomplished by our colleagues at STATISTA.

Our collective, CATPC, is a cooperative of artist-plantation workers based in Lusanga, Democratic Republic of the Congo. Composed of both men and women, CATPC is engaged in a process of buying back land that has been confiscated and exploited for almost a century by the Unilever company, which ran a large monocultural palm oil plantation on it.

After a long overexploitation of nature, and of indigenous people in Lusanga, the company closed in 2011, leaving behind a ruined village and a population living in extreme poverty.

The profits made by this forced labour have been invested in cities in the West, partly to build museums where art and beauty is shown, and where a whole new economy has arisen around these museums.

Nothing of this great fortune amassed – thanks to the sacrifice of the workers – returned to Lusanga. The poverty created by this capitalist system forced people to flee elsewhere in the hope of finding work.

Our group looked at the problem, and thought about how to create new survival opportunities in Lusanga. How are CATPC artists meeting these challenges?

The drawing proposed by one of the CATPC members (Ced'Art Tamasala), better explains this teamwork accomplished by the artist collective in Lusanga.

Plantation workers in Africa supply under difficult conditions – inhuman conditions – agricultural raw products that

are transformed and sold in Europe; none of these profits go back to Lusanga.

Beside this reality, there is us: CATPC. We managed to infiltrate the system. With the support of its partner, the Institute for Human Activities, CATPC manages to:

- show their art, share their ideas with the world (sculptural ideas, reproduced in chocolate derived from the plantation product cocoa, now transformed and exhibited around the world)

- sell art and bring profits back to Lusanga, to buy the land.

On this recovered land, we have achieved many things, the most important of which are:

- an ecologically diverse post-plantation, in harmony with nature.

- a White Cube, and an atelier

- improved living conditions, also for our community.

Since its creation in 2014, CATPC has managed to buy 85 hectares of land, and further negotiations are underway. It is by working together that we have achieved this result. And it is the strength of the collective that guarantees success.

Our most fraternal greetings to fellow artists from Lusanga.

Yours truly,

CED'ART TAMASALA,
Le Cercle d'Art de Travailleurs Plantation Congolaise

Chto Delat: Rosa's House of Culture

WHAT: An initiative of the collective Chto Delat based on commoning and solidarity economies aimed at creating a community of comrades engaging in cultural activity and self-education. Rosa's House of Culture was founded on 1st of May 2015 in Saint Petersburg.

WHY ROSA: A rose is a beautiful and very thorny flower. And, that's the name of Rosa Luxemburg, a great figure in the history of the revolutionary movement, who is one of the few consolidating names for different factions of leftists today who share feminist demands. ROSA's name is a name of solidarity.

WHY A HOUSE OF CULTURE: This project draws on the history of Houses of Culture in socialist countries, the experience of social centers in Europe and Latin America, and the new politics of progressive art institutions that aim to overcome the alienation of the pure display and the passivity of the public. In contemporary Russia, we envision the House of Culture as a model that re-establishes a counter-public sphere (Nancy Fraser), serving as a 'training ground for agitation activities' with the ultimate goal of nourishing new sensibilities that are not always welcome around here, embracing the difference of many different species that may not want to become too visible, and protecting endangered and yet-unborn ideas. The House of Culture is a space for militant cultural environmentalism.

HOW IT WORKS: RHC is a space for running various workshops, reading groups, seminars and circles as well as a space for hosting different kinds of public events (lectures, film screenings, discussions, exhibitions and parties). RHC is home to the School of Engaged Art, as well as a unique publicly accessible library dedicated to contemporary art and activist literature. The activities in RHC are coordinated by a self-management group and general assembly. The work of RHC is supported by the Chto Delat Mutual Aid Fund and by the donations of its participants.

** Self-management Group is an informal open group which has taken over different organizational and programming activities at RHC with the goal of building autonomy and a sustainable safe space for all participants and guests at RHC.

Chto Delat

[1] Collage by Dmitry Vilensky

[2] Image by Vasilina Koshalina

Campus in Camps: How to preserve Statista's temporary collective uses?

Since the 90s, Berlin has been the epicenter of self-organized and experimental temporary uses. Unfortunately, most of these spontaneous interventions have not survived for long or have been appropriated by financial capital for real estate speculation. In the same period, the Karl-Marx-Allee, where the Statista building is located, was listed as a potential UNESCO World Heritage Site. The State of Berlin and the Berlin Senate will appear as applicants in the 2022 UNESCO world heritage nomination of Karl-Marx-Allee and the Interbau 1957 as a unique ensemble of modernity. Will the nomination affect the future uses of Statista? Is it possible to mobilize the notion of heritage for temporary and experimental uses? How to preserve the values of artistic practices that gave the building a new life?

'Steadying'

Temporary manifestations undergoing a process of 'steadying' as a quality which seeks to create a multitude of spatial narratives, slowly consolidating them through time. In allowing incremental developments of various projects to leave their mark, a complexity of multiple ambitions and practices informs the collective future of the site, in which singular visions are displaced by living systems. Supporting a framework in which such projects can be solidified is vital to the practice of keeping space open for new developments, and for the creation of new narratives to be developed within the site.

Collective Organization

Experimentation with organizational structures emerges from the necessities of creating and managing temporary spatial forms. Innovative models of collective assembly and co-ordination are developed in response to the practicalities and realities of the site, and hence are conceived, tested and refined through their application. The site's ability to provide a space to host these collective models is integral to its ability to sustain the possibility of their experimentation and development.

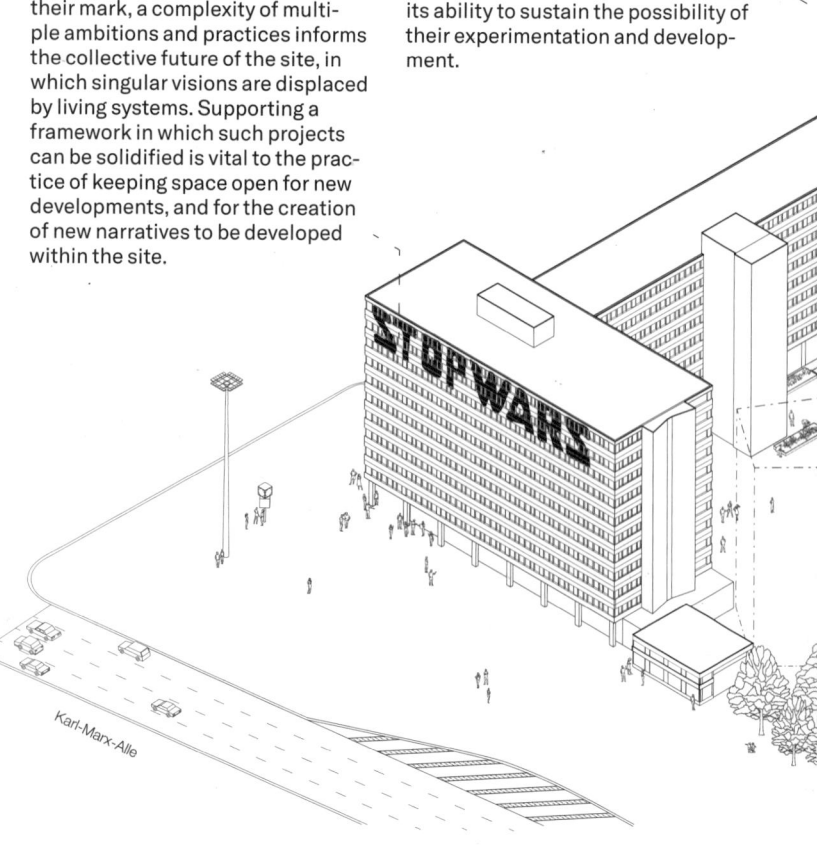

Common Infrastructures

The creation of a common platform constitutes an integral component of the sites, capability to produce new spatial and social typologies. Open artistic and community infrastructures allow for radical new possibilities to emerge, and create a potential framework for the speculation of possible collective futures. These infrastructures function as a form of commons, compelling a collectively engaged, dynamic system to be maintained for their survival, which also informs their structure and outputs in part.

Urban Resistance

Situated within larger systems of urban displacement, privatization and corporate renewal, temporary manifestations have embodied a key typology of spatial resistance, sustaining forms of neglected social productions and generating new collective possibilities within the urban. The ability of the site to act and evolve within the emergence of new social-political contexts is vital for its ongoing contribution in larger urban struggles.

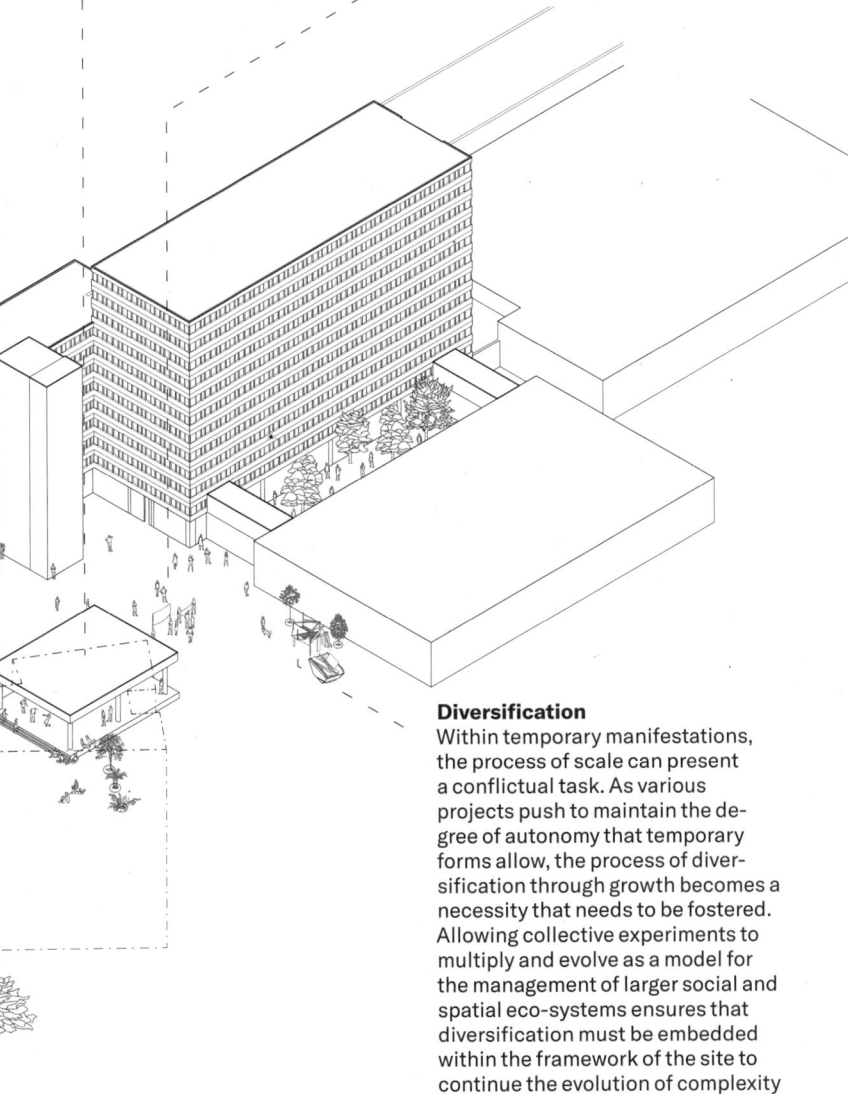

Diversification

Within temporary manifestations, the process of scale can present a conflictual task. As various projects push to maintain the degree of autonomy that temporary forms allow, the process of diversification through growth becomes a necessity that needs to be fostered. Allowing collective experiments to multiply and evolve as a model for the management of larger social and spatial eco-systems ensures that diversification must be embedded within the framework of the site to continue the evolution of complexity and autonomy.

ExRotaprint: How the Heritable Building Right Works

The legal instrument of the heritable building right makes sustainable property management possible by defining the long-term objectives for development and use and guaranteeing an annual interest payment. Heritable building right contracts open up possibilities for both contracting parties to impact the scope and direction of social and city politics without relinquishing forever the space needed to shape community or excluding those segments of the population with fewer financial means from access to space and its uses. They are an instrument for opposing property speculation.

The heritable building right divides up ownership of property by separating the parcel of land from the buildings. The party providing the heritable building right owns the land; the party receiving the heritable building right owns the buildings. A heritable building right is equivalent to ownership with all the associated rights and obligations related to property management. In the heritable building right, the aims and objectives can be specified for types of use, what purposes the management serves, or the scope of the construction. These objectives apply for the duration of the heritable building right and are therefore essential aspects of the contract.

With a heritable building right contract, the landowner leases the parcel of land to the recipient of the heritable building right for an agreed period of time. In return, the heritable building right provider is paid an annual ground rent that is based on the value of the parcel of land and which is freely negotiable. The value of the heritable building right is often higher than the property encumbered with the heritable building right, since the heritable building right recipient makes earnings from managing the property. A loan can be taken out based on the value of the heritable building right in order to invest in building renovations or the construction of new buildings.

If the heritable building right provider does not wish to use the property for other purposes, an extension of the heritable building right may then be negotiated at any time. A premature termination of the contract can only be effected by the insolvency of one of the two contracting parties, a failure to pay ground rent, or a violation of the aims and objectives.

Nachbarschaftsakademie Prinzessinnengärten

[1] [2] [3]
Illustration work by Lígia Milagres

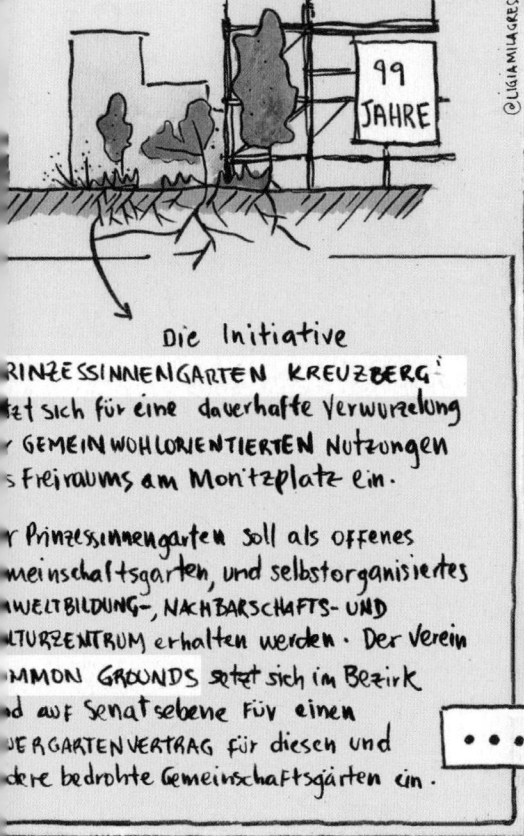

PlanBude–WORKSHOP

Margit Czenki, Christoph Schäfer, Renée Tribble, Lisa Marie Zander

Insbesondere die Nachbarschaft des Haus der Statistik (HdS) ist eingeladen, an einem dreistündigen Foto-Workshop teilzunehmen, der in erster Linie eine Foto-Erkundung in geheime Winkel und ungesehene, vielleicht private Lieblingsecken des Viertels ist. Die Teilnehmer*innen sind eine gute Stunde lang mit ihren Kameras in der Umgebung unterwegs. Zurückgekehrt wählt jede*r drei Bilder aus, stellt diese allen anderen vor und erzählt, warum diese gemacht und warum genau diese Bilder ausgesucht wurden. Foto und Notizen werden als Instant-Poster auf DIN A3 ausgedruckt und vom PlanBuden-Team am Haus der Statistik und in Umgebung plakatiert.

Uns interessiert dabei, die strategische Planung der Moderne mit ihrer suggerierten Übersichtlichkeit und demonstrativen Geheimnislosigkeit mit dem subjektiven Blick der Bewohner*innen, der Gewordenheit und den imaginären Welten des Viertels zu konfrontieren. Oder anders gesagt, im Lefebvre'schen Sinne: Wir möchten die Ebene M (wie Mediation/Vermittlung) der Ausstellung STATISTA nutzen, um die dominante Ebene G des Globalen (der Strategie, der Planung, der funktionalen Trennung) mit der Perspektive der Ebene P (des Privaten, des Taktischen, der Aneignung, der das Funktionale durchbrechenden Vorstellungswelten) zu durchlöchern.
Der Workshop setzt auf das Alltägliche und das daraus entstehende Wissen. Die Einladung und Aufforderung, den eigenen lokalen spezifischen Blick einzubringen, wird an die Hauseingänge rund um das HdS mit blauen, wieder ablösbaren Klebestreifen angebracht. Durch die gemeinsame Diskussion und das Betrachten der einzelnen Fotos werden Blicke und damit die Perspektiven, aber auch das Wissen und die subjektive Wahrnehmung geteilt. Und damit eine gemeinsame Perspektive entwickelt, in der sowohl das Individuelle und Spezifische bestehen bleibt, als auch das Gemeinsame deutlich wird. Dieser kollektive Moment geteilter Perspektiven und geteilten Wissens ist genau der Moment, in dem Planung zur Plattform wird. Wir brauchen Plattformen des Austauschs, des Zusammenkommens und auch der Verhandlung. Des Verhandelns von diversen Aussagen und dem Austausch von Perspektiven. Einen

Raum, in dem die Differenziertheit an Meinungen nebeneinander stehen kann, ohne in der Logik der Stadtentwicklung konsensual abgeschliffen zu werden. Das lokale Wissen ist der individuelle Zutritt, der eine Rolle spielt und von dem der Austausch ausgeht, selbst kreativ zu sein, selbst zu schaffen und dadurch Teil eines Prozesses zu sein, der in einem größeren Zusammenhang durch diesen Austausch entsteht. Nicht Nutznießende, nicht Partizipierende, sondern Produzierende.

Es ist dieser kollektive Moment der Produktivität, der die Plattform des Austauschs ist und zugleich die Bedingung dessen. In dieser permanenten Überlagerung liegt der Reiz und das Besondere, welche es uns erlauben, aus dem individuellen und Partikularinteresse herauszutreten und zu einem gemeinsam formulierten Bild, was Stadt sein kann, zu kommen.

[1]
Dagmar Hutzler, 2018

[2]
Dagmar Hutzler, 2014

[3]
Margit Czenki / PlanBude, 2019

MACAO

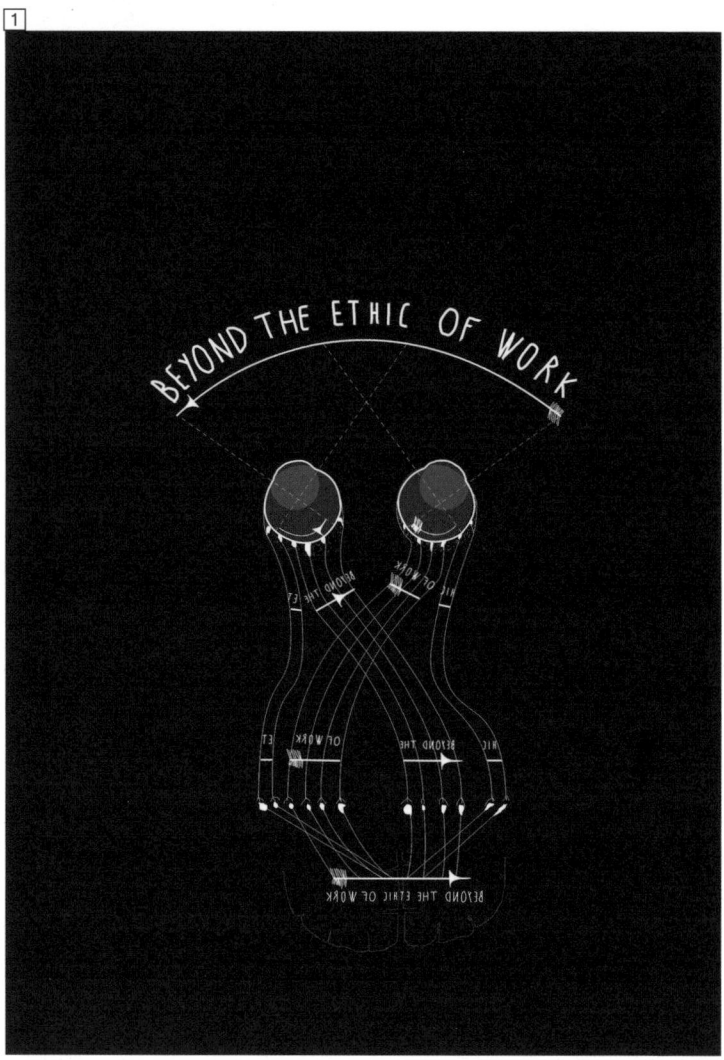

Our social life is a techno-political subject. Society has always organized itself around body-building techniques. What we value and desire has always been linked to a fictional construction technology. The protocols that govern these organizations are social algorithms, as they automate protocols of cooperative behavior. The techniques of patriarchal domination, in which a sovereign decides which type of body has the right to life and death determines (standardizes) the economy of desire within social cooperation. To regulate the economy of desire means to limit the field of fictions to which we can give value. To regulate a given circulation of values, a techno-political financialization is established through the invisibility of the oppressed and a social division of labor. The field of greatest invisibility and current

[1]
Emanuele Braga, '*Beyond the Ethic of Work*'; from 'Possible Spaces', MACAO series #5

[2]
artwork by Maddalena Fragnito, from 'Possible Spaces', MACAO series #5

financialization is social reproduction and care work. The oppressed is who wants another fiction. The oppressed is transsexual, homosexual, migrant, precarious, air and mineral resources, intensive farm animals, agricultural monocultures and burning forests.

There is no neutral Artificial Intelligence, a Biotechnological project or a Social Network to which to entrust the construction of our bodies and energy resources. The technologies of the domain show reassuring luminous screens to hide and render invisible the oppression.

Common intelligence always starts from recognizing the way we are built and from a process of disidentification. It represents our ability to create transversal alliances to build our techno-political body. Common intelligence automates autonomy, it is the constituent space of non-standardized algorithms, in which the circulation of desire is self-organized.

Khalil Sakakini Cultural Center

Meeting #9 15/9/19 Berlin

as defence association solidarity not a means
movements such as Occupy is not enough, solida
freedom and equality) **Solidarity as a**
need to be authentic,
bottom up How do we not romanticise solidarity
struggling with other people, overcoming the br
vulnerability
while at the **Solidarity = Politics**
together Solidaric Economies, e.g. solidarische
systems, we can find modes which are less dest
production, e.g. you share the risk of bad harve
solidarity as affinity with others by belonging
still something deeply enriching in acting toget
about how one acts? Being in conflict with solid
historical transformation of term, expand our u
suffragette movement), and what can it mean in
giving and receiving conscious support Who live
come from, what art do we make? Opening up t
political activism turns it into the commons...
production of it Agriculture and urbanism take
new ways of thinking about cultural production
ways to practice it in cultural ways Solidarity is
infrastructure, ageing population, shouldering t
active **Fear of solidarity** Non-hierar
compositio
songs What came out of spaces that were based
spaces? 90s: frameworks to work collectively i
— known for distribution of resources, non- hie
capitalists, many were eaten up by working toge
How do you manage shared resources? **Work**
infrastructures against precarity Do
produce solidarity? Solidarity needs to be produ
struggle of others? It depends on the mode of n
grants and donations what kind
support?
Does accepting financing make you complicit wi
to act on bigger scales Yet ho
regula
wanting to change the structures? Lobbying is t

Khalil Sakakini Cultural Center

y as means or end? You cannot reach
y without thinking of it as a process solidarity
d, the practicing of solidarity exemplified in
central content of left politics (more than
iod Is solidarity really that voluntary? It
purist, a combustion of feeling from the
an embodiment of solidarity? Generosity of
ween you and the other, involving sacrifice and
es the differences and being in disagreement,
ime there is an urgency of doing something
chaft (with farmers) Even within market
ot a payment for a commodity, but a mode of
tribution of resources there is
when the definitions are different Isn't it more
owing the limits of it and accepting them
ding, what has it meant in the past (e.g.
re Empathy and awareness, the possibility of
he cultural economy? where does the money
the arts and culture to agriculture, urbanism,
scuss economy rather than simply the
erm in thinking about economics, that opens up
t politics as a cultural act and searching for
al issue, we have to share the burden of missing
to maintain the conditions in which we are
uctures in making music, changes of
sical teams in different projects, even between
epts of solidarity, what happened to these
of Berlin in a political context e.g. Botschaft
decision making, lost their bar/house, became
needed to step out to reflect on the experience
ollectively Collective structures and
you need a new challenge to
can it be also the acknowledgement of the
lidarity productive The issue with
re does this
eal with these forms of hegemonic politics?
tivities of the moneygivers? We need
navigate the need to change
lobbying still be an act of solidarity by
privileges which is antithetical to solidarity

[1] poster design based on Sakakini workshop at HdS, September 2019

ruangrupa

A. LUMBUNG diagram

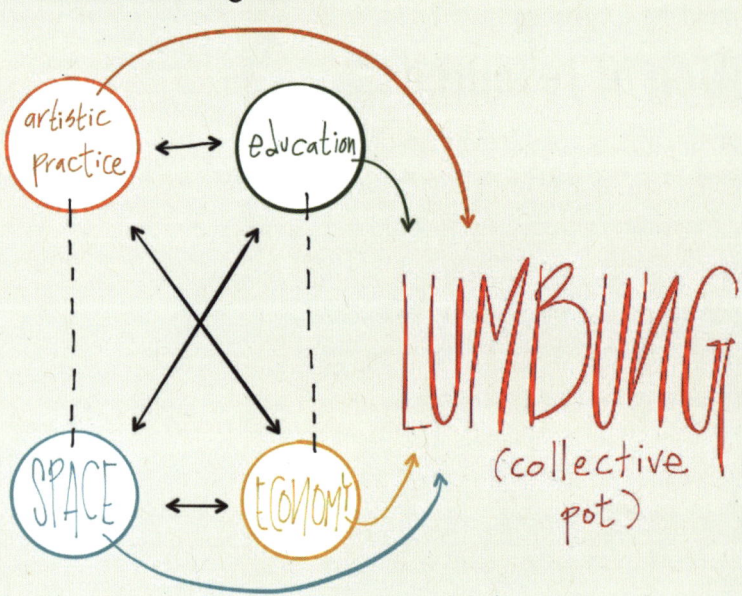

B. PASAR ILMU instructions

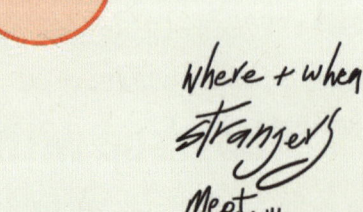

B. PASAR ILMU
instructions

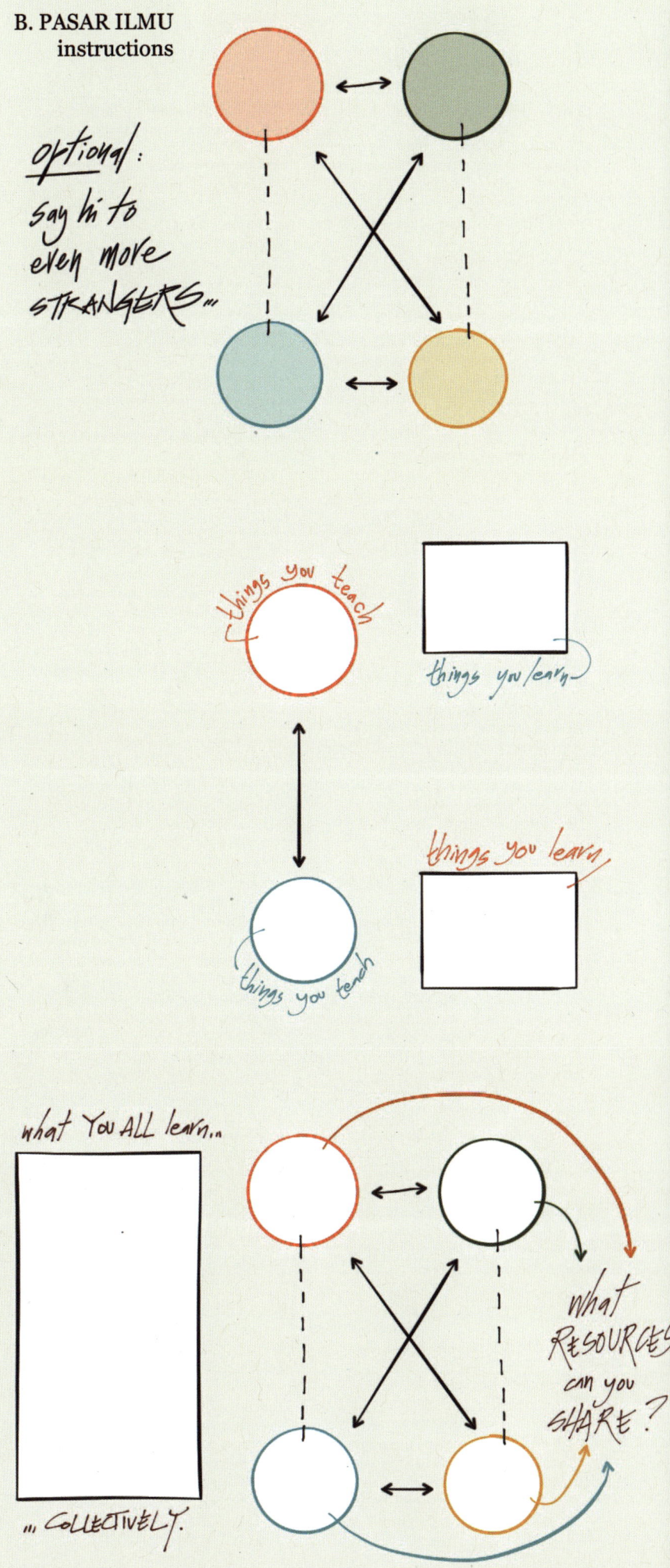

Index

anschlaege.de is a Berlin-based creative agency. Their work centers on communication, design and 'phorschung'. They offer individual solutions for clients with the courage for change. anschlaege.de is an owner-run business founded in 2005 by Axel Watzke, Christian Lagé and Steffen Schuhmann. ▶ p. 154

anschlaege.de ist ein Studio für Gestaltung. Seit 2005 entwickelt es visuelle Systeme und Projekte im Kontext Kultur, Wissenschaft und Zivilgesellschaft. Für seine Arbeit wurde das Studio mit einer Reihe nationaler und internationaler Designpreise ausgezeichnet. ▶ p. 156

Bernadette La Hengst is a Berlin-based songwriter and theatre director. Since 2004 she has developed numerous participative theatre projects, as both a musician and a director, and has founded choirs and written utopian songs with citizens and villagers all over Germany. The 6th solo album by La Hengst Wir sind die Vielen was released in 2019. ▶ p. 94

Bernadette La Hengst ist eine Berliner Songschreiberin und Theatermacherin mit einem Hang zu sozial-politischen Themen. Seit 2004 realisierte sie unzählige partizipative Theaterprojekte und Hörspiele als Musikerin und Regisseurin. Sie gründete viele verschiedene Chöre, um mit Menschen der Stadt- und Dorfgesellschaft utopische Lieder zu schreiben und zu singen. Ihr 6. Solo Album Wir sind die Vielen erschien 2019. ▶ p. 94

Campus in Camps was founded in 2012, and engages with new forms of representation of refugee camps following sixty years of displacement or more. The aim is to provide young Palestinian refugees with the necessary infrastructure and intellectual space to translate their positions and debates into practical community-driven projects. The latter are hoped to initiate new representational practices within and without the camps. Campus in Camps was created as an experimental educational program with Al Quds University (Al Quds/Bard Partnership) and hosted by the Phoenix Center in Dheisheh Refugee Camp in Bethlehem. ▶ p. 178

Campus in Camps wurde 2012 gegründet und befasst sich mit neuen Formen der Repräsentation von Flüchtlingslagern, die nach über 60 Jahren Vertreibung als solche weiter bestehen. Ziel ist, jungen palästinensischen Flüchtlingen die nötige Infrastruktur und den intellektuellen Raum zu bieten, um ihre Erfahrungen und Positionen in praktische, gemeinwohlorientierte Projekte zu überführen. Diese erzeugen im besten Fall neue Repräsentationspraktiken innerhalb wie auch außerhalb des Lagers. Campus in Camps wurde als experimentelles Bildungsprogramm gegründet in Zusammenarbeit mit der Universität Al Quds (Al Quds/Bard Partnership) und dem Phoenix Center im Dheisheh-Flüchtlingslager bei Bethlehem. ▶ p. 178

CATPC (Cercle d'Art des Travailleurs de Plantation Congolaise) was founded near Lusanga, Democratic Republic of the Congo (DRC), August 2014. The grassroots platform is financed by the production and sale of critical art. With the profits, communities buy back their land and build inclusive ecological post-plantations. Members Djonga Bismar, Mathieu Kilapi Kasiama, Ced'art Tamasala, Mbuku Kimpala, Mananga Kibuila, Jérémie Mabiala, Emery Mohamba, and Thomas Leba, are plantation workers from three plantations in the south of the DRC. CATPC president is ecologist Rene Ngongo. ▶ p. 170

CATPC (Cercle d'Art des Travailleurs de Plantation Congolaise) wurde 2014 bei Lusanga gegründet, im Süden der Demokratischen Republik Kongo. Es handelt sich um eine Grassroots-Plattform zur Entwicklung neuer Wirtschaftsinitiativen auf Grundlage von Produktion und Verkauf kritischer Kunst. Mit dem Einführen einer Kreativwirtschaft wird versucht, die wirtschaftliche Situation ihrer Mitglieder und deren Umfeld zu verbessern. Mit dem Gewinn aus ihrer Kunst kaufen sie ihr Land zurück und errichten ökologische Post-Plantagen. Die Gründungsmitglieder Djonga Bismar, Mathieu Kilapi Kasiama, Ced'art Tamasala, Mbuku Kimpala, Mananga Kibuila, Jérémie Mabiala, Emery Mohamba und Thomas Leba arbeiten alle auf den drei Plantagen im Süden der Demokratischen Republik Kongo. ▶ p. 170

Chto Delat (What is to be Done?) was founded 2003 in Saint Petersburg, and merges political theory, art and activism. Activities include art projects, seminars and public campaigns across a range of media, from video and theatre, to radio programs and murals. These resort to alienation effects, surreal sceneries and case-based analyses of concrete sociopolitical struggles. In 2013, Chto Delat initiated the School of Engaged Art in Saint Petersburg, along with the venue Rosa's House of Culture. From its inception, the collective has been publishing an English-Russian newspaper focused on the politicisation of the Russian cultural situation, in dialogue with the international context. ➤ p. 178

Chto Delat (Was tun?) wurde 2003 in Sankt Petersburg gegründet, mit dem Ziel, politische Theorie, Kunst und Aktivismus zusammenzubringen. Das Kollektiv arbeitet mithilfe einer Reihe von Medien wie Videokunst, Theaterstücken, Radiosendungen und Wandbildern. Dies beinhaltet auch Kunstprojekte, Seminare und Öffentlichkeitskampagnen. Die Arbeiten zeichnen sich durch den Einsatz des Entfremdungseffekts, surreale Kulissen, einen großen Wiedererkennungswert und eine kontextspezifische Analyse soziopolitischer Kämpfe aus. Chto Delat rief 2003 eine Lernplattform ins Leben (die „Schule für engagierte Kunst" in Sankt Petersburg), wie auch den Veranstaltungsraum Rosas Kulturhaus. Seit seiner Gründung publiziert das Kollektiv eine englisch-russische Zeitschrift, die sich mit der Politisierung der kulturellen Situation in Russland befasst, im Austausch mit einem internationalen Kontext. ➤ p. 178

Economic Space Agency (ECSA) is a group of finance theorists, computer scientists, software architects, game designers, peer production experts, and decentralized application engineers working on creating the new stack of economic and informational freedom. ECSA is powered by Agoric technology – a next-generation distributed computing, smart contracts platform – that allows for the creation of genuinely decentralized governance. ➤ p. 106

Die Economic Space Agency (ECSA) bewegt sich an der Schnittstelle zwischen radikaler Ökonomie, Finanztheorie, Informationstechnologie, Softwarearchitektur, *Game Design, Peer Production* und dezentraler Anwendungstechnik. ECSA arbeitet mit Agoric-Technologie — eine zukunftsweisende Plattform für dezentrale Datenverarbeitung und *Smart Contracts*, wodurch genuin dezentrale Steuerungssysteme gestaltet werden können. Agoric kombiniert Blockchain-Technologie mit kryptografischen Leistungsvermögen (E-Rights) um widerstandsfähige und interoperable Netzwerke zu generieren, in denen nur Vertragsparteien an der Ausführung, Replikation und Verifikation partizipieren können. ➤ p. 108

ExRotaprint is the former site of the Rotaprint printing press manufacturing plant in Berlin's Wedding district. In 2004, visual artists Daniela Brahm and Les Schliesser formulated a concept for on-site tenants taking over the property. The goal was to develop the location to serve a heterogeneous mix of uses for Arbeit, Kunst, Soziales (work, art, community) and affordable rents for all. ExRotaprint institutes a unique form of ownership and self-organization within a precarious environment. The project is a model for urban development that rules out financial profit through ownership and establishes a heterogeneous, open environment for all community groups. ➤ p. 180

ExRotaprint ist das ehemalige Produktionsgelände des Druckmaschinenherstellers Rotaprint in Berlin-Wedding. 2004 erarbeiteten die bildenden Künstler*innen Daniela Brahm und Les Schliesser ein Konzept zur Übernahme des Geländes durch die Mieterschaft vor Ort. Ziel war eine Entwicklung des Standorts für eine heterogene Nutzung aus Arbeit, Kunst und Sozialem auf der Grundlage von Mieten, die sich alle leisten können. In einer prekären Umgebung bietet ExRotaprint eine einzigartige Form von Eigentum und Selbstorganisation. Es ist ein Modellprojekt für eine Stadtentwicklung, die finanziellen Gewinn aufgrund von Eigentum ausschließt und für ganz unterschiedliche Menschen ein offenes Umfeld schafft. ➤ p. 180

The Hiveeyes Project is a group of beekeepers from Berlin regularly meeting since 2014 to build a collaborative telemetry platform for beehive monitoring. Hiveeyes is an open source, DIY toolkit for building beehive monitoring setups. It is modular and built upon contemporary technologies and components like Arduino, MQTT, InfluxDB and Grafana. With low-cost, low-power hardware, we aim at making non-invasive beekeeping as affordable and comfortable as possible. ➤ p. 112

Das Hiveeyes Project ist eine Gruppe aus Imker*innen, Entwickler*innen und Elektroniker*innen, die als „Elektro-Imker*innen" ihre Bienenvölker elektronisch erfassen. Die an und in den Stöcken gesammelten Daten werden per Funk zu einem Server geschickt, dort grafisch aufgearbeitet und helfen so den Zustand der Bienen kontinuierlich im Blick zu halten. ➤ p. 116

Image-Shift is a graphic design and visual communication studio based in Berlin. The studio is dedicated to – and operates in – social, cultural, political, educational and urban settings. Image-Shift develops communication concepts, strategies and designs for all kind of media formats and distribution contexts. ➤ p. 154

image-shift ist ein Studio für Grafikdesign und visuelle Kommunikation mit Sitz in Berlin. Das Studio widmet sich — und operiert in — sozialen, kulturellen, politischen urbanen Kontexten. image-shift entwickelt Kommunikationskonzepte, Strategien und Designs für alle Arten von Medienformaten und Distributionswegen. ➤ p. 156

Khalil Sakakini Cultural Center (KSCC) is a non-profit organization established in Ramallah 1996. It is dedicated to the promotion of arts and culture throughout Palestinian society, working in the three areas of Visual Arts, Palestinian Identity & Narrative, and public activities. KSCC is also dedicated to rethinking art and culture as economic fields – and of artists and other cultural practitioners as economic actors – in the hope of new political models for collective organization. The self-designed notebooks and tote bags on display are part of a broader, long-term attempt at financial autonomy in a context of politico-economic collapse. ➤ p. 190

Das Khalil Sakakini Cultural Center (KSCC) ist eine non-profit Organisation, gegründet 1996 in Ramallah. Das Zentrum widmet sich der Verbreitung von Kunst und Kultur in der gesamten palästinensischen Gesellschaft und arbeitet in den drei Bereichen visuelle Kunst, palästinensische Identitätsnarrative sowie öffentliche Aktivitäten. KSCC unternimmt hierbei den Versuch, Kunst und Kultur als ökonomische Handlungssphären zu deuten, und Kunstschaffende und andere Kulturarbeitende als ökonomische Akteur*innen zu begreifen. Ziel dabei ist, neue politische Modelle für selbstverwaltete Kollektive zu erzeugen. Die selbstgestalteten Jutebeutel und Notizbücher im Dokumentationsraum sind ein kleiner Teil eines weit gefassten Versuchs, in einem Kontext des politökonomischen Zusammenbruchs finanzielle Autonomie zu erreichen. ➤ p. 190

KUNSTrePUBLIK has been working in public spaces since 2006. The artist collective examines the potentials and boundaries of art as a means of communication and representation of various interests that define public space. KUNSTrePUBLIK's work departs from the spatial and social situations at hand, and creates new intersections between artistic, architectural, spatial-theoretical and political discourses.
➤ p. 42, p. 78, p. 100, p. 112

KUNSTrePUBLIK arbeitet seit 2006 als Künstlerkollektiv im öffentlichen Raum. In seiner Praxis untersucht es die Potenziale und Grenzen von Kunst als Mittel der Kommunikation und Repräsentation von unterschiedlichen Interessen im öffentlichen Raum. Die Arbeit von KUNSTrePUBLIK geht von der jeweiligen räumlichen und sozialen Situation aus und bildet Schnittmengen von künstlerischen, architektonischen, raumtheoretischen und politischen Diskursen. ➤ p. 80, p. 90, p. 102, p. 116

Labor k3000 was founded in 1989 in Zurich by a group of artists, activists, electronic musicians, graphic designers and multimedia designers. Since then, it has served as a platform for transnational research projects, exhibitions and video and web productions on ongoing social, cultural and political transformations. New forms of collective knowledge production and representation are tested in transdisciplinary settings. Since 2008, Labor k3000 has enjoyed a second base in Berlin. ➤ p. 84

Labor k3000 wurde 1998 von Gestalter*innen, Künstler*innen und Aktivisten in Zürich (u.a. von Marcus Maeder, Peter Spillmann, Marion von Osten) gegründet. Das Kollektiv realisiert seither transnationale Projekte, Ausstellungen, Film- und Webproduktionen zu sozialen, kulturellen und politischen Themen, in denen neue Formen kollektiver Wissensproduktion und -darstellung erprobt werden. Seit 2008 hat das Labor k3000 seinen Standort in Berlin und entwickelt neue Ansätze urbaner Gestaltung. Das Projekt *fallingwild* (www.fallingwild.org) wird realisiert von Brian Karl, Marion von Osten, Leonard Lesch, Peter Spillmann, Kolja Venenwald und Franziska Zahl.
➤ p. 85

MACAO is an independent center for culture and research in Milan, currently based in a former slaughterhouse. Its program hosts the visual and performing arts, cinema, design, photography, literature, newmedia, hacking and citizen committee meetings. MACAO is coordinated by an open assembly of artists and activists. Avoiding the creative industry paradigm, and aiming to innovate the old idea of cultural institutions, we consider art production as a space for innovative governance and production models. Our research concerns labor conditions in the creative industry and cultural sector, the right to the city, and new organizational and technological solutions for cultural production. ➤ p. 188

MACAO ist ein unabhängiges Zentrum für Kunst, Kultur und Forschung. Im Versuch, die Paradigmen der Kreativindustrie zu vermeiden, aber auch die Idee der Kulturinstitution neu zu erfinden, wird Kunstproduktion als Prozess begriffen, sozialen Wandel zu denken und politische Kritikverfahren zu entwickeln,

Index

wie auch als Raum für innovative Verwaltungs- und Produktionsmodelle. Der Forschungsbereich untersucht die Arbeitsbedingungen in der Kreativindustrie und im Kultursektor, das Recht auf Stadt sowie neue Organisationsformen und technische Lösungen für Kulturproduktion. MACAO befindet sich momentan in einem ehemaligen Schlachthof nicht weit vom Stadtzentrum Mailands entfernt. Zum interdisziplinären Programm gehören Performances, Kino, visuelle Kunst, Design, Fotografie, Literatur, neue Medien, Hacking und Nachbarschaftstreffen. Die Koordination wird von einem offenen Plenum aus Kunstschaffenden und Aktivist*innen gewährleistet. ➤ p. 188

Moabees is a group of artists and beekeepers founded by Bärbel Rothhaar, Elisa Dierson and Katja Marie Voigt. The project's apiary is located in Moabit at ZK/U Berlin. In participatory workshops, Moabees foster up-close artistic approaches to bees within the city, and to their products: honey, wax, pollen. Imagination, architecture, research and art practices merge. The pilot project Moabees has been funded by the German Federal Ministry of Education and Research since 2013. ➤ p. 112

Moabees ist eine Gruppe von Kunstschaffenden und Imker*innen, die von Bärbel Rothhaar, Elisa Dierson und Katja Marie Voigt gegründet wurde. Am ZK/U in Berlin-Moabit befindet sich der Projekt-Bienenstand. Von dort aus erarbeitet Moabees in partizipativen Prozessen künstlerische Perspektiven auf Honigbienen in der Stadt und ihre Produkte Honig, Wachs und Blütenstaub. Beim Mitimkern zoomt man in die Bienenvölker hinein, kommt ihnen hautnah. Praktiken aus Imkerhandwerk, Architektur, Fantasie und Forschung fließen in die Kunstprozesse ein. Das Pilotprojekt Moabees wird seit 2013 aus Mitteln des Bundesministeriums für Bildung und Forschung gefördert. ➤ p. 116

Nachbarschaftsakademie Prinzessinnengärten is a self-organized platform for urban and rural knowledge sharing, cultural practice and activism. The Prinzessinnengärten itself is a mobile urban garden in Kreuzberg Berlin that allows for farming in a city where most available land is either paved or contaminated. The Nachbarschaftsakademie (Neighborhood Academy) began in 2015, with the program City Country Land. From here on, we complemented our learning platform with a local DIY-network that serves as a living archive, and with the experimental DIY-architecture Die Laube (The Arbor). The collage on display in the Documentation Room, *Trusting Land* (2019), by Brett Bloom & Bonnie Fortune, was developed as part of the program Nachbarschaftsakademie – Aus den Ruinen der Moderne wachsen ("Growing from the ruins of Modernity"). ➤ p. 184

Die Nachbarschaftsakademie Prinzessinnengärten ist eine selbstorganisierte, offene Plattform für städtischen und ländlichen Wissensaustausch, kulturelle Praktiken und Aktivismus. Ihr Schauplatz Prinzessinnengärten, ein mobiler Garten in Berlin Kreuzberg, erlaubt einen ökologischen Anbau in der Stadt, wo der Großteil der vorhandenen Flächen asphaltiert oder kontaminiert ist. Die Nachbarschaftsakademie begann 2015 mit dem Programm „Stadt Land Boden", in dessen Rahmen Themenfelder wie ländliche Resilienz, Gemeingüter, Landpolitik und soziales Wohnen diskutiert wurden. Auf diesem Programm aufbauend wurde die Akademie von einer experimentellen, selbstgebauten Architektur ergänzt (die „Laube"), sowie einem lokalen DIY-Netzwerk, das als lebendes Wissensarchiv der Nachbarschaftsakademie dient. Die ausgestellte Collage *Trusting Land* (2019) von Brett Bloom & Bonnie Fortune wurde entwickelt als Teil des Programms „Nachbarschaftsakademie – Aus den Ruinen der Moderne wachsen". ➤ p. 184

Nascent is an EXIT TECH production studio founded by Max Hampshire and Paul Seidler. Nascent builds infrastructure for institutional or private actors that doesn't rely on surveillance or ad-revenue based income models. Additionally, Nascent consults on tactics and strategies for building a P2P economy via prototyping minimal viable solutions and economic experiments. ➤ p. 112

Nascent ist ein EXIT-TECH-Produktionsstudio, das von Max Hampshire und Paul Seidler gegründet wurde. Nascent baut Infrastruktur für institutionelle oder private Akteur*innen auf, die nicht auf überwachungsbasierte Umsatzmodelle angewiesen ist. Darüber hinaus berät Nascent zu Taktiken und Strategien für den Aufbau P2P-basierter Wirtschaftsmodelle durch Prototyping von minimal tragfähigen Lösungen und wirtschaftlichen Experimenten. ➤ p. 116

openBerlin is a platform and tool for participatory urban development, self-governance, spatial transformation and the production of ideas. It connects projects with open spaces, accompanying them from the initial idea to the final concept. One aim is to sustainably generate

Index

the highest possible social, cultural, ecological and financial value for the city at large. Successful projects share the knowledge acquired, taking responsibility with regards to the city. Our priority is the permanent safeguarding of open spaces as public property, in order to prevent speculative exploitation. ▶ p. 100

openBerlin ist eine Plattform und ein Werkzeug für partizipative Stadtentwicklung, der Selbstverwaltung, der räumlichen Transformation und Ideenproduktion. Sie vernetzt Projekte, Projektsuchende und städtische Freiräume und begleitet sie von der ersten Idee bis zum finalen Konzept. Wichtig ist, durch die mit Unterstützung entwickelten Projekte nachhaltig einen möglichst hohen sozialen, kulturellen, ökologischen und finanziellen Mehrwert für die Stadt zu generieren. Bereits erfolgreiche Projekte teilen ihr Wissen und übernehmen damit Verantwortung gegenüber ihrer Stadt. Größtes Augenmerk liegt dabei auf der dauerhaften Sicherung der Freiräume als öffentliches Eigentum, um spekulative Verwertung zu verhindern. ▶ p. 102

Penny Rafferty is a writer and visual theorist based in Berlin. Her theoretical essays and creative texts have been commissioned for *Cura, Kaleidoscope* magazine, Keen On, NRW Dusseldorf, Rote Fabrik and Flash Art amongst others. She frequently draws on antagonistic lines of critique, popular culture and ideas surrounding cosmic depression aka paradise without utopia. ▶ p. 157

Penny Rafferty wohnt in Berlin und schreibt über Kunst und visuelle Theorie und zwar für Cura, *Kaleidoscope* Magazine, Keen On, NRW Dusseldorf, Rote Fabrik, *Flash Art* etc. Sie bezieht sich oftmals auf Spannungsfelder im Bereich Kritik, Popkultur und „kosmischer Weltschmerz": *cosmic depression aka paradise without utopia.* ▶ p. 160

PlanBude is a transdisciplinary office, organizing the planning and participation for a 28,000 square meter ensemble of houses that are to replace the former Esso-Houses on Reeperbahn, St. Pauli, Hamburg. Kicked off by an independent citizen's assembly in the Ballroom of St. Pauli F.C., the team consists of planners, artists, architects, cultural scientists, DJs and community workers. It is now developing innovative planning tools to involve neighbours in the overall planning process. ▶ p. 186

PlanBude ist ein transdisziplinäres Planungsbüro, das die Planung und das Partizipationsverfahren des 28,000 Quadratmeter großen Gebäudekomplexes organisierte, das die ehemaligen Esso-Häuser auf der Reeperbahn im Hamburger Viertel St. Pauli ersetzen sollte. PlanBude wurde im Ballsaal des FC St. Pauli von einer unabhängigen Bürgerversammlung gegründet, die aus Stadtplaner*innen, Kunstschaffenden, Architekt*innen, Kulturwissenschaftler*innen, Djs und Sozialarbeiter*innen bestand. PlanBude entwickelt innovative Planungsinstrumente zur Einbeziehung der Anwohner*innen in den Planungsprozess. ▶ p. 186

raumlaborberlin, founded in 1999 in Berlin, works between the fields of architecture and public art. raumlabor means 'space laboratory', and creates projects based on events, performances and theatre. Collaboration with specialists is a key part of the strategy, including engineers, sociologists, ethnographers and common citizens. raumlaborberlin partakes in a utopian tradition of 1960s architecture, including, in particular, the work of Yona Friedman, Buckminster Fuller and Haus-Rucker. ▶ p. 94

raumlaborberlin sind acht ausgebildete Architekt*innen, die sich zu einer kollektiven Netzwerkstruktur zusammengefunden haben. Sie arbeiten seit 1999, ausgehend von Berlin, an den Schnittstellen zwischen Architektur, Stadtplanung, Kunst und Intervention. In ihrer Arbeit adressieren sie Raum, Stadt und Stadtbau als kulturelles Projekt und als Prozess. Schwierige städtische Orte ziehen sie förmlich an. Orte, die zwischen verschiedenen Systemen, Zeitabschnitten oder Planungsideologien aufgerieben wurden und sich nicht anpassen. Orte, die aufgegeben sind, die übrig bleiben, aber für die Stadtgestalt eine nicht unerhebliche Relevanz haben. Diese Orte sind ihre Experimentierfelder. ▶ p. 96

ruangrupa (est. 2000) is a Jakarta-based collective working in contemporary visual art and beyond. Since 2016, together with Serrum & Grafis Huru Hara, ruangrupa has been playing with the notion of a collective of collectives. Its latest iteration is Gudskul (est. 2018), an informal educational platform focusing on collectivity and ecosystem building. ▶ p. 192

ruangrupa ist ein 2000 gegründetes indonesisches Künstlerkollektiv aus Jakarta, das im Bereich der zeitgenössischen bildenden Kunst arbeitet. Mit dem 2016 ins Leben gerufenen Serrum & Grafis Huru Hara spielt ruangrupa mit dem Begriff des Gemeinschaftskollektivs. Seine neueste Form findet dies in Gudskul (2018), einer informellen Lernplattform, die sich auf die Schaffung von Kollektivität und Ökosystemen richtet. ▶ p. 192

Index

sub_ʇxǝʇ is an itinerant platform for sonic knowledge production. It produces and distributes radio, programmes across a thematic spectrum ranging from investigative reporting to experimental sound and music. Designed as an inherently collaborative platform programmes are developed with artists and practitioners through on-the-ground research and dialogue. sub_ʇxǝʇ is a partner project of Threads Radio in Tottenham, London. ➤ p. 166

Die Konferenz wurde dokumentiert und ausgestrahlt von sub_ʇxǝʇ, einer Plattform für akustische Wissensproduktion, deren Spielfelder von Enthüllungsjournalismus bis hin zu experimenteller Musik reichen. sub_ʇxǝʇ steht in Partnerschaft zu Threads Radio in Tottenham, London. ➤ p. 166

**Credits
Bildnachweise**

p 14, 27, 80, 81, 95, 97, 100, 107, 109, 115, 120, 124, 126, 128, 130, 132, 134, 136, 140, 142, 146, 148, 150, 155, 168, 169
© Victoria Tomaschko

p 39, 41, 48, 57, 88, 90
KUNSTrePUBLIK

p. 31 © Bundesarchiv, Günter Weiß
p. 31 © Bundesarchiv
p. 69 Torsten Arendt
p. 79 © Dirk Lehnartz
p. 84 Labor k3000
p. 85 Labor k3000
p. 97 Raquel
p.101 openBerlin
p. 103 Leona Lynen
p. 113 © Karl Hillert
p. 119 © Karl Hillert
p. 122 © Harald Hauswald
p. 138 Labor k3000
p. 144 Leona Lynen
p. 155 © Bundesarchiv, Hubert Link
p. 162 Ishtar Gate
p. 172 CATPC
p. 177 Dmitry Vilensky
p. 177 Vasilina Koshalina
p. 178 Campus in Camps
p 180–183 ExRotaprint
p 184/185 Nachbarschafts-akademie Prinzessinnen-gärten
p. 186 © Dagmar Hutzler
p. 187 © Dagmar Hutzler
p. 187 PlanBude, Margit Czenki
p. 188 © Emanuele Braga
p. 189 © Maddalena Fragnito
p. 190 Khalil Sakakini Cultural Center
p 192/193 ruangrupa

**Project imprint
Impressum Gesamtprojekt**

STATISTA
Towards a Statecraft of the Future
Staatskunst am Haus der Statistik
ZK/U – Zentrum für Kunst und Urbanistik
KW Institute for Contemporary Art

Artistic Directors / Künstlerische Leitung: Matthias Einhoff, Philip Horst, Harry Sachs (ZK/U)
Curator/Kurator: Tirdad Zolghadr (KW)
Technische Leitung / Production: Konrad Braun
Coordination/Koordination: Olesia Vitiuk, Stephanie Holl-Trieu
Design: anschlaege.de, Johannes Wilke (beecoin.de)
Web Programming: Lars Hayer, Nascent
Press/Presse: Denhart v. Harling
Social Media: Dr. Sylvia Metz
Documentation/Dokumentation: Victoria Tomaschko, Simone Häckel

Mit freundlicher Unterstützung von / funded by:

Colophon ZK/U
Directors/Direktion: Matthias Einhoff, Philip Horst, Harry Sachs
Communications/Kommunikation: Dr. Sylvia Metz, Kristina Miller
Residency Coordination/ Koordination Künstler*innen-residenz: Lotta Schäfer
Research/Forschung: Miodrag Kuč
Coordination/Koordination: Dennis Lindenau
Technical Management/Technik: Gustavo Sanromán Vázquez
Design: Hannes Mitterberger

Colophon KW
Director/Direktor: Krist Gruijthuijsen
Office Manager to the Director/ Assistenz des Direktors: Friederike Klapp
Head of Production/ Produktionsleitung: Claire Spilker
Design: Marc Hollenstein
Head of Press and Communication/ Leitung Kommunikation: Karoline Köber
Project Management/ Projektmanagement: Duygu Örs
Head of Administration/ Administration: Silke Krummel